MEDIA EXPERIENCES

Media Experiences: Engaging with Drama and Reality Television travels across people and popular culture, exploring the pathways to engagement and the various ways in which we shape and are shaped by the media landscapes in which we move. This exploration includes the voices and bodies, sights and sounds of audiences as they experience entertainment through television drama, reality TV, at live events and within digital television itself as actors, participants and producers. It is about the people who create the drama, live events and reality entertainment that we experience. This book traverses the relationships between producers and audiences in shared places of a media imagination.

Annette Hill's research draws on interviews and observations with over 500 producers and audience members to explore cultures of viewing across different genres, such as Nordic noir crime drama *The Bridge*, cult conspiracy thriller *Utopia*, and reality television audiences and participants in global formats *MasterChef* and *Got to Dance*. The research highlights how trends such as multi-screening, catch up viewing, amateur media and piracy work alongside counter-trends in retro television viewing where people relish the social ritual of watching live television, or create a social media blackout for immersive viewing.

Media Experiences bridges the divide between industry and academia, highlighting how producers and audiences co-create, shape and limit experiences within emerging mediascapes.

Annette Hill is Professor in Media and Communication at Lund University, Sweden, and Visiting Professor at Kings College London, UK. Her research focuses on audiences and popular culture, with interests in media engagement, everyday life, genres, production studies and cultures of viewing. She is the author of eight books, including *Reality TV: Key Ideas* (2015).

MEDIA EXPERIENCES

Engaging with Drama and Reality Television

Annette Hill

LONDON AND NEW YORK

First published 2019
by Routledge
2 Park Square, Milton Park, Abingdon, Oxon OX14 4RN

and by Routledge
711 Third Avenue, New York, NY 10017

Routledge is an imprint of the Taylor & Francis Group, an informa business

© 2019 Annette Hill

The right of Annette Hill to be identified as author of this work has been asserted by her in accordance with sections 77 and 78 of the Copyright, Designs and Patents Act 1988.

All rights reserved. No part of this book may be reprinted or reproduced or utilised in any form or by any electronic, mechanical, or other means, now known or hereafter invented, including photocopying and recording, or in any information storage or retrieval system, without permission in writing from the publishers.

Trademark notice: Product or corporate names may be trademarks or registered trademarks, and are used only for identification and explanation without intent to infringe.

British Library Cataloguing-in-Publication Data
A catalogue record for this book is available from the British Library

Library of Congress Cataloging-in-Publication Data
A catalog record for this book has been requested

ISBN: 978-0-415-62535-7 (hbk)
ISBN: 978-0-415-62536-4 (pbk)
ISBN: 978-0-203-10353-1 (ebk)

Typeset in Bembo
by Taylor & Francis Books

Printed and bound in Great Britain by
TJ International Ltd, Padstow, Cornwall

To Peter, a star constellation that shines in the night sky; and to my family and friends for their ever present love and support.

CONTENTS

List of figures   *viii*
Acknowledgements   *x*

1 Pathways to engagement   1
2 An analytic dialogue   15
3 Roaming audiences: *The Bridge*   30
4 Spectrum of engagement: *Got to Dance*   53
5 The cool heart of Nordic noir   72
6 Illegal audiences: *Utopia*   94
7 Embedded engagement: Reality talent shows   121
8 Authentic reality TV: The case of *MasterChef*   138
9 Warm up acts   163
10 Audiences as pathfinders   184

Appendices   *193*
References   *209*
Index   *219*

FIGURES

1.1 Pathways, places and people: going to the launch of *Bron/Broen* season three Malmö Live, Sweden 2015. Photograph Tina Askanius   2
1.2 *Bron* is on: launch event for third season at Malmö Live, Sweden. Photograph Tina Askanius   7
2.1 On location of *Bron/Broen* season three. Photograph Tina Askanius   16
2.2 On the set of *MasterChef Denmark*. Photograph Tina Askanius   17
2.3 At the offices of Filmlance. Photograph Tina Askanius   23
3.1 Right to roam: the Heather Scarecrow Festival. Photograph Ian Calcutt   31
3.2 Storyboarding *Bron/Broen*. Photograph Tina Askanius   39
3.3 Topographies of the self and fans. Photograph Tina Askanius   49
4.1 An invitation to engage: scarecrow festival in England. Photograph Alison Calcutt   54
4.2 Heather Scarecrow festival. Photograph Ian Calcutt   55
4.3 Scarecrows, Heather Scarecrow Festival. Photograph Ian Calcutt   59
4.4 'Strictly Crow Dancing', Heather Scarecrow Festival. Photograph Ian Calcutt   70
5.1 Distressed landscapes for *Bron/Broen* season three. Photograph Tina Askanius   73
5.2 Stand-in Saga: at the production offices of Filmlance. Photograph Tina Askanius   87

6.1 Cult drama *Utopia*, on the wall at Kudos. Photograph
     Annette Hill   95
6.2 The Network is watching: *Utopia* on the wall at Kudos.
     Photograph Annette Hill   106
7.1 Auditions for *Got to Dance* Photograph Tina Askanius.   122
7.2 Researching *Got to Dance*. Photograph Tina Askanius   128
7.3 At the *Got to Dance* venue. Photograph Tina Askanius   130
8.1 *MasterChef* participants. Photograph Tina Askanius   139
8.2 Behind the scenes at *MasterChef*. Photograph Tina Askanius   149
8.3 Backstage at *MasterChef*. Photograph Tina Askanius   151
8.4 Playing with *MasterChef*. Photograph Tina Askanius   158
9.1 Live reality entertainment. Photograph Tina Askanius   164
9.2 At the auditions for *Got to Dance*. Photograph Tina Askanius   172
9.3 Behind the scenes at *Got to Dance*. Photograph Tina Askanius   176
10.1 Pathways: on the set of *Bron/Broen*. Photograph Tina Askanius   185
10.2 Pathfinders: mapping Mother of Three at *Bron/Broen* fan
     meeting. Photograph Tina Askanius   187

ACKNOWLEDGEMENTS

The research in this book is based on a three-year project and I would like to thank the Marianne and Marcus Wallenberg Foundation for the research support and funding, alongside Lund University, Sweden. I would also like to thank Endemol Shine for their collaboration with the research in this book. In particular, my heartfelt thanks goes to Douglas Wood, Head of Audience Research and Insight, for his generosity in time and energy for a collaborative project, and his enthusiasm for audience research.

The project team provided rich empirical research, and were a continuing source of ideas and encouragement. A big thank you to Tina Askanius, Julie Donovan, Koko Kondo, and Jose Luis Urueta, without whom there would be no book such as this – you are all amazing and thank you so very much for travelling with me on this journey. A special thank you to Ian Calcutt who conducted invaluable research for the project. My thanks also to the advisory group, Göran Bolin, Raymond Boyle, John Corner, Jeanette Steemers, and Douglas Wood. A special thank you to Jeanette Steemers for arranging the symposium on 'Media Experiences and Engagement' in London where we debated all things related to engagement and co-edited a publication for the journal *Media Industries* that was a great help in preparation for this book.

I thank my colleagues in Media and Communication at Lund University, and heads of department Mia Marie Hammarlin, Patrik Lundell and Tobias Olsson for their support and encouragement. In particular, a special thank you to Peter Dahlgren for always offering such good advice and inspiring me to think more on media engagement; to Joanna Doona and Michael Rubsamen for bouncing ideas around and managing the annual symposiums at Lund University which have been a source of inspiration for this book; thank you to Zaki Habibi for his inspiration in photography as research, and to the postgraduate students on the M.Sc. in Media and Communication who generously debated issues with me and wrote such strong dissertations on media engagement and experiences. A heartfelt thanks goes to John Corner, Joke Hermes and Jane Roscoe for our March conversations; those meals at Govindas and the drinks at Grand helped sustain me through the project and writing of the book; long may those March moments continue.

Some of the sections and ideas in Chapters 4, 5 and 7 appeared in the following publications 'Saga's Story: Emotional Engagement in the Production and Reception of Nordic Crime Drama' in *Crime Pays: Contemporary Global Television Drama*, editors Kim Toft Hansen, Sue Turnbull and Steven Peacock, Palgrave Macmillan (2018); 'Live Reality Television: care Structures for Live Experiences' (with Tina Askanius and Koko Kondo) in *Critical Studies in Television* (2018 in press); 'Reality TV Engagement: Reality TV Producers and Audiences for Talent Format *Got to Dance*' in *Media Industries*, volume 4, issue 1 (May 2017).

Above all, I must thank the executive and creative producers who generously gave up their time and shared their ideas on the craft of television drama and entertainment at Endemol Shine, Filmlance International, Kudos, Princess, Endemol Shine Nordics, and Shine. In particular, Anders Landström and Lars Blomgren were a delight to work with and I want to thank the Filmlance production team for trusting us in this collaboration; I also want to thank Princess for the full access to their talent show which was inspiring to study. A special thank you to the warm up acts who generously shared their experiences for the project; and finally to all the audiences and fans who shared their thoughts and creative expressions on media that matters to them: thank you so very much.

1
PATHWAYS TO ENGAGEMENT

The Bridge entangles you and it's difficult to leave.
(30 year old Mexican-Colombian male lawyer)

Media Experiences is a book about people and popular culture, about the pathways and tracks people make as they criss-cross the media landscape. We can imagine producers, including executives, creatives, performers and participants, creating byways and highways for audience orientation, making pathways to engagement with media content in national and transnational settings. We can also imagine audiences in topographical terms as roaming around storytelling, including viewers and listeners, fans and consumers, who are not only following pathways but acting as pathmakers in their media experiences. 'Roaming audiences' is a metaphor that captures the dynamic practices of people as they experience storytelling that takes place across dispersed sites of production, distribution and reception. This way of thinking about the media as an imaginary landscape shows the regions, borders, and contours of the cultural terrain, the enclosed spaces for commercial uses and the public byways for common land: in such a way we are shaped, and in turn shape, the media landscapes in which we move.

There has long been interest in the relations between places and people, where landscape is connected to storytelling that helps to create a feeling of belonging. Nature writer Robert Macfarlane has written about the experience of walking, talking about the strong bond between people and places. In his book *The Old Ways*, for example, he sets off on ancient byways, thoroughfares and barely-there tracks across Britain, reflecting on what he calls a bio-geography (2012: 32). By this, Macfarlane is referring to a topography of the self as a means of understanding our relationship with landscape and nature, and the wider significance of movement, stillness and imagination as a means for self reflection. He writes about how we can use walking through the landscape to make interior maps to help us

FIGURE 1.1 Pathways, places and people: going to the launch of *Bron/Broen* season three Malmö Live, Sweden 2015
Source: Photograph Tina Askanius.

navigate these psycho-social terrains (2012: 26). He explains: 'we think in metaphors drawn from place and sometimes those metaphors do not only adorn our thought, but actively produce it' (ibid.).

MacFarlane observes that whilst we are fairly adept at asking what we make of places, we are less confident about asking what places make of us (2012: 27). This is a useful way of thinking about media landscapes – as places that shape and are shaped by us. Media landscape is a metaphor that works in two ways: Bolin (2017: 46–47) maps the metaphor as referring to both technological landscapes, such as the material dimensions of television aerials and satellite dishes, and symbolic landscapes, such as representations, values, and ideologies within media content. This is a metaphor drawn from place, and following Shaun Moore's (2012) analysis of mobility and media in everyday life, the emphasis here is on the cultural, spatial and temporal work of placemaking as telling us something about lived experience.

As audiences roam around entertainment content, the pathways and tracks they make are shaping their experience of television and related social media. People's movements say something about what kind of media matters to them and how they reflect on these experiences. This symbolic power of media is connected to the social imaginary. Charles Taylor's idea of a modern social imaginary is 'a broad understanding of the way a given people imagine their collective social life' (2004: 23). What is important for Taylor is that the way ordinary people imagine their social surroundings is not through theories but 'carried in images, stories, and legends' (ibid.). This is suggestive of the cultural work of audiences in their various understandings of the social imaginary within popular culture. There is an affective relationship, a sense of legitimacy, where people have an emergent sense of rights to roam across media storytelling. The movement of roaming audiences is played out in mobile media spaces and across geographical and economic boundaries. A right to roam thus evokes a sense of television storytelling as open to all, and if we watch and share content, or remix stories into new narratives, then we help to shape a shared collective experience that is determined and sustained by use.

The laws and regulations surrounding content and communicative rights do not allow audiences to freely move across public service and commercial platforms and across national television and transregional content. The business model for television is to restrict access and monetise audiences, both in the interests of the political economy of media institutions and as a means to measure audience engagement through ratings and social media analytics that are collated within national boundaries. For those who resist these media laws and regulations, they are trying to generate an alternative vision for what Deborah Chambers (2016) calls a media imaginary where these technologies enable freedom to watch without restriction. Thus, there is a symbolic power to a right to roam media without economic barriers, time constraints or geographical borders. These kinds of roaming audiences are disrupting the ability of media industries to monitor and monetise consumers and users, and they are doing this in the spirit of first release media citizenship (Lobato and Thomas 2015).

This media landscape is a story of place and belonging, but to something that is changing. We hear talk of television institutions in decline, amateur media on the rise, platform players dominating the global market, and algorithms and wearable technologies telling us what to eat, who to date and when to sleep. This is a restless viewership for a digital age (Boyle and Kelly 2012), a fickle audience no longer loyal to broadcasters, channels or timeslots. We might think that being an audience today is all about the new. But when you listen to people and observe their cultural practices you often find a mixing of past and present in their various ways of experiencing media. As Macfarlane (2012) observes, our pathways and thoroughfares lead outwards to society and culture; track backwards to history; and inwards to the self.

There are the old ways, the traditional experience of television and radio, books and print media, in the home; the old ways are visible in those moments when people sit down on the sofa with a cup of tea to watch their favourite show, or curl up in bed with a crime novel. This is an image of audiences fixed in one place and time and transfixed by storytelling in the media. Nowadays, this old school mode stands in stark contrast to the always online, streaming, play all mode. Television, radio, print and social media are part of connected viewing (Holt and Sanson 2014), typified by people multi-screening and multi-tasking; picture an image of the audience in forward motion. A mother ship TV show connects with a branded universe of social media, gaming, and fan remixing. This is an image of audiences with freedom of access, choice of screen culture, and agency to fit favourite shows into personalised schedules. It's a promise of limitless media and opportunities for creation, but there are restrictions to access, distribution and consumption, with subscriptions for video on demand services, monthly fees for high speed internet access, data roaming charges for mobile users, and gated content for regional audiences. Not everyone has the resources (money, time, skills, support) to experience a streaming, play all mode of engagement.

New ways of experiencing media suggest audiences are moving in multiple directions at the same time. For example, there's an underground piracy culture that captures the latest TV series, films, music and sporting events and shares such content in a deliberate act of first release media citizenship. A black market exists for live television, where for a monthly fee you can watch content from your homeland in your hostland, unlocked from geoblocking. Informal routes to screen culture abound, through the sharing of friendly passwords, clouds and sticks. Most of us know someone who knows how to freely roam the digital landscape, a technologically savvy friend who can get us into media spaces with 'no trespassing signs' and security fences. Alongside these new ways of experiencing media, there's a need to slow down and take time out from binge watching, snacking and multitasking. One example is the social media blackout, a new way that draws on the old ways of watching television without interruption, making 'me time' (Nowotny 2018) where the mobile is turned off and media devices are in sleep mode – a still moment out of the slipstream of life.

Push-pull dynamics

All these ways of engaging and experiencing media are connected to how institutions and creative producers craft content for audiences. One means of theorising and analysing both production practices and audience engagement is to try to find concepts that enable an integrated approach to both areas of study. One such concept is push-pull dynamics. There is a push and pull to the dynamics between producers and audiences. There is a way cultural production pushes audiences into content, for example through distribution and branding for television drama across live transmission or subscription services. And there is a way audiences are pulled into the here and now of storytelling, for example through strong characterisation and multi-layered narratives in serial drama. Another dimension relates to how audiences pull different kinds of content and artefacts into their everyday lives, for example by choosing to engage with a specific television series over another one, or embedding material into their family routines. Such push-pull dynamics offer insights into broader changes in the media industry. This push and pull between producers and audiences works both ways, as restless consumers and users can push back, for example through alternative fan practices, disengaging with content, or illegal viewing. Thus, the idea of push-pull dynamics is understood as complicated power relations in the transactions between media industries and audiences.

For example, in the case of television drama we find varieties of experiences depending on the systemic power of television in public service and commercial environments, subscription video on demand services, and illegal distribution flows. If we take the case of the American-Mexican adaptation of the crime drama format *The Bridge* (FX and Fox Mundo 2013–2014) we can see the push and pull of the relations between institutions, producers and audiences generates problems for the performance of the format (see Hill 2016a). The original Scandinavian drama *Bron/Broen* is a Nordic noir drama that thrives in public service environments, with immersive viewing for Danish and Swedish audiences. But remakes suffer in commercial markets for more dispersed audiences and users, and the series was axed after the second season due to poor ratings. In particular, the constitution of commercial television in America and Mexico pushed viewers away from live screening towards catch up and illegal viewing. Here was a drama at the forefront of a DVR revolution in America, and part of illegal downloading in other regions, and yet the dominant audience information system of overnight and consolidated ratings could not capture the diversity and strength of audience and fan engagement. FX needed patience for the kind of viewers who streamed, downloaded or recorded, and stored up the show to watch in a quiet moment in their busy lives. Months after the show aired, viewers were finding the drama and spreading the word on *The Bridge* Facebook groups. They started 'bring back *The Bridge*' campaigns on social media. One fan summed up the reasons for its cancellation: 'I was amazed that it was cancelled. I think their problem was that they didn't wait, they didn't have patience' (23 year old American male swimming pool maintenance worker). He thought the show could have been like FX's *Breaking Bad* (AMC, 2008–2013), gathering audiences over time for binge watching and catch up viewing. He felt FX sabotaged the show with 'horrible advertising … when you do that it is like you are going towards failure no matter how good the show is'. In a performance of power, we witness audience practices that resist how the television industry measures and understands its viewers. This particular case illustrates a push–pull dynamic strained to breaking point, where structural factors work against producer–audience relations.

A key point is that the push-pull dynamics of producers and audiences underscores the particularities of power for media industries and audiences. Coleman urges researchers to think of 'power in performative terms' (2010, 127) in order to understand the contradictions and mediation of cultural performance. Push-pull dynamics highlights what power looks like within the cultural production and reception of television. The argument put forward here is not an overwhelmingly negative one of power relations as one way, flowing from institution, to producer, to audience. Nor is it a reversal where all the power is in people's hands. This is the particularity of power as it is performed in the push and pull of producer–audience relations, showing us a story of the reality of power and the struggle over how producers and audiences make sense of transnational media.

The idea of a push-pull dynamic poses challenges for research that explores production and audience studies. It's a challenge because as previous studies have shown, there are points of connection, disconnection and contradiction between cultural production and engagement (see Mayer et al. 2009). For example in relation to reality television, there are points of connection with the constitution of television, such as commissioning, distribution and marketing, which push audiences towards multi-platform entertainment experiences, from television to second screen, from apps to pop up events. Alongside commissioning decisions, or branding and marketing campaigns, producers craft content that immerses audiences in storytelling. For points of disconnection, poor scheduling can sabotage a reality series, and in the case of global formats there is the added complication of territorial distribution, where different versions of the format may be showing in the same region, hampering the chances of success of an adaptation when the original is already available. And in terms of contradictions, audiences are fickle. A reality television series can engage audiences, but just as easily people disengage. As such, we see how audiences can pull creative content into their viewing routines, making a series part of social rituals in the home, and we see how audiences can push back against broadcast television, turning to other content and streaming services that better suit their own personalised schedules.

Spectrum of engagement

In a similar way, engagement is another means of simultaneously analysing and reflecting on production practices and audience research as integrated, rather than separated, within different fields of research. By focusing on the notion of media engagement we can address industry definitions and refine the dominant ways of thinking about and measuring audiences so that academic theories of attention, interaction and engagement can enhance ways of understanding media engagement in a more holistic fashion. Perhaps more importantly we can address how audiences actually engage with a wide range of media through formal and informal routes, learning more about their multi-faceted ways of engaging with popular culture.

Media engagement is a broad term for research into how we experience media content, artefacts and events, from our experience of live performances, to social media engagement, or participation in media itself. Media engagement explores the dispersed connections across industry contexts, cultural forms, and audience experiences. We want to understand industrial contexts for engagement, including performance metrics, production practices and policy discourses; and we want to understand people's shifting and subjective relations with media as live audiences, catch up viewers, illegal users, as consumers and users, fans and anti-fans, contestants and participants. Media engagement thus encapsulates research on audiences, fans or producer-users, and the ways these different groups co-exist with those making content and driving policy and politics (see Hill and Steemers 2017).

The concept of a spectrum of engagement captures how integral engagement is to transformations in digital media production and audience experiences. It's a term that highlights how audience engagement is changing currency, combining ratings and social media trends with cultural resonance. A spectrum of engagement shows the cognitive and affective work of audience engagement; where engagement is experienced in myriad ways, and extends across an emotional range so that people switch between positive and negative engagement, or disengagement. A spectrum of engagement also works across different contexts, such as time, including fleeting engagement with a live event, or long form engagement with a brand on broadcast schedules; and space, including live venues, distribution and digital spaces, and the spaces of everyday life.

There is a dynamic interplay between producers and audiences about the value and meaning of media engagement, something played out in the contexts of the format industry, distribution and everyday routines. When power is slipping from the constitution of digital television to disparate sites of media content across multi-platform environments, producers risk disrupting an all-important dialogue with audiences. People wish to be treated as intelligent viewers, performing and participating, streaming and binge viewing; in short, people feel they have a right to experience content in their own way. Overall, the research argues for the soft power of audiences who push beyond commercial frames, engaging with culture in ways that complicate, frustrate and outpace traditional media.

Researching media experiences

This book arises from a big picture project that explores what it means to be an audience today in a digital media age. What follows are some reflections on how

FIGURE 1.2 *Bron* is on: launch event for third season at Malmö Live, Sweden
Source: Photograph Tina Askanius.

the project is situated in a qualitative approach to the study of people and popular culture, an approach that is embedded in my own experience as a researcher. Some of the lessons learned from doing this project, and collaborating with industry professionals and other researchers, have enabled me to conceptualise roaming audiences for contemporary mediascapes, thus shaping the arguments in the book overall.

A brief personal reflection on academic industry research helps to frame this book on media production and cultures of viewing. I started out with a small scale study of media violence, which was my doctoral thesis on how and why people liked to watch violent movies. The book *Shocking Entertainment* (1997) was my first foray into audience research and I liked the look and feel of this kind of approach where you listened to people, and learned that respect is a vital part of research. I moved on to work with David Gauntlett on the *TV Living* (1999) book which was based on the British Film Institute's five-year longitudinal mass observation study of television and everyday life. I learned there that big data is not something to be afraid of, as people wrote over three and a half million words in hand written diaries about everything and anything to do with living with television. From that study I became interested in the genre of reality television, which began a long relationship with this tricky entertainment genre. So far, I have written three books that deal with factual and entertainment audiences, including *Reality TV*, and *Restyling Factual TV*, and a key ideas book called *Reality TV* (Routledge 2015), all of which explore a large amount of quantitative and qualitative data with over 15,000 audiences over a 15-year period.

Throughout this period I have made a commitment to work with media industries – the British Film Institute and their mass observation study, Channel 4 on *Big Brother*, ITV and the BBC on reality television; I worked closely with former regulatory bodies the Independent Television Commission and Broadcasting Standards Council, now merged into the Office of Communications, and media industries in other countries, for example public service broadcaster YLE in Finland did a one year study in television and everyday life; or research on *Big Brother* in Finland used parts of my survey with the ITC and BSC on reality television. All of this was important in building the groundwork for production research. The need to conduct production research came from a sense of a knowledge gap on my behalf, a deep interest in audiences, but an ignorance of who made the content for audiences. I met two people then working at Fremantle Media, and we established a team that would explore how to do production and audience research, combining industry and academic perspectives. Douglas Wood and Julie Donovan taught me the value of this combined approach. It took two years of talks, but finally we were able to work together on a project.

The project was called Media Experiences and Rights, and was funded by the Marianne and Marcus Wallenberg Foundation and Lund University. The project team of senior researchers, consultants, and young scholars worked over three years (2013–2016) with the industry partner Endemol Shine, in particular Douglas Wood (Head of Audience Research and Insight), and a formats consultant Julie Donovan, who both offered generous insights and helped shape the project from an industry perspective. The team critically examined media experiences and rights by combining analysis of production and audience perspectives in three key countries: Sweden, Denmark and the UK.

Our cases included a range of drama and reality television, specifically *The Bridge* crime drama format (Filmlance International), *Utopia* cult drama format (Kudos), *MasterChef* reality entertainment format (Shine) and *Got to Dance* reality talent format (Princess). The project used multi-method and multi-site research where each television series was treated as a fit-for-purpose study. We used a range of qualitative interviews, focus groups, participant observations, social media analytics and analysis of scheduling and ratings. In total, there were 108 production interviews with creative and executive producers, actors, performers and below the line workers; 25 days of production observations; 33 interviews with reality television performers; 336 interviews with audiences and fans, and participant observations of live events with crowds of up to 6,000 at venues. Further details about the research can be found in Chapter 2 and in the Appendices.

For a project such as this, it was important to adopt a pragmatic and flexible approach to the research for each of the reality entertainment and drama formats we studied. This approach included participant-orientated and context-dependent methodological routines for the research design and analysis. In particular, the pragmatic sensibilities of looking at cultural practices within situated contexts meant that attention was given to how parts and linkages connect with the whole (Seale et al. 2007: 6). Different types of original qualitative research and existing data were used in the fieldwork, including data collected by marketing teams which is used to consider performance metrics, alongside interviews with executive producers and creatives working on the series. The pragmatic approach of the fieldwork is connected with the analytic strategy of subtle realism adopted throughout the research (Hammersley 1992); subtle realism enabled the building of reflexive knowledge about how media is constructed within certain values and assumptions around audiences. When working on the interviews, participant observations and fieldnotes, there is a depth of analysis that comes through a reflexive way of building, circling and re-analysing the material to build an overall picture. This multilayered analysis enabled an interpretation of the data across the sites of production, circulation, content, event and audiences (see Rose 2016), offering an all-round perspective of producer practices and audience engagement and experience.

To reflect on the research, this is an approach to the study of creative producers and audiences, where agency is given to people and their interpretations of and reflections on their experiences (Hammersley 1992). The aim is not to be critical of the people who took part in our study but to ask critical questions of the subject of the research and the context to their experiences. The research addresses the production context of media experiences as a means to understand the values of media production within the larger framework of socio-cultural values within everyday life (Corner and Roscoe 2016: 162). And the research addresses the reception context as an equally valuable data set to analyse the shaping of media experiences and what audiences do with media in their everyday lives.

A pragmatic means of understanding media experiences involves considering the experience of being within media content, that is to say the experience of watching a television drama in the moment of live viewing, and the experience of reflecting through media content, as this experience becomes embedded in people's daily lives, dreams, and memories (see Frosh 2011). At its core, human experience can be understood as 'a co-performance of a number of different, interactive and evolving individuals, species and processes' (Szersyznski et al. 2004: 3). Applied to the media, people's experiences involve both individual and collective performances that include experiencing within and through the media, often in multiple ways. Audience experiences are therefore defined here as performative and interactive practices, and empirical data, such as interviews, focus groups, or participant observations, can be analysed within the framework of sense and performance. Sense refers to multiple modes of engagement (thinking, sensing, feeling) that make up media experiences; performance refers to individual and collective practices as embedded in social life. Sense and performance is an analytic frame that works both in respect of identity and sense of self (Goffman 1959; Vannini et al. 2013), and affect, emotions and social relations (Hochschild 2003, Stewart 2007).

This tradition of work on media experiences connects with the work by Margaret Wetherell on affective practice. She explains: 'affective practice focuses on the emotional as it appears in social life and tries to follow what participants do. It finds shifting, flexible and often over-determined figurations rather than simple lines of causation, character types and neat emotion categories' (Wetherell 2012: 4). For Wetherell, affective practice includes the meaning of practice as forms of order, habits, expression of emotions and actions, and the meaning of practice as what could be otherwise, thus how we might imagine ways of being, or alternative relations (ibid.). An important aspect of affect and emotion is the attention paid to both individual and social relations, so that these ways of addressing subjective experiences allow us to consider the individual-personal and the collective social affective practices within popular culture.

John Corner (2011) argues that when researching subjectivity it is best to assume less and investigate more. As such, this book offers a quiet manifesto regarding the power of exploratory, qualitative research to say something about the big issue of human experience. The research connects with work by Hesmondhalgh and Baker (2011: 65) and their research on media industries and what constitutes working practices and the aspiration to produce quality television entertainment and drama. In a similar way to their book, the research here has a theoretical and normative underpinning provided by Raymond Williams' notion of the communication of experience as both objective and subjective, where creative producers craft entertainment experiences for audiences, and audiences in turn 'formulate, describe and communicate' their experiences of this creative work (ibid.). As Stuart Hall (1980: 63) notes, Williams' contribution to cultural studies was precisely in the interweaving of social practices in an understanding of culture: this sense of human praxis underlies the interconnections and conflicts around the meanings and values of popular culture in production and reception contexts.

Outline of the book

Chapter 2 deepens the discussion of the introduction to this book by looking at the processes of empirical production and audience research. An analytic dialogue highlights the value of listening and respect (Sennett 2002) in the cultural conversations across creative production–audience practices. In this way, researchers listen to the voices of producers and the values they create alongside the voices of audiences and their experiences. As such, academic researchers become a bridge across the industry–audience divide, humanising audiences so that alongside ratings performance and social media analytics, we get a sense of engagement as cultural resonance. The innovative type of production and audience research for the project enabled an internal understanding of creative values in Endemol Shine production practices; for industry stakeholders, engagement means a variety of connection points in order to capture a spectrum of engagement with cross-media content. The research also highlighted a revaluation of audience engagement and experience with content across a spectrum of platforms, including formal and informal media economies (Lobato and Thomas 2015). From a more theoretical perspective the intense relationship work of the research suggests a new semantics of engagement to understand the cultural resonance of television for future audiences (Hill 2016, 2017).

Chapter 3 addresses how audience research faces a challenge in understanding our fluid experiences with media today. Audiences are often described as fragmented, or nomadic, moving around media in mobile contexts. This chapter argues that people roam around storytelling within cross-media content. Roaming implies people's movements involve a certain degree of planning, or following of existing byways, and tend to involve an anchoring in the tradition of wayfaring, meeting other people roaming the same pathways, and the co-operative endeavour of keeping these pathways open to the public. The activity of roaming is one where people traverse the media landscape, following pathways and becoming pathfinders themselves. Roaming audiences is a metaphor that captures the dynamic practices of audiences as they experience storytelling that takes place across dispersed sites of production, distribution and reception. The chapter uses a geo-cultural approach to audiences, drawing on a qualitative study of transnational drama production and reception for Nordic noir format *The Bridge*. What sort of movements are possible for roaming audiences in contemporary mediascapes? There are affective, temporal and geographical relationships, where people have an emergent sense of right to roam across boundaries. Thus, there is a cultural dynamics of roaming audiences, as people's movements are shaped through media institutions and legal structures, and as it is experienced by audiences in mobile media spaces and across geographic and economic boundaries.

Chapter 4 presents the concept of a spectrum of engagement. When we use the term media engagement it is most often meant in a pragmatic sense as audience attention. My argument is that there is a spectrum of engagement that includes emotional and cognitive modes, switching between positive and negative engagement, to disengagement. Positive engagement typically might include emotional identification, inviting sympathy and empathy, voting for the underdog, or sending encouraging tweets. Negative engagement might involve emotional dis-identification, closing down sympathy, or trash talking on Twitter. These emotional modes often work in tandem, and professionals and performers are fully aware of how to craft both positive and negative emotions even in the same character, thus inviting intense feelings from audiences, fans, consumers and users who emotionally invest in storytelling in popular culture. Disengagement can be sudden, a brusque disconnect with a series, or it can happen gradually, an increasing awareness that the presence of a series in your life is gradually becoming an absence. Disengagement is a means of interpreting how audiences disengage with popular culture on a regular basis, sometimes due to the simple fact there isn't enough time in the day and they need to make room for other content and experiences, but also due to disaffection and even anger with a story, character or entertainment brand. A spectrum of engagement is a concept which addresses engagement as relationships between producers and audiences, formed over time, and something that can be easily broken in the viewing cultures of today. Various chapters in the book explore the dynamics of engagement in relation to emotions, the context of time and space/place, including media distribution and digital spaces, local, national and transnational places, and the spaces of everyday life.

Chapter 5 examines emotional engagement with crime drama. The chapter uses a cultural approach to the issues of genre, affect and emotion, exploring how executive and creative producers, artistic performers, and audiences all perform specific practices that in the end come together in a co-production of intense engagement with this crime drama. The character of Saga Noren in *Bron/Broen* is a rich site of analysis for research on affective structures and emotional engagement, as this female detective struggles with the very notion of emotion in her drive to solve crimes (see Turnbull 2014). From the small details of what sound Saga's footsteps make, to the physical performance of the actress, and the director's understated storytelling, we see the specific practices that make up the overall characterisation, ordinary affects (Stewart 2007) and emotional tone associated with Saga. For the production company, *Bron/Broen* has become Saga's story across four seasons, a character that symbolises relationship dynamics, moral dilemmas, and political and cultural tensions. The way to tell Saga's story did not emerge fully formed, but was the result of collaborative creative and emotional labour. This research on the crafting of affect and emotional engagement is combined with the work of audiences. Many viewers in this study had a love–hate relationship with Saga in the first two seasons because of her lack of empathy. But for season three audiences empathised more with this character's personal struggles, seeing Saga as the emotional hub of the storytelling; viewers reflected on the details of the script, lighting, performance, and music that affected their character engagement. In short, they learned to react to Saga through serial engagement over time.

Chapter 6 explores the practices of illegal viewing. Media industries face the pressing problem of unmeasured digital viewers. The case study of cult television drama series *Utopia* is used to explore the lived reality of the unmeasured audience, analysing formal and informal relations across production and reception practices. *Utopia* attracted underground digital audiences. The drama's dialogue about geopolitics and subversive tactics resonated with those digital viewers who accessed the drama through illegal routes. Rather than picturing the unmeasured audience as one big, immovable problem, we can see the many faces of piracy in the activities of *Utopia* fans. We may consider these fans as self-informing media citizens, consumer choice advocates, de-centralised media sharers, and activists. They see themselves as intensely engaged fans who like being treated as intelligent viewers and who want to watch drama in their own way, streaming and binge viewing without commercial breaks or subscription payments.

Chapter 7 considers a form of embedded engagement where people form relationships with drama or reality entertainment over time, and in the context of their everyday lives year on year. The case of reality talent shows is used to explore the value and meaning of the live events as a temporary experience, and the more enduring collective-social experience of the series. There is a strategic privileging of the temporary over the durable experience of live reality events for media industries, in the form of performance metrics such as ratings and social media. The performance metrics for live television signal the primacy of the now; this flow of power to the live shows and the constitution of television obscures the sense of community and viewer agency that is built up over time through the embedding of these series in everyday routines. There is a power chronology at work in the temporal relations between television itself and audiences.

Chapter 8 offers an analyisis of audience engagement with *MasterChef* as authentic reality television. When audiences engage with what they perceive to be authentic reality television they are signalling a culture of viewing that embraces positive values, the pro-social side of reality television as enriching their lives in someway, somehow. This is a form of engagement that runs counter to what they routinely describe as the negative, commercial world of reality television with its tendency towards what they call 'emotional porn'. This specific cooking talent show uses the imaginative spaces of storytelling to reflect and engage with food culture, to explore healthy eating, self-identity, and professional work ethics. Indeed, the significance of audience engagement with authentic reality television highlights what happens beyond engagement, as we find people connecting their reactions to and reflections on reality television with their everyday lives and the habits and values of food in their lived experiences.

Chapter 9 addresses an unusual aspect of live entertainment by focusing on the way warm up acts shape an affective climate for live experiences. Warm up acts and comedians offer a craft of live audience management that is hard won through years of creative and precarious labour practices (in theatre, comedy television, and leisure industries), and yet they are invisible in television production and academic research. Warm up acts are an absent presence in television industries. This chapter thinks through the paradox of the high recognition of warm up acts by crowds at live events and at the same time their hidden work in the production industry and on screen. Recognition of creative value is fleeting at best; the actual value of the warm up act and their relationship with live audiences is lost in industry's obsession with celebrity stardom. But the warm up performer is someone who creates a meaningful connection with audiences and understands the value of cultural experience in entertainment television. The warm up act shines a light on the cruel optimism of recognition and stardom in the creative industries.

Chapter 10 reflects on the pathways and tracks of audiences, with trends in multi-screening, streaming and snacking on content; the downloading and sharing of illegal television within informal media economies; and a sense of the right to roam across storytelling and geographical and temporal barriers, highlighting the myriad ways people engage with screen cultures today. However, the speed and variety of screen culture also leads to counter-practices, such as anti-streaming television, local viewing cultures, and old school television – the ritual of watching and enjoying live television with others. Here then, the future of audiences is set within a strong hold on the past and a nostalgia for social ritual viewing. The movements of roaming audiences tell us something about mobility and stillness, about the constitution of audiences in mediated spaces and in the physical places of homes, public settings and live venues, and this tells us about the importance of storytelling to digital media and how this is a profoundly social experience.

2
AN ANALYTIC DIALOGUE

> To peel back the layers of audience engagement beyond the traditional boundaries reveals a universe that is rarely explored or reported.
> *(Douglas Wood, Director of Research and Audience Insight, Endemol Shine)*

This chapter offers a reflection on the value of dialogue across media industries and academia in enhancing understanding of audience engagement and disengagement with screen culture. The basis for this reflection is an industry-academic collaborative project between Lund University and Endemol Shine. The Media Experiences project conducted production and audience research on a range of drama and entertainment during a three-year period in several countries, primarily Sweden, Denmark and the UK, with smaller offshoot studies in Japan, Colombia, USA, and Mexico, and one case study which included transnational audiences from around the world (2014–2016).

The project was designed to look at the connections across media industries and creative production, genre, and audiences. It builds on an innovative approach where production research intertwines with the crafting of genre and aesthetics within particular texts and live events, and crosses over into audience research that explores people and their experiences of these genres, texts and events. This way of conducting multi-site and multi-method research is a means of taking seriously production values for creative content, such as the various ways people craft sonic and visualscapes, use costume design and locations to enrich symbolic meaning, or edit a drama to generate an affective climate; and it is a means of taking seriously everyday lives, such as the various ways people engage with these texts, and embed their engagement with entertainment into the fabric of their lives. There are many studies that offer rich empirical and theoretical analysis of production, or genre and aesthetics, or audiences, but few studies that offer an all-round picture of production, genre and text, and cultures of viewing – one example is Bolin and Forsman's (2002) holistic study of *Bingolotto* as national television entertainment.

16 An analytic dialogue

FIGURE 2.1 On location of *Bron/Broen* season three
Source: Photograph Tina Askanius.

This approach of a dialogue highlights the value of listening and respect (Sennett 2002) across creative production and audience practices. The researchers on the project listened to the voices of producers and the values they created alongside the voices of audiences and their experiences. As such, we became a bridge across the industry–audience divide, humanising audiences so that alongside ratings performance and social media analytics, producers could get a sense of engagement as cultural resonance (see Chapter 4). From a more theoretical perspective, the intense relationship work of the research suggests a new semantics of engagement to understand the cultural resonance of television for future audiences (Hill 2017). For industry stakeholders, an engagement portfolio has several connection points with audiences in order to capture the interplay between varieties of audiences and publics, users and consumers, fans and participants, and their spectrum of engagement with cross-media content.

The Media Experiences project

The Media Experiences project conducted production and audience research on a range of television content. The project team included: Professor Annette Hill; Julie Donovan, a creative content consultant with twenty years' experience working in the media industry and interests in the international formats business; Dr Tina Askanius, a Danish-Swedish media researcher with interests in social media;

FIGURE 2.2 On the set of *MasterChef Denmark*
Source: Photograph Tina Askanius.

Dr Koko Kondo, a Japanese-British audience researcher with expertise in qualitative research; and Jose Luis Urueta, a Colombian-Swedish researcher with a passion for audience research. We worked closely with Douglas Wood, Director of Research and Audience Insight, Endemol Shine.

Endemol Shine Group is a producer and distributor of factual and entertainment content, including reality entertainment formats such as *Big Brother* and *MasterChef*, drama formats such as *Broadchurch*, *The Bridge* and *Utopia*, and entertainment brands such as *Mr Bean*. According to its website,

> Endemol Shine Group works on a unique local and global axis, comprised of 120 companies across all the world's major markets, dedicated to creating content that enthralls and inspires … In 2017 Endemol Shine Group produced more than 800 productions, in 78 territories airing on more than 275 channels around the world.
>
> *(Endemol Shine 2018)*

Shine was our partner in the project from the start, and the case studies of *Got to Dance*, *MasterChef*, *The Bridge* and *Utopia* were selected from the Shine portfolio of content, alongside local production companies who were interested in working with an academic project. Douglas Wood was head of audience research at Shine. After the merger of Shine with Endemol in 2015, Wood went on to head up a

Research and Audience Insight group in the newly merged company; the continuity of the relations across the industry and academic partners was crucial to the way cultural conversations arose within the research.

The case studies were chosen on the basis of casting audiences for the project. Early on in the design of the project a short document was produced for the industry partner on the aims of the research, access to information, local production companies, industry ratings and social media analytics data, and so forth, as well as the potential outcomes, including industry workshops, internal reports, and academic conferences and publications. Certain formats were identified as of particular relevance to the project. The *MasterChef* format offered the possibility of researching entertainment audiences at home, a typical show for family viewing; the global format also offered transregional audience research for Northern Europe. The *Got to Dance* format offered the possibility of both participants in a reality talent competition, live audiences and crowds at televised events, and audiences at home reacting, interacting and voting; in this case several performances of audiences and participants would be observed in one show, in particular the live experience for an entertainment event. *The Bridge* format offered drama audiences in different regions, a transregional audience for original drama and adaptations of drama for public service and commercial broadcasters. *Utopia* offered cult drama audiences, in particular transnational audiences for the drama accessing it both through formal media economies by the national broadcaster, and informal media economies by streaming the drama and watching online. In all, the range of audiences included reality entertainment audiences at home, reality talent show participants, entertainment events and live audiences and fans, crime drama audiences and fans in transregional viewing cultures, and conspiracy drama audiences and fans in transnational online cultures of viewing.

In this project, we asked a simple question: 'How do creative producers craft content for audiences and how do audiences actually engage with this content?' We used qualitative, flexible research to explore this question across production practices and cultures of viewing. The research analysed drama and entertainment formats within particular production companies, including *The Bridge* (Filmlance International and Nimbus Film), *Utopia* (Kudos), *MasterChef* (Shine), and *Got to Dance* (Princess), and across Endemol Shine global audience research trends; and the findings allowed us to unpack the idea of audience engagement and experience and of how different meanings of this idea can be of value across academic and industry research.

Project design

The project used multi-method and multi-site research where each television series was treated as a fit-for-purpose study. We used a range of qualitative interviews, focus groups, participant observations, social media analytics and analysis of scheduling and ratings. In total, there were 108 production interviews with creative and executive producers; 25 days of production observations; 33 interviews with reality

TV participants/performers; and 336 interviews with audiences and fans. Please see the Appendices for full information about each case that was designed as a fit-for-purpose study.

In brief, the production interviews included executive producers, line producers, actors and performers, to below-the-line workers, and participants, including contestants and family/friends supporters. This production research has been analysed using qualitative data analysis, where the descriptive and analytical codes have been situated within the site of the research, for example the specifics of being a line manager on a reality entertainment series, or the experience of being in the auditions, reflections on fair treatment, the production staff, the judges, and so forth.

Several internal workshops with production staff were conducted with each case study. An internal report was written and circulated to each relevant production company, and Douglas Wood at Endemol Shine, in advance of the workshops (see Hill and Askanius 2015). Producers' feedback on the industry reports was generated from the research, alongside feedback from audiences to the producers. For example, when asked what they wanted to say to producers of *MasterChef Denmark*, audiences resoundingly agreed that they valued the series as 'friendly TV', but that they were experiencing format fatigue and wanted more focus on food rather than competition; above all viewers highly valued the respect given to participants by the judges and producers: 'Of course you can tell that some people are better than others but at no point do they expose these people or belittle them' (48 year old Danish male IT consultant). In such a way we carried through the idea of a dialogue across the production context into the spaces of audiences and their cultures of viewing, exchanging information, opinions and critical reflections.

We also made available some of the reports to audiences. For example, the *Utopia* report was circulated to participants of the study and made available as a free PDF download (see https://mediaexperiences.blogg.lu.se/). Comments on this report by the writer, composer, director and actors of *Utopia* were shared with the producers at Kudos and audiences for this drama, creating a space for the voices of creative producers, and audiences and fans, to be heard and recognised by each other. Take this comment on the industry report for *Utopia* by the actor Alistor Petrie (2015):

> I was in shock after reading this report. To see the analysis of the drama and responses from the fans is terribly humbling and endorses my sense of privilege of being a part of this unique drama. The relationship between *Utopia* and its fans is special, long term and a wonderful alchemy. *Utopia* invites its audiences to look hard at themselves and the world around them; and they do this in a way that is curious, sometimes surreal, often emotional but also with humour. The fans have taken ownership of it in the best way, embracing the drama and continuing its legacy. Perhaps its greatest pay off is that people talk of *Utopia* in the present tense when they discuss it. Fans say '*Utopia* is this or that' not 'was this or that'. On it lives as well as the questions it asks.

We can see in his comment the recognition of the value of fans and a respect for their sense of ownership of this series.

To briefly look at the audience research, the samples involved self-defined viewers and fans for different genres in different countries (see Appendices for the socio-demographics of each sample). The research took place in a combination of individual hour-long interviews, focus groups, short interviews at a launch event, exploratory interviews at fan events, and participant observations of viewing for at-home audiences. Most of these interviews took place face to face, in coffee shops, offices and homes, with a few occurring via the telephone or Skype. Face to face interviews were a priority in the research in order to understand viewing cultures in context, including attending fan events, showing clips from the series in interviews, playing music, and watching episodes in people's homes.

The team took part in different participant observations, depending on the case studies, taking notes, keeping diaries, and taking photographs and short videos as visual aids for the analysis of the data – these photographs are used in the book as illustrations of the sites of research and case studies. Members of the team discussed the participant observations in several periods of reflection during and after each production day was over. This continual reflection and analysis of the ongoing fieldwork allowed for flexibility in the data design, as each day the participant observations would be attuned to the production environment, and if relevant the different kinds of participants at the live venues. For example, in relation to the live shows of *Got to Dance*, participant observations involved shifting attention to the backstage rehearsal space for the dance groups alongside the spaces for friends and family which were semi-backstage, and the main venue for audiences. Production practices for the participants, family supporters and crowd management worked across these production and reception zones. Such observations supported the theory building and analysis of the care structures within the production of a live reality event (see Hill et al. 2018).

All interviews were transcribed and analysed using qualitative data analysis, where descriptive and analytical coding was combined with critical reflection of interviews in the context of fieldnotes and participant observations (Seale 1999). This multilayered analysis enabled an interpretation of the data across the sites of production, live and catch up viewing and audiences' reflections on their experiences. For example, the theme of emotional engagement in the data on *The Bridge* emerged in the pilot research and the design of the fieldwork, and in the initial data analysis, drawing patterns across the interviews on responses to key characters and linking this theme with the concept of engagement, where deeper analysis suggested that the cognitive and affective work of audience engagement with the characters related to the crafting of affective structures related to performance style, directing, editing and sound design within the drama and the audience's emotional identification with Saga. This data analysis allowed for a more theoretically informed argument about emotional engagement and genre work that features in Chapter 5.

A note on formats

All of the case studies in this project are global formats, including drama and reality entertainment genres. The formats chosen for this project address what Albert Moran and Karen Aveyard (2014) call the 'geo-cultural paradox' of international formats. This paradox refers to the inherent contradictions in the quintessential 'go anywhere' value of a global format that works alongside an appeal to local audiences. Moran and Aveyard (2014: 20) call on researchers to 'explore the characteristics of these multi-layered geographic interrelationships'. Some of the cases in this book address the geo-cultural paradox and aim to understand how television format producers attempt to engage both local and transnational audiences; see for example *The Bridge* or *MasterChef*. Interviews with executive producers connect with research on the pressures of global television formats to perform in a high risk business (see Oren and Shahaf 2011, among others), or industry trends in multi-platform content for diverse audiences and users (see Holt and Sanson 2014). The research indicates the tensions surrounding adaptations of drama and reality entertainment in different cultures and regions.

For example, the original *Bron/Broen* as a Danish–Swedish drama and the adaptation of *The Bridge* as an American–Mexican drama highlight the different values and ratings success of the format in public service and commercial environments. *The Bridge* is uniquely positioned for a critical analysis of the geo-cultural paradox of international television formats. The 'go anywhere' value of a global format means a television drama risks being any place and no place at the same time. Producers of *The Bridge* strategically use the specificity of place by embedding the storytelling in geo-cultural politics. In this way, producers attempt to engage local/ transnational audiences through a sense of place that works in various ways, for example through distinctive landscape and locality, or genre, characters and emotions, that grabs viewers and keeps them in the here and now of specific stories.

But, there is no clear-cut path to the ways producers of *The Bridge* construct a sense of place as a mode of address and the various ways audiences engage with this drama format. A problem that arises from the empirical research is the ambiguity of contemporary drama formats. Is *The Bridge* a drama format, an adaptation, or an original production? It is all of these things, and yet runs the risk of being neither one thing nor the other with audiences. This ambiguity creates problems for a format with a go anywhere quality. Although the specificity of place is one way for the format trade to overcome a geo-cultural paradox, it can backfire with audiences. For example, the international success of the original version of the drama format *Bron/Broen* as part of the contemporary wave of Nordic noir (see Waade and Jensen 2013) was not replicated in the American–Mexican adaptation. *The Bridge* (FX 2013–2014) had a schizophrenic identity as a drama that was trying to be both a format with global appeal and a local adaptation with regional appeal, and was cancelled after its second season. The reasons for the success and failure of original drama and adaptations highlight the entangled relations between the production and reception of *The Bridge* and the complex notion of place within our understanding of global formats. There is a balancing act between a sense of place as a reason to engage international audiences – a British curiosity about Scandinavian culture for example – and a sense of place as a source of pleasure for local audiences. A global drama format treads a fine line between a successful original production and an adaptation that struggles to find a secure place and audience following in contemporary media.

In another example, the production of reality entertainment format *MasterChef* in Britain, Denmark and Sweden involves three different broadcasters for the format, and three models: public service media (BBC in the UK), hybrid public service and commercial media (TV4 in Sweden), and commercial media (TV3 in Denmark). These three broadcasters are quite different in terms of their values and strategies, and the influence of television itself on the local productions and audience engagement can be seen in the research (discussed in Chapter 8). Across the research on this format, we find intra-regional audiences for the Scandinavian series, a national audience for the British series, and transnational audiences for the various versions of the global format, such as the American or Australian series, also shown in Scandinavia and Britain. The different audiences for the local versions of the format share similar ways of engaging with this food talent show as authentic, signalling a wider counter-trend in the reality genre for pro-social television that goes against the grain of most commercial shows. Yet audiences also relate to the local versions as best reflecting the distinctive nature of their food culture, underlining the significance of place in a local audience's engagement with what it perceives as authentic; this is not a universal sense of authenticity but something that speaks to local experiences.

This supports the way successful global formats are 'made to measure' for local audiences (Hill and Steemers 2011). The format is owned by Endemol Shine, but some latitude is given to local production companies in how they adapt the format for their regional audiences. What we see in action is the geo-cultural paradox that Moran and Aveyard (2014: 19) note as so distinctive to formats: 'On the one hand television formats are highly transferable, and on the other hand these formats possess specific qualities that appeal to particular audiences.' The research in Chapter 8 shows how food talent formats can have a go anywhere quality, and create a sense of locality and regional specificity for what are perceived to be authentic food cultures.

Values of a production and audience study

The idea of an analytic dialogue across production and audience studies came about through discussing the value of qualitative audience research. Initial conversations took place during project meetings and were expanded to include industry speakers at academic symposia; these included international symposia on media producers and audiences, media engagement and experiences, media and passion, and media and transgression, which took place over the course of the project. From the panels, keynotes and discussions, ideas emerged for ways of conducting academic

FIGURE 2.3 At the offices of Filmlance
Source: Photograph Tina Askanius.

and industry research. One of the key issues to emerge on engagement, for example, was how industry research on engagement is as a measurement of interest and a performance metric for creative values in the television industry; whereas academic qualitative research on engagement approaches this as shifting subjective positions by fickle audiences for television, social media and pirated content. It is critical to the future of audience research across industry and academic settings that we find useful ways of researching engagement that capture both performance metrics and the relationships between people and media content. As Uno Forsberg (2015), Head of Analysis and Research at EndemolShine Nordics, notes: 'In statistical research you can provide quite sophisticated and fancy answers to who?, how much?, when? and nowadays even how?, but the most important question of them all still might be why?'

The notion of a dialogue has been addressed in public service media and public engagement. Public service media are adapting to contemporary media eco-systems by rethinking production practices and audience engagement. This raises implications of the constraints on voice for the values of public service media, such as accountability and governance. The understanding of 'voice' offered by broadcast and new media firms is controlled and filtered; there is little involvement or public participation in the design of new public service platforms and services, the development of media policy, or in citizen and audience engagement. Apart from an improved complaints procedure there have been few opportunities for exploring innovative facilitation of the public voice. For example, research on Estonian public service media suggests that producers working in legacy media tend to foreground old paradigms, one of which is a low level of reciprocity or engagement between producers and audiences (Nani 2018). For Lizzie Jackson (2013) and her research on producer and audience interactions, one way forward is to include the public in the design of new services that incorporate digital media user-centred design practices. There is a potential for greater dialogue between creative producers and publics in shaping the future of public service media.

The focus on dialogue came about because of a difficulty early on in the research collaboration, where I was having trouble explaining the project to various local producers within the parent company. The biggest obstacle to overcome was the absence of qualitative research as a regular part of the organisation. Priority was given to audience engagement as a quantitative measurement of interest, with performance metrics for ratings and social media, and internal surveys for specific series. My first problem was that creative producers were unfamiliar with academic qualitative audience research, and I lacked the language necessary to make this work seem accessible to professionals within the media industries. I recall the moment when the approach started to take shape, whilst talking to Julie Donovan, the industry consultant on the project. I was on a call whilst walking in the Swedish winter forest in Ydre; I had climbed to a hotspot to get a 3G signal and had listened to Julie tell me that I needed to change my language if I wanted to be heard; in essence she encouraged me to listen more. Retracing my route through this white and silent landscape, I realised that at its core the research project was about listening, really listening closely to producers and the values they create in their work, and then listening closely to audiences and their actual engagement with this content. To start with a cultural conversation, then, is to begin with the basic approach of listening and having respect for creative production and cultures of viewing. Our role in the project was to be the bridge between the two, analysing where dialogue flows, or breaks down, when producers are listening to audiences and when audiences feel ignored, or sense a disconnection. In essence, our role was to humanise the audience for creative producers. The approach of an analytic dialogue is a means to explore and critically analyse the meaning of audience engagement in different settings, across media industries and everyday life, that can widen our horizon of understanding of engagement and experience.

As Jane Roscoe (Hill et al. 2017: 3) notes: 'there are often different languages and value systems at play, such as pragmatism in the industry and creative explorations in academia'. Academic research can identify some of the gaps and some of those shared moments where we can expand and explore engagement further. The value of the research for Endemol Shine was explained by Douglas Wood (Hill et al. 2017: 2):

> In the commercial world you rarely have the opportunity to do this type of research, typically in our research you go in with a problem that needs to be answered – 'why isn't this storyline working?' We would never analyse the

creative process itself: it's alien to us. So, it was fortunate to have a third party come in and explore this process of talking to creatives and audiences. It was a unique opportunity to understand what we do internally and how that relates to our audiences, and to think about the future of those audiences and where they may be in five or ten years' time.

Someone we worked closely with in maintaining relations across industry and academia was Julie Donovan. She noted (Hill et al. 2017: 3):

> The conversation from the academic perspective was to listen more and ask less questions, 'We are looking into this, and how do we find it?' There is a different language. If you are going to maintain relationships across academic and industry sectors, then you have to make sure the conversation is dynamic and fluid.

The feedback we received from the producers supports this perspective of the value of dialogue for stakeholders in commercial and public service media sectors. Here is a range of comments on the collaborative work:

> You are the person in the whole machine who has the most contact between the producer and the audience. We need you … It is really hard to know what signals you communicate to the audience. People might love Saga but there are so many details within that. This goes beyond *Bron*, what is it in storytelling that moves us?
>
> *(Patrick Austen, editor of* Broen/Bron*)*

> It is so nice to have everything that you think and hope that you are doing right actually confirmed. It is exactly what you want to hear. All the ideas we have, that we fight over, we are right! And the viewers actually get it. It is so nice to get this, rather than statistics where you are told your viewer is a 47 year old woman from Jutland. This is really really, really helpful.
>
> *(Thomas Velling, Series Producer,* MasterChef Denmark*)*

From my perspective, relationship management is central. At each step in the process our relationships with the creatives, within the team, and with audiences were a constant presence. As such, I began to understand that engagement within the industry is about the meaning of the term as relationships, the collaborative experiences of creatives working together to produce a drama for example, and our relationships with these writers, directors, or actors and extras. Then, I also slowly understood the tensions surrounding the relationships between the creatives and the executive producers and broadcasters, ones based on trust, but where trust can be broken by decisions from on high about marketing or scheduling. And finally this kind of engagement within the industry connects with audiences, fans, and consumers, as the relationships across production and reception contexts make or break the overall success of a show.

The project highlighted how there is a re-evaluation of the meaning of engagement. According to Wood (Hill et al. 2017: 3):

> We are moving away from a single currency of engagement ... we are in a situation where engagement may mean a very different set of criteria depending on how you judge success. Faced with this audience fragmentation, as producers we are increasingly being asked for platform defining content, something that is unique, something that will find a voice and have cultural impact.

Drawing from this, I explored within the empirical research the meaning of engagement as relationships, looking to capture the subjective positions of varieties of people, such as producers creating content that engages us, professionals promoting and marketing content for mass and niche audiences, and fans as producers and users.

The playoff between engagement as performance metric and cultural resonance is a sign of the tensions around the very meaning of the term 'engagement' within media industries. If we see engagement as a performance indicator for economic targets then this is a one-dimensional understanding of the term. The television industry has dominated the definition of engagement as economic targets, and it is time we changed the conversation to include the socio-cultural value of engagement as well. Creative producers experience the tensions between these kinds of targets all the time. There is the cultural value of their work, which they know and understand – it's a language of emotion and storytelling and aesthetics – and then there is the economic value placed by the industry on their work, which is communicated by ratings in a way that is often hard to understand.

Take for example, global drama format *The Bridge*. As Uno Forsberg (2015), Head of Analysis and Research at EndemolShine Nordics, noted:

> We all know that *Bron* is a unique product in our portfolio. We can easily count the number of territories it has been sold to, the ever increasing ratings and even the amount of articles written about it. But, why this particular production and not any of the others? How is this product's unique DNA composed? How is a monster created? That's what you're really after.

Thus, engagement as cultural resonance unpacks the why within the success of a show, offering an analysis of the unique DNA within a drama format. For the production team, the kind of academic research that we have done underscores the significance of creative values in drama, supporting all those decisions and budget lines that put creativity and quality at the heart of the production. Lars Blomgren (2015, Executive Producer, Filmlance) reflected on the research reports and workshops we conducted throughout the project: 'What is so important about this report is that it strengthens our belief in quality drama, and justifies the working method within Filmlance to maintain quality at all costs.' Producer Anders Landström (2014) echoed this point about quality drama, where all the 'hard decisions and choices we have made during all seasons really makes a difference and that our audience both appreciates and notices even the smallest of details'.

In another example, on the cookery format *MasterChef* we found local audiences loved home grown versions of the series. So in Denmark, *MasterChef* follows the brand and the building blocks of the competitive cooking show, but what audiences valued most about this local variation was its focus on Danish food and the national habit of using all the scraps. People talked a lot about how the show was relevant to them because it symbolised a down-to-earth approach to food in family life. We spoke with the production team about this kind of engagement as embedded in families' everyday lives. For viewers, food comes first and the competition second. On the value of food, a crucial issue is that the programme promotes 'decent and honest food' (30 year old Danish male, self employed). This woman explained: 'the food is the most important part to me … It is not what kinds of funny things are said along the way, it's the result on the plate you could say' (45 year old Danish female secretary). This attention to honest food gives the home grown brand a strong cultural resonance with Danish viewers. A father explained:

> Food means a lot to me. It really does. It has to be proper food and by that I mean good ingredients. It doesn't have to be gourmet or fine dining but it has to be honest food. And that means something to me because I know that everything we put in our mouths matters. If you put diesel in a car running on gas that doesn't work either. It needs to be suitable for us humans. I just had a boy and I think a lot about what he eats. Food is what sows the seeds for everything we do and become. That's what it means to me.
>
> *(48 year old Danish male IT consultant)*

One food blogger reflected on how a series like this can be part of a collective dialogue about the economic crisis:

> I think when the crisis started this *do it yourself* trend emerged. We realise we could go back to home cooking and save money … There has been a shift in focus from quantity to quality … and in the process I think people realised just how delicious it is, how cool real, home cooked, authentic food can be.
>
> *(30 year old Danish male musician)*

All of this was in stark contrast to the celebrity version of the format, which people felt was overly commercial and not honest at all. They told producers: 'Do not underestimate us!' – a rallying cry for a more inclusive and participatory approach to creative production and reception.

The significance of engagement as about both economic and socio-cultural values is never clearer than the case of the cult drama *Utopia*. Channel 4 took a risk with this experimental drama, knowing it would appeal to niche audiences. It marketed the drama in such inventive ways, pulling in a cult audience that would come to that channel for unique drama like this. The broadcaster also knew that many of its viewers would watch the drama on catch up and it made the series available for free over a long period of time to allow for binge watching and catch up audiences. All of this would suggest the broadcaster understood the relevance and impact of this series for niche audiences of cult drama in the UK. And yet the numbers did not add up. The drama was too cult for national audiences. In our research on *Utopia* we found the drama had global appeal, with a long tail of really engaged audiences around the world. *Utopia* is popular in countries like Chile or Russia for example, where they are watching the drama illegally, an invisible audience, and yet we can say they are intensely engaged, and from an industry perspective the drama had very high cultural resonance. There is a paradox here, where the new currency of engagement includes cultural resonance and yet the measurement systems are out of step with this development. The recently announced adaptation of this series for Amazon Prime, with showrunner Gillian Flynn, suggests that streaming services are more than aware of the significance of unique drama that has long lasting cultural resonance not only in one region, but for transnational audiences and VIP subscribers.

Reflections

The type of research exemplified by an analytic dialogue across creative production and cultures of viewing aims to make an intervention in media industries so that we open up the language of engagement to include socio-cultural as well as economic values. Engagement is more than capturing the attention of audiences, it is making a connection, and in some cases making a real difference to people's lives. We have studied drama where producers have wanted to make that connection with audiences and felt they failed because of low ratings. We were able to show producers that not only did they make a connection but their work had a lasting impact on audiences, in their daily lives, memories, and dreams. What is the value of dreams? This is what academics can offer industries in the new currencies of engagement.

According to John Corner (2017: 3), 'around each media product a variety of levels of engagement/involvement will be generated across audiences who bother to attend at all, ranging from intensive commitment through a cool willingness to be temporarily distracted right through to vigorous dislike'. This spectrum of engagement can be charted back in time to a series of decisions made at the planning and production phase, the distribution flow, branding and promotions, through to the actual moment of engagement, something 'realised' in the relationships generated across the range of audiences engaging with screen culture (ibid.). Corner (2017: 4) calls this an engagement profile, where producers can '*anticipate* the likely profile of a product – the cultural take-up across different platforms and demographic groups with its consequences for product success and future product development'; this is a means of 'second-guessing the "engagements to come" as it were, using a variety of predictive resources, including the record of past success and failure'.

Corner's point about the relationships between media producers, products and audiences is pivotal. This way of researching engagement sees the interface between media structures, content and processes, as difficult to identify and research but significant to our sense of the media producer–audience relationship. In particular, the role of academic research can be to creatively explore engagement in a variety of forms. Indeed, by considering the value of media for both creative producers and audiences, the research can be a form of public engagement, where we as academics can add cultural and social value to the existing forms of ratings and social media analytics. By opening up the meaning of audience engagement and experience we can glimpse how the media add value to our lives. Corner (2017: 5) describes this kind of engagement as a resource for living, a means to improve the conditions for social and cultural equality. Here then, moving beyond conventional forms of engagement can highlight the long view of engagement as a cultural resource for lived experiences.

3

ROAMING AUDIENCES

The Bridge

> It's a feeling of belonging, suddenly you're at home in the story.
> *(51 year old Swedish female office manager)*

Audience research faces a challenge in understanding our fluid experiences with media today. Audiences are often described as nomadic, moving around media in mobile contexts. Silverstone refers to nomadic audiences and asks 'what sort of movements become possible?' (1999: 8). Similarly, Athique (2016) researches transnational audiences, noting how audiences wander anywhere and everywhere, but in doing so they risk becoming placeless. My argument is that rather than see audiences as nomadic, I want to suggest that people roam around storytelling within cross-media content. A key question to ask is what sort of movements become possible for roaming audiences in contemporary mediascapes? To answer this wide-ranging question I am going to explore qualitative audience research for transnational crime drama *The Bridge* to highlight the practices of roaming audiences. The ways in which audiences experience storytelling for this television drama tells us something about the cultural work of audiences as a 'spatial and mobile process' (Chambers 2016: 11).

As discussed in Chapter 1, the metaphor of roaming audiences suggests that people take different pathways and tracks through the media landscape. Some of these pathways are made by television itself, including broadcasters, social media, marketing and so forth; and some of these pathways are made by audiences, as fans and producers of content, for example. I prefer to see audiences not as static entities, or malleable masses, but as pathmakers (Macfarlane 2012: 17). Here, we see a sense of roaming audiences where people have agency as they navigate their way through television and its storytelling across different media (the TV, iPad, laptop, mobile phone, books, radio, newspapers), different places (home, work, trains, buses and planes, public and private spaces), and different times (live, catch up,

FIGURE 3.1 Right to roam: the Heather Scarecrow Festival
Source: Photograph Ian Calcutt.

across seasons, binge viewing, illegal viewing, and part of everyday routines). As I noted at the start of this book, the nature writer Robert Macfarlane argues that 'people understand themselves through landscape' (2012: 26), creating what he calls a topography of the self, where we move around, shape and produce a social imaginary. 'Roaming audiences' is a term that helps us glimpse how people understand themselves through mediascapes, a narrativising of the self and a sense of belonging that is experienced through television as storytelling and social ritual.

The kinds of movements that audiences make are restricted; people are not free to roam no matter how much this romantic image appeals to us. There are commercial constraints, censorship, surveillance tracking of audiences and users by algorithms, geoblocking for content restricted to regional audiences, signalling a range of political economic, legal and ethical issues around access, content and comments. Nevertheless, audiences push against these constraints, for example through illegal streaming or using getarounds for geoblocking, and they pull content into their everyday lives, choosing a particular drama series, for example, as a favourite narrative to watch with friends and family in a shared social ritual. Thus audiences are pathmakers, roaming around storytelling as viewers, users and producers. Their movements suggest a right to roam. These are rights of way determined and sustained by use, referencing the old ways of footpaths imagined as worldly, open to all (Macfarlane 2012). A right to roam thus evokes a sense of television storytelling as worldly, and if we watch and share content, or remix stories into new narratives, then we help to shape a shared collective experience that is determined and sustained by use. The case of *The Bridge* is used to think through audiences' affective, geographical and temporal relationships with television. 'Roaming audiences', then, tells a story that is played out in mobile media spaces and across geographical and economic boundaries.

Imagining audiences

'Roaming audiences' is a creative way of thinking about television audiences that can help us understand the duality of the material object of the television and screen devices drawing audiences to one place and timeframe, and the symbolic power of television to move people through images and sounds. A metaphor transfers meaning from one thing to another; the TV billboard connects the meaning of television as a technology and the way it is a commercial space designed to sell us something. A metonymn is a word that is a substitute for something with which it is closely associated: 'gogglebox' describes the quality of looking at a box-shaped object that we associate with television and its economy of attention. As we can see, these are value-laden metaphors or metonyms for television experiences. We want to shift the meaning of television audiences by using a different metaphor that helps to differentiate the geography of audiences, and their experience of screen culture in a particular place and time, with the imaginative world of storytelling within television and related media content.

Metaphors for audiences can be found in histories and theories of television experiences. In *Armchair Nation* (2013) Joe Moran notes how early adopters of television sets in 1930s Britain would invite family and friends to watch television as a social activity; one farmer, for example, invested in a television and found over a hundred locals flocking to his home to watch their favourite programmes, some settling in the house, others watching through the window. The metaphor of the electronic neighbourhood is apt for this 1930s English farmer (see Buonanno 2006). Some American accounts of television picture it as a billboard, highway, or shopping mall. For example, Lawrence Grossberg (1987: 31) described television's affective economy as a 'billboard to be driven past' on the freeway. Margaret Morse (1990) also described television as a freeway, with audiences driving through urban settings and yet dislocated from this experience. Inspired by Raymond Williams' idea of mobile privatisation, which is a means of describing the industrial development of television, Morse depicts the television experience as 'mobile subjectivity' (1990: 26, 202) which is suggestive of television symbolising an illusion of freedom in consumer culture.

Another metaphor for audiences is that of the nomad. Joshua Meyrowitz in *No Sense of Place* (1985) looked at the changing social and political landscape of 1980s America, a time of Reaganist politics and the neo-liberal project of privatisation and individualisation. Briefly, neo-liberalism is connected to an entrepreneur culture that focuses on economics and deregulation of the finance sector, and a politics of the individual rather than society. Meyrowitz argued that Americans had a changing sense of place. The pun was intentional: 'sense' referred to 'both perception and logic' and 'place' referred to 'social position and physical location' (1985: 308). He saw television and electronic media as having a 'tremendous impact on Americans' sense of place': an evolution in media had 'changed the logic of the social order by restructuring the relationship between the physical place and social place and by altering the ways we transmit and receive social information' (ibid.). 'Nomadic' audiences gather information to consume immediately without reflection on other knowledge or ideas; there is little attention given to distinct social spheres or physical settings: in short 'our culture is becoming essentially placeless' (1985: 317).

This metaphor of nomadic audiences being placeless, or homeless, has been the subject of much debate. Buonanno argues against this criticism of the de-localisation of social life; they suggest television is about 'seeing far' and 'going far' (2006: 17), both symbolic and imaginary departures, travels and arrivals, taking place in the 'dislocative character of the televisual experience' (2006: 29). They explain:

> Watching television also resembles an experience of displacement, of moving away, of mobility, which is accomplished, or rather 'takes place', in the framework of the dynamic relationship between localised context of places … and the distant contexts of where, for their part, the events on screen are taking place.
>
> *(Buonanno 2006: 17)*

In describing this ambiguous relationship with television, they are drawing on Paddy Scannell's discussion of radio in modern life as a doubling of place (1996: 91). In a similar argument about placemaking for media in everyday life, Shaun Moores (2012) also uses Scannell's notion of the doubling of place. He argues that in the disruptive environment of mobility, with audiences on the move across the media landscape, they create a sense of place that is not determined by geography or structure, but is a meaning of place as experiential, involving the body, affect and sensuous experiences.

In *Why Study the Media?* Roger Silverstone noted that audiences are wanderers, moving across media environments, sometimes being in more than one place at once. For Silverstone, the concept of nomadic audiences is a means to explore the blurring of boundaries between public and private spheres, or local and transnational mediated spaces. Silverstone argues for a conceptualisation of audiences as grounded in 'the reality of experience, that experiences are real, even media experiences' (1999: 9). Here then, relations of presence and place become caught up in ways of understanding audiences.

It is this sense of audiences and their experience of media, time and place, that is helpful to contemporary audience research. Adrian Athique (2016: 11) notes how place has been somewhat missing from accounts of audiences:

> Like the diasporic migrant or the crossover cosmopolitan, the transnational web surfer is granted the privilege of being anywhere and everywhere, but tends to end up being nowhere in particular … the human geography of audience studies fails to account adequately for the specifics of place.

Athique argues that transnational exchanges within local, national and global flows are now ordinary experiences for audiences around the world. The context of transnational media content, distribution platforms and varieties of representations creates a media matrix where Japanese horror is remade in Hollywood, or Korean pop music is a cultural fusion of different styles. Athique challenges the meaning of transnational, often seen as technologically deterministic, with assumptions about a break with the nation state. Instead, the transnational is a messy overlay of local, national and global, or intra-regional flows, where 'national imaginaries provide key staging grounds for transnational practices' (2016: 15). Thus, we engage with a range of global content from our own standpoint of where we live now, suggesting media experiences take place somewhere, sometime.

Roaming

Roaming signifies audience access to media through myriad ways; viewers and users can watch their favourite drama on TV, iPad, laptop, mobile phone, read related content and reviews, and take part in discussions in radio, newspapers and social media. Audiences engage with media in different places; viewers and users can choose to watch their favourite drama at home, in the lunch break at work, on the train to visit friends, on the bus to work in the morning, or during a long haul flight on holiday. And audiences engage with media at various times in the day, week, and season; viewers and users can watch live TV, watch or re-watch on catch up services, binge view drama on subscription video on demand services, play all on DVD box sets, stream through illegal sites to watch on first release, or upload and share on illegal sites with fan subbing. Thus the roaming signifies the affective, temporal and placemaking practices of audiences for a range of storytelling.

The idea of roaming audiences connects with broader changes around the relationships between the material object of television and its audience. The box in the corner used to be a fixed and stable object, literally a piece of furniture that people would position and polish, and a symbolic object of friendship, a reliable member of the household which was always there if you needed it. People used to put objects of value on top of the television, such as family portraits, or ceramic figurines, turning the box in the corner into a household shrine to display memorable items. This more working-class practice stood in contrast to affluent homes that tried to hide televisions behind wooden cabinet doors, to be revealed on suitable occasions. Some people had portable televisions, often black and white, which they could move from room to room, or park in the garden, say to watch Wimbledon whilst sitting on their lawn. Today, people position slim TVs in the corner of the room, or hang them on the wall; you can get television projected onto a screen to give the appearance of being in the cinema; and you can watch television from hand held devices and computers anywhere you want, as long as you have charged batteries, an electricity supply and reliable internet access. Holt and Sanson (2014: 2) use the term 'connected viewing' to refer to the 'multi-platform entertainment experience', where we see a 'migration of our media and our attention from one screen to many' and changing directions in 'the flow of entertainment content in new patterns' (ibid.). They argue that connected viewing is about both digital distribution for multiplatform brands and new forms of user engagement with cross media content.

In a discussion of transmedia storytelling Elizabeth Evans (2011: 148) writes of armchair schedulers, referring to the ways downloading and streaming television drama alters the temporal relationship with television itself. In her interviews with pirate viewers in the mid-2000s, they described how the institution of television and its broadcast schedules had failed to account for their everyday routines; there was an erratic element to their lives where they liked to be able to watch their favourite drama when they wanted to, without interruptions, or advertising. These viewers also described a temporal and geographical freedom; they did not have to sit down in a specific place at a set time prescribed by broadcasters:

> downloading offered them the opportunity to counteract the moments in which television failed to fit satisfactorily into their lives. The technology offers them greater agency and control, the chance to act as their own schedulers rather than having to rely on broadcasters.
>
> *(Evans 2011: 152)*

For roaming audiences, the ability to be your own armchair scheduler is no longer a transgressive act but rather a ubiquitous experience as so much television content is available across digital platforms. The technological affordances of streaming services, catch up TV and piracy sites heighten the temporal and geographical freedom of audiences to roam. Indeed, the instability of viewers' daily lives is perhaps even more pronounced now than when the study was done a decade ago; precarious working conditions, the pressure to manage time productively at work, home, on the train and waiting in line is a feature of neo-liberal economics and the politics of late modern life. There are also the economic and social pressures of play-all television viewing. As we shall see, in this media environment, the broadcast television schedule can actually be a place to rest in the busy on demand world of connected viewing.

As audiences are roaming around entertainment content, the pathways and tracks they make are shaping their experience of television and related social media. People's movements say something about what kind of television matters to them and how they reflect on this experience. This symbolic power of television is connected to the social imaginary. Charles Taylor's idea of a modern social imaginary is 'a broad understanding of the way a given people imagine their collective social life' (2004: 23). Theories are often 'the possession of a small minority, whereas what is interesting in the social imaginary is that it is shared by large groups of people' (ibid.). Perhaps, most important of all, 'the social imaginary is a common understanding that makes possible common practices and a widely shared sense of legitimacy' (Taylor 2004: 23).

As mentioned briefly in the introduction to this book, Taylor's use of the term 'legitimacy' is useful when thinking about the right to roam. This phrase refers to the old ways of footpaths that were imagined as 'worldly', that is to say open to all, in countries such as Britain and Sweden. Macfarlane explains: 'as rights of way determined and sustained by use, they constitute a labyrinth of liberty, a slender network of common land that still threads through our aggressively privatised world of barbed wire and gates, CCTV cameras and "No Trespassing" signs' (2012: 16). The Swedish custom of *allemansrätten* (the rights of everyman and woman) allows citizens to roam across uncultivated land provided they do not cause harm; people can forage for food, or swim in any watercourse if they so choose (ibid.).

The emphasis on 'a sense of legitimacy' is significant because the laws and regulations surrounding content and communicative rights do not allow audiences to freely move across public service and commercial platforms and across national television and transregional content. The business model for television is to restrict access and monetise audiences, both in the interests of the political economics of media institutions and as a means to measure audience engagement through ratings and social media analytics that are collated within national boundaries. Deborah Chambers (2016) notes how households domesticate and keep up to date radio, television, computers, smart phones, and wearable technologies, contributing to what she calls a 'media imaginary', where she draws on Taylor to explain how technologies become part of 'society through a series of policies, design and marketing strategies' which works alongside 'popular cultural visions' (2016: 12).

As for those who resist the laws and regulations of television, they are trying to generate an alternative vision for a media imaginary where these technologies enable freedom to watch without restriction. In their book *Informal Media Economies*, Lobato and Thomas (2015) show how formal media economies mix with informal ones, such as sharing friendly passwords, watching television within piracy sites, or using a getaround for geoblocking. They describe audiences who use informal media economies for their favourite television shows as first release media citizens, wanting to watch *Game of Thrones*, say, with no delay, no adverts, and no legal or economic restrictions. This feeling of a right to roam is a subjective experience, a sense of legitimacy that suggests how audiences can work around barriers put in place by television industries and the big platform players.

For example, Lobato and Meese (2016) untangle the notion of internet freedom and geoblocking in thinking around global screen culture. They note how much of the debates on internet freedom focus on political activism and the division between free and unfree countries. They argue that geoblocking has little to do with a digital divide, or a Western sensibility of developed and undeveloped regions for free communication; instead geoblocking is linked to infrastructures, class and other social demographics, and the resources to unblock content. They also point out that not all geoblocking circumvention is related to political activism or resistance to state censorship; there will also be mundane reasons for wanting to stream and share illegal content. In what they see as a 'shortcoming in the internet freedom literature' there is little attention given to illegal audiences and fans and 'the everyday politics of pleasure and consumption' (2016: 19). The empirical audience research here, and particularly in Chapter 6, contributes to this intervention in the practices and pleasures of roaming audiences who use getarounds for geoblocking to create an entertainment experience.

Juan Llamas-Rodriguez (2016) is interested in geofences for screen culture; he differentiates between above ground channels for legitimate screen content and tunnelling as a network practice that exists below the ground level, creating channels of interconnected tunnels, through VPNs for example, as methods of circumventing geoblocking. 'Tunnels' is evocative of what we might call underground audiences and users; similar to cultures of music for underground sounds, these more politicised practices involve a certain type of intensive engagement and form of audience activism that can often be related to political cultures and social movements. With the metaphor of roaming audiences, these practices are mainly concerned with overground activities, suggesting a more mundane and normalised way of accessing screen culture through formal and informal routes. The fact that audiences are using methods for circumventing geoblocking deserves close attention, including how audiences imagine themselves, as underground tunnellers or overground pathfinders.

What kinds of rights talk might we find amongst audiences? Andrew Calabrese explains how 'the public articulation of rights claims in liberal democracies often is based on egalitarian appeals to reason as means of securing the legitimacy of rights'; 'whether it be the sovereignty of the individual, the pursuit of happiness, or respect for human dignity, to name a few rationales, rights claims typically have an underlying philosophical framework that offers a foundation for their legitimacy' (2017: 99). The moral philosophy of 'the good life' or moral recognition and distribution of human needs in liberal democracies are examples of the public articulation of rights claims for transnational public spheres (ibid.). Although the rights talk of roaming audiences is different to this traditional sense of communicative rights, there is a symbolic power to their wish for access to television without economic barriers, time constraints and geographical borders. Audiences articulate how their favourite drama series contributes to their happiness and sense of belonging –expressed quite simply as 'this is my show', and 'it makes me happy'. If their freedom to watch favourite drama is restricted due to time constraints for live broadcasting or catch up windows, censorship of content, or bad translations, then audiences not only express their unhappiness but find ways around these restrictions.

This sense of rights is articulated in several ways that suggest changing temporal, economic and geographical relationships with television. There is a temporal freedom; audiences create personalised schedules that fit with their routines, reflecting Evans' (2011) point that viewers feel television broadcasters are failing to be in tune with their everyday lives. There is a geographical freedom; audiences bypass geoblocking put in place by broadcasters and media companies to limit viewing to specific regions that have paid for the transmission rights, and these getarounds allow transnational audiences to access the global flow of media content (Athique 2016). There is an economic freedom; illegal viewers are uploading content to piracy sites, or streaming drama via informal sites, some of which charge for this black market service, and for these audiences anti-commercialisation and distrust of global capitalism is a significant driver in their informal media engagement. These kinds of roaming audiences are disrupting the ability of the television industry to monitor and monetise consumers and users through information systems and advertising revenues. The unmeasured audience is a focus of Chapter 6, but here we see rights talk most clearly articulated by consumer choice advocates, TV watchdog communities that share information on how to stay off the radar of piracy detection, and activists for first release media citizenship.

There are strictures that come alongside these subjective feelings of a right to roam. An illegal viewer in Evans' research noted how their informal media practices 'liberated me from the schedule', and yet they still felt a 'slave to the television' (Evans 2011: 155). Criticism of fan labour as exploitation, or the immaterial labour of fans for television and social media, is especially relevant here. The argument that audiences face a digital enclosure, rather than a democratic space, is reflected in viewers' and users' movements within the economically and geographically bounded mediascape (see Lee and Andrejevic 2014). Even if audiences are resistant to being measured, and use various tactics to avoid detection, they still know that their practices are part of an attention economy. And there are economic and time strictures on audiences: watching television costs money, whether this is through subscription services, high speed internet access, or upgrading mobile devices; and having the time to watch television can feel both a privilege (this is my time to relax), a guilty pleasure (should I be doing something better with my time?), and worthless time spent doing nothing (think of the coach potato). We can see that there is freedom and stricture in the idea of audiences roaming across dispersed sites of production, distribution and reception.

To get a grasp of the freedoms and strictures of roaming audiences I turn to an unusual example of the work of French cultural critic Roland Barthes. In his essay 'Dining Car' Barthes (1979) reflects on the experience of eating on a French train. This is an elaborate dining experience. He describes a table covered with 'a cloud of napery', a starched linen tablecloth, lots of napkins. There is the illusion of eating out at a fancy restaurant, with glamorous names attached to dishes that emerge from an invisible galley kitchen. The menu consists of five courses designed to take you through a long train journey. Barthes meticulously counts thirteen 'waves' in the experience, beginning with being seated at the table, the aperitifs, the drink orders, the uncorking of the bottle, the five courses, the coffee, and ending with asking for the bill and then paying it. All of this provides a heavy materiality to the journey, everything is designed to produce a 'mirage of solidity'(1979: 141); 'the traveller should consume at the heart of his [sic] journey everything constitutively opposed by the journey' (ibid.). The mirage conceals contingency, displacement, and movement. He writes: 'each constraint seems to produce its contrary freedom' (1979: 141). Whilst the suburbs and shipping stations slip by, we participate in what he calls 'transported immobility' (1979: 143).

His idea is richly suggestive of the contrary freedom of roaming audiences. We find audiences making pathways and tracks through media landscapes, feeling a sense of a right to roam, and we also find audiences experiencing constraints on this freedom, in the form of economic, temporal and geographical barriers. But to add to these cultural practices, we also find audiences creating an illusion of immobility so that they can feel at the heart of their journey through the media landscape things that are at odds with this movement. In the next section we look at the case study of crime drama *The Bridge* to understand this cultural work in action.

Roaming audiences for *The Bridge*

This section addresses *The Bridge* in Scandinavia, Great Britain and America, and asks: what kinds of movements are possible for roaming audiences? A brief note is necessary on methods for the use of empirical research in this chapter (for detailed information see the Appendices). *The Bridge* is a format based on the original crime series *Bron/Broen* (2011–2018, SVT and DR) located in the border territory of Sweden and Denmark. There are two adaptations of the original series set across Britain and France (*The Tunnel* [Sky], *Le Tunnel* [Canal Plus, 2013–2016]), and America and Mexico (*The Bridge*, FX 2013–2014); a recent adaptation is set across Estonia and Russia (NTV, 2017). The original *Bron/Broen* has aired in 157 countries around the world, and the third season won a Crystal award for the best TV drama series of the year in Sweden. In this chapter, the focus is on the original drama *Bron/Broen*, which means 'the bridge' in Swedish and Danish, and the American–Mexican adaptation *The Bridge*. To avoid confusion '*The Bridge*' is used

FIGURE 3.2 Storyboarding *Bron/Broen*
Source: Photograph Tina Askanius.

when viewers refer to the American–Mexican version, or when British viewers refer to the original version that is translated as *The Bridge* when screened in this country, and '*Bron/Broen*' is used when referring to the original version, respectively called *Bron* by Swedish viewers and *Broen* by Danish viewers.

The case study as a whole involved production and audience research, working with the makers of the series in a collaborative academic and industry project. The production research is analysed in other chapters in the book, and here is used as contextual knowledge that enhances the audience analysis, for example of the craft of storytelling. The audience research took place from 2014 to 2016, for seasons two and three of *Bron/Broen*, and season two of *The Bridge*. There were 185 interviews in total, with interviewees aged from 18 to 65 and a gender breakdown of 127 females to 58 males, reflecting the mainly female target audience for crime drama (see Turnbull 2014). In Chapter 5, crime drama is addressed in an analysis of the character of Saga Noren and emotional engagement with this genre. Respondents ranged from students, unemployed, office workers, sales assistants and swimming pool attendants to IT workers, business owners, lawyers, teachers, artists and retired people. For details about the fieldwork please see the Appendices.

All interviews were transcribed and analysed using qualitative data analysis, where descriptive and analytical coding was combined with critical reflection on the interviews in the context of fieldnotes and participant observations. This multilayered analysis enabled an interpretation of the data across the sites of production, live and catch up viewing as well as the audience's reflections on their experiences. For example, the theme of social ritual in the data emerged in the pilot research, the design of the fieldwork, and in the initial data analysis, drawing patterns across the interviews and observations in homes, and at fan events, where viewers reflected on the collective experience of watching the drama. This theme was linked with the concept of placemaking (Moores 2012), where deeper analysis suggested that this format, which is built on a strong sense of location and the border as a place of political and social significance, speaks to audiences from their site of reception and their ritual practices for *Bron* Sundays. This data analysis allowed for the more theoretically informed argument about mobility and place, and immersive drama and social ritual in this chapter.

Social rituals

A common way of watching television drama is through subscription video on demand services such as Netflix or HBO Nordic, or through catch up services. Viewers talked of not having a television due to the hassle of multiple contracts and restrictions on global content: 'I've failed as a television viewer for a few years, I don't even have a TV set' (35 year old Swedish male clerk). Most disliked advertising and preferred to stream content in order to watch television when and how they wanted. The dominance of streaming television was clear to see in viewers' accounts of how they watched shows such as *Homeland* on Netflix, or *Game of Thrones* on informal websites. Binge viewing was common: 'We love binge watching TV... We cut class. We love TV shows. That's just how it is' (22 year old Swedish female student). Binge watching is part of the routinised habits for this generation – 'that's just how it is' – highlighting how 'media is becoming an increasingly important feature in the experience of generations' (Bolin 2017: 4).

Some viewers in Denmark and Sweden started watching *Bron/Broen* after its original transmission, hearing about the show through friends or family, then binge watching seasons on Netflix so they could catch up with the event television of the latest season:

> I watched it on Netflix, the first season is on there. I watched all the episodes at once. I worked evenings and watched *Bron* during the days. All of it. My boyfriend told me that he had seen the first season and that he thought I would like it. It took a while to catch up since we watched it on SVT Play. But now we've had two or three Sundays which have been *Bron* Sundays. It's been so cosy on Sunday nights at nine o'clock .... We'll have some food, things like that, enjoy ourselves and watch *Bron*.
>
> *(26 year old Swedish female supermarket worker)*

A recommendation by her boyfriend led this viewer to binge watch during her downtime from work, using the public service catch up function to watch 'all of it'; but once they reached the timeline for the new season on television they adjusted their routines to a cosy night in on Sundays, the classic ritual television viewing experience.

The routines of scheduling Sunday evening drama on public service media SVT and DR established this series as a resource in people's everyday lives: chores were finished, food was prepared, children put to bed, all in time for Sunday night crime: 'Sunday night TV is a bit of a tradition. I grew up with watching together with the family at 8 p.m. on Sundays. It is a bit of an institution in Denmark. All of the large Danish productions we have always watched together in my family' (27 year old female Danish social worker). Audiences across Sweden and Denmark reserved time to gather together: 'it's at home on the sofa with the family. Everybody watches. Everyone is focused on the show' (25 year old Swedish female till operator). The live experience was significant, not only as an appointment to view, but a reason to be on the sofa during the darker months of the year in Scandinavia: 'It is that time of year where you feel like curling up on the sofa and watching television' (63 year old female Danish clerk). Audiences described the drama as stripped down viewing during the winter months: 'Somehow it feels very raw, at home, lying on the sofa, watching something creepy on TV' (23 year old Swedish female student).

Audiences arranged their weekend so it would end with this show: 'I always watch it on TV, unless there's some disaster preventing me from watching. I want to watch it on Sunday night, on my sofa' (50 year old Swedish female project manager). And this way of reserving time for television drama stood out as unusual, making it one of the few shows people watched together as a live audience: 'I stream a lot ... there is something about this show that makes us want to see it together' (41 year old Danish female copy editor); '*Broen* is the only one I watch every week' (37 year old Danish male advertising worker). The power of live broadcasting generated a sense of togetherness, in the living room, and through social media chatter after the show: 'I find that there is a bit of a Sunday ritual around it, I also like knowing that other people are watching it at the same time' (23 year old Danish female student). 'Nine o'clock, we have to watch and you can't be doing anything else. We watch *Bron* on TV, there's a gang of us, we get some popcorn and we watch *Bron*. And then you write something on Facebook, you talk about the episode' (23 year old Swedish male law student).

The narrative traits of crime drama help to shape an attentive viewing experience (see Chapter 5 for a discussion of narrative engagement). One viewer described the immersiveness of the show as 'what happened now? I barely have time to breathe' (72 year old Swedish retired female). The mesmerising nature of the drama drew loyal viewers every week: 'You don't want to miss a single episode. They're really good at creating that sense you're not going to miss it on a Sunday' (45 year old Swedish female head of communications). The drama was addictive, rewarding viewing. For example, this student described watching with friends: 'As soon as it's up on SVT Play, we watch it. Sometimes we pause: "What's going on? It's crazy. Oh, it's brutal, the people who wrote this must be sick." And then we keep going' (21 year old Swedish female student).

In Britain, something similar occurred in the way audiences watched the original version of *Bron/Broen* (translated as *The Bridge*), finding out about it through friends and family, streaming and playing catch up with the drama, and then falling into the routine of watching live on Saturday evenings, when BBC4 scheduled two episodes a week. For example, this viewer explained: 'We started watching all episodes of *The Bridge* season 1 on my iPad all day with my friends and then we went to a pub to try to calm down for a few hours. Then, for season two, we watched two hours a week' (24 year old British female casting assistant). *Bridge* Saturdays became a social ritual, an alternative to the typical reality talent show programming scheduled on the main public service and commercial channels: 'last Saturday we were very cool; we watched two recorded ones from the week before and watched two live' (27 year old British male teaching assistant). BBC4, home to more middle-class and older viewers, offered an evening with 'Scandi Noir', building up a taste profile for foreign drama: 'I think it is a good slot on BBC; before *The Killing* we didn't have this ritual on Saturday evenings, so it wasn't really special before, so over the last few years, the slot has became almost sacrosanct for us' (48 year old British male manager).

For those who worked over the weekends, or missed the live broadcast, the drama became event television, making time for binge watching with food and wine, and good company. In one household observation, a couple watched the entire season three of *The Bridge* in two Sunday sittings as their own event television: they had stored up six episodes on their DVR box, watching in one sitting, and then completing the final four episodes on a winter weekend. Each time an episode started, they would sing along to the opening music, and in between the episodes, try to figure out whodunnit. Although these viewers were not watching live on Saturdays, they created their own special occasion during the winter months.

In America, a different picture emerges of *The Bridge*'s adaptation and social ritual viewing. There were examples of live television viewing, finding drama in the flow of content on offer with network and cable television: 'My boyfriend and I were just flipping channels and it happen to be on and it looked really good so we watched it, and we both fell in love with it so we just continued to watch it' (35 year old American female office worker). But the typical way viewers found the drama was through word of mouth, then locating it on a streaming service within formal and informal media economies. For example, this viewer explained:

> I pretty much watch everything online. I have a TV upstairs but my computer is downstairs so I tend to spend more time downstairs, I mean I do sometimes watch something in the bedroom live but most of the time I just find it more convenient to watch it online and it is available, I mean everything is available online.
>
> *(46 year old American female unemployed)*

Although this viewer had a television set in the bedroom, it's the computer that dominates the everyday viewing experience, one characterised by easy access and unlimited availability. In another example, a fan downloaded the show from iTunes: 'I participate during and after the show, I'm a member of the Facebook *Bridge* FX club, not through FX but through other members that like *The Bridge* and are interested in it' (46 year old American female retail owner). She avoided watching it live on FX and avoided official social media so that she could create her own pathways to engage with the drama and share this with other fans.

We found audiences accessing the show whenever and however they wanted, an example of consumer choice advocates in action. One viewer watched with his father, recording the drama at a time that suited them. He explained:

> There are so many dramas on TV that, unlike before, like ten or five years ago even, you couldn't record or stream so you had to watch the show when it came on, and then if you missed it you were screwed. You could not watch the next episode. But nowadays you can watch them whenever.
>
> *(23 year old American male swimming pool attendant)*

In this instance the old ways of watching television put viewers in a time bind with network and cable schedules; 'nowadays' two different generations of father and son have the freedom to immerse themselves in television drama in ways that fit with their everyday routines. The way he describes this viewing experience supports Bolin's point that media generations can be understood as both temporal and spatial localities (2017: 96), with an emphasis on how the current technological changes in the media landscape offer a temporal freedom that enhances an immersive drama experience in households.

A viewer watching in Mexico mixed formal and informal media economies in their media experience: 'I download from Internet. I do the pay-per-view thing if there are any subtitles available for the download, and lately I have learned that I can download the subtitles separately from the shows' (30 year old Mexican-Colombian male lawyer). In the case of *The Bridge* they downloaded an illegal version of the series without dubbing as they wanted to enjoy the drama with the original meaning of the language and script. Their way of watching tells us how a right to roam works in practice; they speak about the ways they access television through informal routes and then describe the value of storytelling to their personal experience: 'When I watch a series it is like a prize for a hard day's work, before bed I put on an episode of any series I'm following. If I do not feel too sleepy, I see two episodes or sometimes repeat episodes that I like' (30 year old Mexican-Colombian male lawyer).

Although some audiences resist live viewing, seeing it as a time bind, for others the live transmission pulls viewers into the week-by-week drama experience, rationing out their engagement into a manageable amount of time. One person explained:

> I can commit myself to an hour every week but two hours, for me it is too much … It is like a book, you know, it is like instead of telling you a story in two hours they are telling it to you in ten hours with a lot of detail … I wouldn't have gotten attached to this Mexican cop if it weren't that I follow him for three months! I didn't watch it on Netflix so I had to wait every week to watch it, so, in my mind I would think about the show, you know, I would be on the bus and be like 'ok, what's going to happen? What did he say?' You know, like when you read a book, it is exactly the way I felt.
>
> *(40 year old Canadian female civil servant)*

For her, each episode is like reading the chapter of a book, with spaces in between to reflect on characters and storytelling. The line producer Patrick Markey (2014) reflected on how the second season of the drama was shaped to create this kind of experience, letting the drama 'unfold like reading a book … you get this experiential sense of living it very much as if it is in real life; there are good things and bad things, wonderful things that are also terrible and in that mix we might find the truth'. This slower pace of narrative engagement shapes a more enriching drama experience that this viewer carries with her at home, on the bus, and in between transmission times.

Social media blackout

If we return to Scandinavia, we find audiences roaming around storytelling in *Bron/Broen*, immersing themselves in the drama, and at the same time placemaking through social ritual. An example of a Danish fan helps to put this way of watching into context. Rachel was a 40 year old freelance journalist and blogger who lived with her husband and three children in western Denmark. She ran a site where she gave vent to her passion for crime fiction in all shapes and forms. Although the blog had only been active for little more than a year when we spoke to her, Rachel was an old hand in the art of blogging, one of the 'web-veterans' who remembered when it was still called web logs and the phenomenon was something that required an explanation to everyone but hard core techno-geeks. Rachel was a dedicated fan of *Bron/Broen* and she blogged and tweeted extensively on the characters, themes, and plotlines. Ideally, she wanted to stay online at all times, even when the show was transmitted live. She explained her passion for the crime series: 'It's excitement. It's fascinating because the story is so great. I've read the writer's books, Hans Rosenfeldt. He has written some great crime novels … It is a pleasure to watch really. It makes me happy.'

But this always-online drama experience was not so popular with her husband; this was the only series they watched together on Sunday evenings and, after some disagreements, she agreed to ban electronic devices during the show:

> I think it annoys my husband sometimes when I film when it's on. I am often using my iPhone or iPad when watching. He gets a bit stressed so we agreed I would stop. You know he gets a bit … and I guess it is really a bad habit because you are not present in the moment when you have too many devices going on at the same time. But, sometimes I just have to check Twitter.

Every Monday when the children had been sent off to school and her husband had left for work, she curled up on the couch and revisited Sunday night's episode to ensure that she had not missed any important details in the detection of the crime or in the characters' development. She would be lost without her favourite crime series: 'It feels a bit sad that it's coming to an end. It leaves a void. You miss it somehow.'

Here we see a good example of roaming audiences using different media technologies to enhance their experience; Rachel reads crime novels, blogs about the crime genre, watches Nordic noir drama series, and integrates different social media with her experience, sharing this with other fans in the moment. Evans (2011: 178) describes three forms of engagement with transmedia storytelling, and although this is a traditional TV drama narrative, Rachel's practices across media content and different storytelling (novels, television, blogs) relate to Evans' discussion of engagement as immersion, agency and immediacy. However, her husband resists the pressure of roaming across different media content, wanting to create a social ritual that is about the two of them, not online fans and followers of her blog. She gets around this contested site of viewing by making extra time before and after the live show to be active on social media, capitalising on the value of immediacy as a fan blogger, and by finding time in her everyday routine when she can watch without familial restrictions – the morning after the night before.

Rachel and her husband could have timeshifted, or binge watched, to avoid this conflict, but they resisted that way of experiencing the drama, choosing live event television:

> There is something nice about not controlling it ourselves. I remember looking at my watch yesterday and thinking 'yes another ten minutes left' phew, because I thought it was ending. So that countdown and the suspense … Binging lacks these aspects of the traditional TV experience, the waiting for next week. But sure there is something great about binging as well. When I was sick, and really not allowed to watch television, I watched twelve episodes of *House of Cards* in a day.

She describes her temporal relationship with television; public service media controls the private scheduling of the drama in her household, pulling her into the appointment to view and slowing down her enjoyment of this crime drama, 'that countdown and suspense'. When she describes a 'traditional TV experience' there is a nostalgic reference to her memory of watching live to the nation TV together; this slower pace of viewing and collective experience is a counterweight to binge speeding through an entire series in 24 hours. The politics of waiting is significant, enhancing a sense of time and place for television drama.

Her experience was not unique. Retro television viewing was a pattern across the empirical research. The speed with which streaming television has dominated the market in Sweden and Denmark has had an impact on an anti-streaming trend. Younger audiences described how social ritual around the show and its event status was something they associated with the past, chatting with school friends about what you watched on TV last night. For this generation *Bron/Broen* offered a retro experience of 'old school television':

> When you watch shows on television when it is aired, you can discuss it with your friends in school the next day. That is not so easy now as people stream shows a lot more. The atmosphere around that has kind of disappeared.
>
> *(24 year old Danish female student)*

> It's funny because this has been lacking since I was a kid, seeing your friends at school and someone would ask if you'd seen the latest episode of *Friends* and you'd start talking about that … I haven't experienced that phenomenon since the nineties. And I like that it's coming back.
>
> *(32 year old Swedish male receptionist)*

In the above comments, a younger generation of viewers reflect on the affordances of media technologies to stream content, associating this with their everyday experience; and yet they nostalgically look back to the 1990s, when watching *Friends* the night before became the topic of conversation at school the next day. That atmosphere of old school television helps to create a sense of belonging.

In the following conversation from a focus group, some Swedish students discussed the social value of public service drama:

It's almost like going back to the old way of watching TV, it's like a ritual … Old television. With other shows, you barely know when they're on, but with *Bron* you do.

(23 year old Swedish female student)

I agree that it feels like when you were young. If you watch Netflix you plough through all the episodes.

(24 year old Swedish male student)

The pressure of "I've seen all of it now." *Bron* is the only show we watch together on TV at nine o'clock. Everything else is streaming when you have the time.

(23 year old Swedish male student)

It's more of an emotional and an intellectual investment to watch *Bron*. You have to make an effort. *Paradise Hotel* is okay to watch at work or while you're texting someone … It's not the same with *Bron*. Sometimes I pick up my phone, and I stop myself – 'no, I need to focus.'

(24 year old Swedish male student)

When you pick up the phone while watching *Bron* you stop yourself because you need to invest so much of yourself in the show and you get so much in return … We have a friend who plays computer games while he's watching, and he doesn't get much out of it, other than knowing who the killer is. I watch because it gives me so much more than that.

(23 year old Swedish male student)

Bron/Broen is an antidote to the pressures of streaming television drama in blocks, checking social media and multi-screening. The time pressures are clear to see in the phrase 'ploughing through all the episodes', it becomes a chore to play all; the split screen pressures are also evident in the admonishment to stop automatically checking a mobile, almost a muscle memory, and focus on the story, investing time and emotion in the drama.

Something similar was happening in Britain for *The Bridge* Saturdays on BBC4: a social media blackout, but this time for a somewhat older audience.

We watch together. We don't talk. We are really focused. It's a big deal! Big deal! We have Saturday nine o'clock.

(58 year old American male web designer)

It became a ritual … We have a Yam Yam dinner and we have to concentrate on the subtitles because the plot is difficult and if you lose a bit you get confused … If you phone me up when we are watching, I would tell you 'we are watching *The Bridge*, call me later.'

(44 year old Italian female architect)

This ritual of *The Bridge* Saturdays is marked by blocking time to watch together, making the TV series 'a big deal'. The crime drama's complex plotlines and subtitling demand attentive viewing. One woman gave *The Bridge* the ultimate accolade: it was so gripping she had to put down her knitting.

In America and Mexico the technological infrastructure for commercial television meant that if people wanted to create an immersive drama experience then they had to either record and timeshift, or watch through informal routes. One of the most common complaints against the live schedule was intrusive advertising. For example, 'I stream everything ... because I hate commercials!' (55 year old Canadian male academic). The father and son who watched the show at their own pace also chose to do this to avoid advertising: 'There was tons of commercials all over the network. Usually we would record it and then watch a little later, or on demand, so we could not watch commercials' (23 year old American male swimming pool attendant). Another complaint was about dubbing the show for Mexican viewers, meaning that those who wanted to watch the original version would have to remix the series using piracy sites:

> The thing is that sometimes the episodes available for download on the internet do not have subtitles available and even though I can speak English I still miss a lot of things so I rather to watch them with the subtitles, never dubbed, I do not like that.
> *(30 year old Mexican-Colombian male lawyer)*

When American viewers felt they were in a time bind, immersing themselves in this crime drama was a highlight of their week, and adverts were to be avoided at all costs: 'I have one or two hours in the evening to relax and the rest of my day is "forget it!" fully booked, so that little bit of time that I have by then, when my eyes hurt and everything hurts, *The Bridge* is relaxation for me' (42 year old American female sales director).

Topographies of the self

Bron bootcamp is the kind of unusual encounter that can take place for audience researchers, finding a Facebook fan group and then participating in a *Bron* dinner party. This fan group began between two friends in Stockholm, Katarina (51) and Karin (47), both office managers. It moved online to a Facebook group, gradually including more and more people passionate about *Bron*. Whether in online spaces, apartments or bars these meetings had one common purpose: to find out whodunit. The group had an acronym for all possible suspects, so 'mother of three' in the second series became MOT and the fans mapped possible characters for who could be mother of three. 'We take each other's analyses very seriously ... it's not often that someone says: "No, no, no", rather it's the other way around: "Okay, let's test this hypothesis. What happens then, what consequences would that have?"' (Katarina). She reflected on the value of the drama:

> It's like an escape, a free zone. We were joking about it, it's like a legal drug. You get to escape reality and everyday life, all the musts and important things.

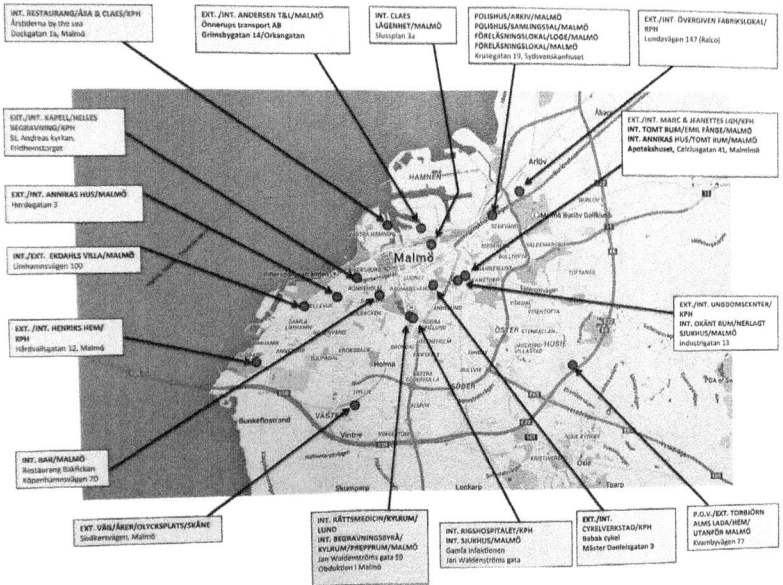

FIGURE 3.3 Topographies of the self and fans
Source: Photograph Tina Askanius.

And you enter something that somehow becomes serious, even if you know that it isn't. And it's solving, it's about solving relationships, their relationships with each other. You want to understand, before it happens. You want to be one step ahead, be able to read the codes. It's like this riddle. But it's also a way for us to channel our creativity, and enter a world of fantasy.

Katarina was aware that her experience of *Bron* says much about her identity, an example of Erving Goffman's (1959) idea of the performance of self in everyday life, where the drama is a prop for performing identities: 'I don't think we're really talking about *Bron*, I think we're talking about ourselves. But we do it through fiction.' The group dreamed of going to a *Bron* bootcamp for ten weeks to devote themselves to solving the mystery: 'We would all love it … if we basically could go to camp during these ten weeks …. To have an agenda, to only be allowed to talk about this. It would probably be impossible, but that's what we long for, we really only want to talk about this.'

What we see in the above example of a *Bron* bootcamp is fan engagement with the drama as a creative product, one that pulls these fans into its complex narrative and creates a strong affective investment in solving the puzzle of the crime. The dream of a ten-week camp, where each live transmission on Sundays would lead to intensive problem solving, code cracking, and alternative theorising sessions, signals just how important the public service schedule is in shaping an immersive experience that is similar to a novel, each chapter unfolding with space in between to reflect on what this means within the imaginary world of the drama. The fans roam around inside the story, and use other media to enhance their experience: information gathering online, reading crime novels, watching other crime series, podcasts and films, meeting online and offline to co-create this social imaginary for Nordic noir. Perhaps this dream of the *Bron* bootcamp also signals the symbolic power of storytelling to say something about themselves, making pathways through the imaginary world of *Bron* as a means of self-reflection. A *Bron* bootcamp places these fans in an enclosed space, giving them room to create parallel stories in which characters take on a life of their own. Imagine what could happen to mother of three if they only had a name? Set against their everyday lives and working week, the dream shows an imaginary zone where they are free to roam within the storylines. As Katharina explained: 'it's a feeling of belonging, suddenly you're at home in the story'.

Macfarlane's reference to a topography of the self is useful for seeing a media landscape as interior maps to help us navigate psycho-social terrains (2012: 26). Landscape, 'to borrow George Eliot's phrase, can "enlarge the imagined range for self to move in"' (2012: 26). What we find in the *Bron* bootcamp is that fans create a topography of the self within the media landscape and their everyday practices. They follow the pathways within the storytelling of the drama, and also become pathmakers, co-creating new storylines inspired by the drama. Whilst we might wonder what those new storylines entail, the ways these fans reflect on their experience tell us much about the stories of audiences. We have seen how audiences move in a fast paced media environment, constantly checking mobile phones, pressing play all and ploughing through every episode of a series, and at the same time working long hours, dealing with the day-to-day needs of looking after a family and running a household. We have also seen how audiences make time for their favourite drama shows, just before they go to sleep, cutting class, taking Fridays off work.

And when given the chance, people slow down the pace of viewing to watch in a quiet, still, and reflective way, the contrary freedom that Roland Barthes described in 'Dining Car' (Barthes 1979). The cultural dynamics around social ritual for *The Bridge*, the creation of a social media blackout, and the dream of the *Bron* bootcamp, are all examples of the ways in which displacement is transformed into stability. Take the TV as a material object: viewers claim they don't even have a TV anymore, and yet for this drama they position screens in such a way to make them appear more solid, and they position themselves in ways that make them feel more at home, cosy on the sofa. Or, look at the ways people describe a timebind, with viewers lamenting their lack of time and how they only have an hour or two to devote to their favourite drama – 'that's it, I'm fully booked!' When this 'my time' occurs they slow down the temporal experience, make a time bond with the drama. The *Bron* bootcamp is the ultimate mirage of solidity, fans finding each other online and offline and dreaming of transforming the constraints of everyday life into ten whole weeks of engagement, reflection and creation of all things *Bron*. This dream gives us a glimpse into the narrativising of audiences themselves, making storylines that weave the dramatic world with the real world of our lives.

Conclusion

People's experience of screen culture today can be characterised as roaming around storytelling within cross-media content. Audiences roam across the media landscape as dispersed sites of production, distribution and reception, where the meaning of television as screen culture is being shaped and reshaped by public service and commercial institutions, private companies, policy bodies, and audiences. There is freedom and stricture to the kinds of movements that audiences make when they roam around media, such as commercial constraints, or geoblocking for content restricted to regional audiences. Nevertheless we can see an emergent sense of a right to roam, referring to the ways audiences create a feeling of ownership of the content they want to watch in their own time, in their own way. This sense of rights suggests changing temporal, economic and geographical relationships with screen culture, such as a temporal freedom to stream content, an economic freedom to avoid advertising or access content through informal media routes, and a geographical freedom to engage with content that is gated for regional audiences.

In the case of *The Bridge* we see how roaming audiences find out about this crime drama through personal recommendation, or social media chatter, locate the first series on streaming and catch up services, try out the series in stages, first one episode, then another, until they have seen 'all of it'. This route to the show highlights how pathways to engagement are shaped by television streaming services and creative production, where an immersive drama pulls audiences into storytelling, and then keeps audiences in this imagined place through narrative, characterisation and setting – 'when's the next one on? And then we were hooked.' What is also apparent is an emotional and time bond that is created by producers and audiences, an example of affective and temporal relationships with television. The time bond is so strong that audiences go against their routinised viewing of streaming and binge watching to make a date with the drama, week by week. This is something viewers reflect on as unusual in their everyday lives, a nostalgic way of 'waiting for the next episode', so that this generation of streaming, play-all viewers has to slow down its media experiences.

A social media blackout is a cultural practice that offers an antidote to the pressures of working life, streaming television drama in blocks, checking social media and multi-tasking. It's a practice shaped across several generations, including students, parents and full time workers, and people in early retirement, but it is most apparent as an anti-streaming trend by a younger generation now so habituated to streaming and binge viewing. The deliberate move to enjoy this drama live on public service media is at odds with the fast moving, time shifting, media landscape they associate with their everyday routines. The social ritual of *Bron/Broen* Sundays acts as a still moment, a place to rest, where they give themselves permission to roam within the storytelling of the crime drama, not in the media landscape as a whole. The fact that public service media enables this social media blackout tells us something about the power of live television as social ritual and a sense of belonging, in particular when there is no advertising to interrupt an immersive drama experience. In a commercial television environment we see audiences having to record, stream, and remix the drama in order to re-create the feeling of '*Bron* is on' that Scandinavian and British viewers enjoy.

These various practices highlight the significance of stability in a media landscape constructed around contingency, the illusion of stability in a fast paced environment, showing what Roland Barthes calls a contrary freedom (1979). The creation of social ritual and a social media blackout also tells us something about the symbolic power of storytelling and the idea of a social imaginary. For *The Bridge* audiences there is pleasure to be taken in investing something of yourself, time, emotion and energy into the series. They describe the viewing experience as a social contract, an emotional and intellectual investment between the producers and audiences in creating quality drama that is worthwhile.

4

SPECTRUM OF ENGAGEMENT

Got to Dance

> *Got Talent*, if someone goes on and tries to blow bubbles out of a dog's bum, it ain't talent!
>
> *(30–40 year old female viewer)*

A scarecrow festival involves people creating, sharing and then burning scarecrows in a collective event (normally in fields to see off the crows, these scarecrows are situated outside people's homes). When you visit a festival you get a map with the scarecrows dotted along people's gardens, and you can vote for your favourite 'Idol'. For example in the guide to the 15th Heather Scarecrow Festival which took place over an August bank holiday weekend in 2015, there were 74 scarecrows scattered across the village, which was just outside Leicester; you could pop along to Belcher Close to see the '50 Shades of Hay' scarecrow, a playful re-mixing of erotic fan fiction and the vampire brand *Twilight* (Stephanie Meyer, 2005–) with a scarecrow. On Swepstone Road there was a 'Strictly Crow Dancing' scarecrow at number 59 (a riff on the BBC's ballroom reality show); and if you walked along the street and turned into Blackett Drive you would find 'Winter Is Coming Jon Crow', a reference to the television series *Game of Thrones* (HBO, USA 2011–).

The photographs taken at the Heather Scarecrow Festival (Figures 4.1–4.3) illustrate the relationships we form when we individually and collectively engage with popular culture. The normally private places of people's homes become public spaces of creative expression, there are even signs saying please step on our lawn during the festival. The scarecrows cheekily communicate our relationships with media by inviting us to engage with the myths and narratives, the characters and settings, of popular culture. In this photograph there is an invitation to engage with a popular hate figure in the talent and music industry by throwing eggs at a scarecrow Simon Cowell – vent your anger at a rotten egg. It perfectly illustrates

FIGURE 4.1 An invitation to engage: scarecrow festival in England
Source: Photograph Alison Calcutt.

the range of emotions in how we engage with media – a creative expression of the good, the bad and the ugly in entertainment.

This chapter seeks a purchase on engagement, exploring how production and audience research can offer a situated and contextual understanding of the various and often contradictory ways in which people engage and disengage with entertainment. Engagement is a seemingly simple term, referring to people's interest in media content of one kind or another, and yet it is a slippery concept, as it captures the subjectivity of people's relationships with media. When we say we are engaged with the media, we do not simply mean we are paying attention to a podcast, or sharing a link for a drama we just watched. When engagement happens it is a powerful thing. Engagement is a form of agency, something that is a crucial dynamic in how we form meaningful relationships with popular culture. John Corner (2017) has suggested that we understand engagement as an interplay between communicative engagement, that is to say looking, listening and reacting to a text, and a more immersive engagement, when we are participating, making and doing something beyond the text itself. This way of understanding engagement takes us beyond a pragmatic meaning of the term towards a more nuanced interpretation of engagement as a site of agency for audiences and their affective and media practices in everyday life.

This sense of engagement as multiform is used to explore the idea of a spectrum, where engagement is based on core elements, but experienced in diverse ways. A spectrum of engagement includes the cognitive and affective work of producers and audiences, and extends across an emotional range where people switch between positive and negative engagement, or disengagement, for example switching from positive identification with performers to negative identification with judges in a reality talent show. A spectrum of engagement also works across different contexts, such as the context of time, including fleeting engagement with a live event, or long form engagement with a brand on broadcast schedules; and the context of space, including live venues, television distribution and digital spaces, and the spaces of everyday life. A spectrum of engagement, then, is a concept that captures the multidimensionality of engagement within industry settings and reception contexts, pushing the meaning of the term beyond audience attention and ratings metrics where there is a primary focus on economic value, to also include social and cultural values, where engagement is understood as cultural resonance. As such, the concept makes space for both the economic value of screen culture and audience engagement as a measurement of interest, and the socio-cultural value of creative content that is meaningful to people in their lives.

The meaning of engagement

The meaning of engagement within the television industry encapsulates a more pragmatic, goal orientated understanding of the term as audience attention, measured through ratings data and social media analytics. Douglas Wood, Director of Research and Audience Insight at Endemol Shine, argues that there are new currencies of engagement that include audience measurement and cultural resonance

FIGURE 4.2 Heather Scarecrow festival
Source: Photograph Ian Calcutt.

(see Hill et al. 2017). This broader notion of engagement is something executive and creative producers have long understood as part of the cultural impact of television in society, but the tools to research this type of value of engagement are still in development within industry audience information systems. Here, the prime focus remains on engagement as economic value, with performance metrics for live and consolidated television viewing, and social media trends connected with sharing content and sparking public debate. Undoubtedly short form engagement takes priority for much live television – overnight ratings, consolidated figures for a seven-day window for catch up viewers, Twitter analytics, audience appreciation indexes: all frame engagement as fleeting, here today and gone tomorrow. Much media content relies on being re-commissioned on the basis of its ratings performance, interactive voting, and social media buzz.

It is worth unpacking the term to fully appreciate the subtleties of engagement as both economic and socio-cultural relations co-created by producers and audiences. To mix money with emotions is not a new notion; the history of sports and popular culture tells us of the long tradition of connecting economics with feelings. Terms such as emotional economics, or the experience economy, highlight the business trends in this area; work by economic sociologist Viviana Zelizer (2013) on what she calls economic lives makes a strong case for how subjective feelings are mixed up in legal and economic matters in so many industries, be they the caring industry or the media. But when it comes to engagement there has been little academic attention given to the core meanings of the term as economic and socio-cultural relations, the lives hidden within the ratings data.

Affect and emotions are often associated with the term engagement because these concepts address subjectivity and social relations. Broadly speaking there are two approaches to affect theory and research. One is associated with 'psychosocial texture' in social and cultural analysis, so that the meaning of affect as to act upon or influence something is researched in relation to 'how people are moved, and what attracts them' to media and culture, how people develop feelings and memories for cultural experiences (Wetherell 2012: 2). Another approach is associated with a theoretical and philosophical standpoint of post-humanism and process based perspectives; influenced by the work of Gilles Deleuze, Baruch Spinoza and others, this conceptualisation of affect is part of a philosophical project that rejects formal objects of study, such as institutions or identities, and is critical of discourse, instead drawing attention to 'a process of making a difference', the process of becoming, potential, encounters, and impact (Wetherell 2012: 3). Margaret Wetherell usefully blends approaches to affect and emotion in her discussion of affective practice. She draws upon research in psychology and neuroscience, critical social theory, cultural studies and the sociology of emotions to find a pragmatic way of thinking about affect and emotion. She explains 'affective practice focuses on the emotional as it appears in social life and tries to follow what participants do. It finds shifting, flexible and often over-determined figurations rather than simple lines of causation, character types and neat emotion categories' (Wetherell 2012: 4). For Wetherell, affective practice includes the meaning of practice as forms of order, habits, expression of emotions and actions, and the meaning of practice as what could be otherwise, thus how we might imagine ways of being, or alternative relations (ibid.).

In writing about popular culture, affect and emotion, the work of Raymond Williams and his notion of 'structures of feeling' is significant. This poetic term touches on the structural and relational connections between industries, artists and performers, and people. In his early writing on a structure of feeling, in *Preface to Film* (1954: 21), Williams explains the term thus: 'the dramatic conventions of any given period are fundamentally related to the <u>structure of feeling in that period</u>'. He goes on to say how we can examine each element within culture, but every element is part of a lived experience of the time, so the elements are an inseparable part of a complex whole.

According to Sharma and Tygstrup (2015: 2) the idea of structures of feeling 'complements the analysis of the social and material infrastructure of reality with a third layer: that of affective infrastructure'. They go on to suggest that affectivity is 'what tinges or colours the way in which we take part in the environments we find ourselves placed into' (2015: 14). For Williams (1978), structures of feeling give expression to prevailing cultural currents and moods of a given historical moment; they are implicit and inchoate, yet can still impact on people's experiences. Thus, structures of feeling refers to affective structures, patterns or scripts that we might find in personal and social histories.

For Wetherell, the concept poses some problems in social science research. She notes that structures of feeling are difficult to detect: 'personal and social life flows on and is endlessly evolving, so that it is often only when a structure or pattern is changing and disappearing that its grip becomes evident' (2012: 104). Another problem is that 'structures of feeling are embedded in practical consciousness and usual streams of activity', but we also 'live our practices quite obscurely, often not fully knowing the choices made and the implications' (ibid.). Structures of feeling refers to affective structures and practices which take place in broad daylight but at the same time can be difficult to see, often precisely because these practices are so much are part of our everyday day routines – hiding in plain sight, so to speak. Williams spoke of the concept as 'all it can do and all the difficulties it still leaves' (1978: 159), offering a tantalising and yet elusive thread for researchers to unravel in their own analytic procedures of forms and conventions.

Despite the difficulties in the concept, <u>structures of feeling</u> is still perhaps one of the most fruitful ways into researching media industries and audience engagement. The plural of structures opens up the multidimensionality of the concept to contemporary media environments, forms and narrative conventions, and, coupled with feelings, the concept becomes a sensuous form of knowledge about media and our relationship with it. There is a significant sociological and cultural dimension to structures of feeling that 'marks the plurality of frameworks of feeling at work in the same historical moment and amongst the same demographic group' (Corner 2015: 1). Certainly an approach to researching affective practice would benefit from looking at cultural practices shaped by popular culture, and which in turn shape popular culture (Calhoun and Sennett 2007); this would be a means to research the dynamics of media engagement in our lived experiences.

A note on experience is relevant. Experience is a process, yet its consequences become part of our psychic archive, our memory and identities. For Frosh (2011) there are broadly speaking two kinds of experiences: there is the lived reality of the moment and our thoughts, feelings and sensory responses within the experience itself; and there are the memories of our experience, what stays with us, what we archive and talk about and reflect on after the experience itself. These ways of understanding experience intertwine with each other over time, so this becomes a process of experiencing reality and reflecting on our experience of reality, which sometimes can be in harmony and at other times in conflict with each other. In relation to engagement, it is how this process feeds into our experiences both before and after the present moment that concerns us in this chapter. Corner (2017: 5) writes:

> It is the experiences, both shaping and shaped, which variously precede, inform and then follow media engagements that are often the real matter at issue. Research into media engagement is often, if only partly, an inquiry into the realm of the experiential and its contemporary cultural resources, with all the challenges that implies.

Corner urges researchers to study engagement in all its forms, including what happens beyond engagement, such as participation in the media, or creating content from our engagement with texts.

A final note on participation is also relevant here. Sometimes engagement is understood as a precondition of participation, in particular political participation within the theoretical framework of media and democracy. 'Participation mostly involves forms of communicative action – that derive from the emotional experience of engagement. Participation becomes thus the realization of the pre-state of engagement' (Dahlgren and Hill 2018; see also Dahlgren 2009). When we consider political participation, forms of engagement need to connect with power relations and the struggle for maximalist participation in democracy (Carpentier 2011). In this understanding of the term, 'the subjective state of engagement can be treated as a prerequisite for observable acts of participation' (Dahlgren and Hill 2018: 4). This interpretation of engagement helps in understanding the connections across interaction, engagement, participation and experience, all different elements of our relations with media formed over time.

If we want to focus on popular culture then the subjective state of engagement needs to be given more thought. Engagement becomes situated between interaction and participation, but we do not want to pass through this stage of the process when the present moment of engagement is quite often the raison d'être of popular culture. This slow looking at engagement itself as a form of audience agency is explored in the next section. The intention is not to over-complicate the idea of engagement more than it already is.

Our struggle to semantically corral the notion of engagement – whether from the perspective of politics or popular culture – is of course difficult: humans are slippery and complex creatures, and our concepts ultimately are rather clunky tools trying to grasp very subtle inner processes.

(Dahlgren and Hill 2018)

Having said that, the meaning of engagement within entertainment ought to do justice to the affective practices of audiences. What we shall see is that <u>people put a lot of time, energy and emotion into their engagement with media</u>.

A complex semantics of engagement

To get a purchase on the meaning of engagement let us turn to Raymond Williams (1981) musing on the meaning of culture by playing with words that rhyme with it. He says there are two words – vulture, a carrion bird that feeds on dead flesh; and sepulchre, associated with tombs and monuments to the dead. So, we have culture rhyming with vulture (culture vulture) – and sepulchre (the death of culture). Williams mournfully notes how the good has been drained from the meaning of culture. This riff on culture can inspire a play on words that rhyme with engagement. Sometimes coming at a word from an unusual angle widens our horizon of understanding. What words rhyme with engagement? The first that comes to mind is arrangement – a coming together, something composed of various parts. A second rhyme might be that of enragement – provoked to fury, livid

FIGURE 4.3 Scarecrows, Heather Scarecrow Festival
Source: Photograph Ian Calcutt.

with anger. A third rhyme is estrangement – a state of having been broken apart, a loss of affection. Here, then, we have rhymes illuminating a complex semantics of engagement, suggesting a coming together, bursts of positive and negative energy, and a pulling apart. These rhymes are suggestive of the core relationships, the interconnections between people and media that underpin the meaning of engagement with entertainment.

This play on rhyme (arrangement, enragement, estrangement) signals the different affective, emotional and cognitive elements within audience engagement. If we use Peter Dahlgren's (2009) definition of engagement as an energising internal force then we can see the varieties of intensities, dispositions and modes that work across a spectrum of engagement. Corner (2011) describes this process as stages of engagement, exploring how we can 'conceptually configure the relation of individuals to media' (2011: 91). Before engagement there is exposure to media content, ranging from a chance contact to an appointment to view, indicating 'just how wide, various and continuous the profile of daily exposure to the media now is within many societies' (Corner 2011: 91). At the moment of engagement there is a purposive relationship formed with media content; this is where our chance look at a newspaper headline turns into a sustained cognitive and emotional focus on the newspaper article itself. Engagement can 'vary in intensity', sometimes 'casual and intermittent', at other times enduring and long-lasting; and these stages of engagement involve different intensities of 'cognitive and affective work' (2011: 91). Intense engagement forges a meaningful bond between media artefacts and the subjective domain (2011: 92).

From this conceptual discussion we can chart the foundation to a spectrum of engagement in three ways of researching this area; there is Williams' structures of feeling for a way of researching the multidimensionality of media production and audiences; there is Wetherell's approach of affective practice as embodied meaning making, what she refers to as the practices of feeling in empirical research; and there is Corner's suggestion to see stages of engagement as a conceptual configuration of the relations between individuals and media in society and culture. This analytical purchase on media engagement establishes a way of seeing it as relationships between producers and audiences, and this analysis balances the personal-individual with collective social media engagement (see Corner 2011: 93). In such a way we can address the socio-cultural dynamics of engagement in the context of media industries, texts and their communicative mode of address, and audiences and their embodied meaning making in everyday life.

The affective practices of engagement work across a short and long timeframe, so that we are looking to see affective practices in the build-up to engagement, what we experience in the moment itself, and what happens beyond engagement. Kathleen Stewart (2007) calls this 'ordinary affects', where she argues for attention to the affective dimensions of everyday life. Similarly, Wetherell (2012: 78) considers how to situate affect, seeing affective practices as something we perform on a daily basis; she explains that patterns of affective practices occur through our embodied conduct in scenes of daily life, these ordinary, demotic, affective actions often happen without meta-commentary, and yet they are significant to our overall understanding of affective performances in everyday situations. Wetherell notes how situated affective active is difficult to research, posing methodological challenges to social science and its continuing debates about how to research subjectivity. Nevertheless, she argues that an analysis of affective moments, and what happens after these moments, is important if we want to understand the familiar, intuitive patterns within society and culture.

In a production context, affective patterns can be seen in the physicality and sensations associated with a live television experience, for example. Paddy Scannell's (2014) work on live television highlights the care structures within live events, where he argues that electronic media organise the living moment for us and reduce the existential strain of existence. The intensity of a live audience, the adrenalin-fuelled participation of a large crowd and their immediate reactions to performers on stage, is crucial to a reality spectacular; this is what drives a live talent show and is part of its entertainment appeal. These events are carefully managed and the care structures established by the production team include affective practices in audience engagement. For example, crowds want to feel they are treated with respect, from the way they are seated to how they are invited to vocalise their feelings; crowds expect to see a duty of care from the presenter and judges, to the performers. This is the affective element of the care structures of live reality television and it is a very significant means of crafting positive engagement from crowds participating in live television (see Chapters 8 and 9 for further discussion of live events).

Affective practices can also include the construction of performance and authenticity in production contexts. Erving Goffman's (1959) early research on pragmatic impression management is helpful to understanding the cognitive and emotional work of engagement. In his landmark study of the presentation of the self in everyday life, Goffman highlights how we perform different selves, a frontstage and backstage self, that project public and private aspects of our identities. This performative frame is very prevalent in the production of reality talent shows. There are performers on stage, and also the backstage experiences of these people and their emotional journey through the competition; there are the reactions of family and friends to these performers, adding another layer of the performance of supporters of reality contestants; there are the performances of the judges, including their professional opinions, and the whispered asides caught on camera and microphone; and there are the performances of audiences themselves, either in the live venue, or at home and through social media, reacting to themselves watching a live event. For producers, the casting of performers is crucial, especially the balance of skill and personality in a talent competition. For audiences at the live venues, at home and on social media, critical evaluation of the professional performances of contestants, and the public and private personas of these same people is also crucial. This genre knowledge of the value of performance and reaction within reality television is significant to critical modes of engagement.

For the site of audience engagement itself, there is a spectrum that includes affective, emotional and critical modes, switching between positive and negative engagement, to disengagement. Positive engagement typically might include emotional identification with a character, inviting sympathy and empathy, voting for the underdog, sending encouraging tweets, for example. Negative engagement might involve emotional dis-identification with a character, closing down sympathy, voting to eliminate, trash talking on Twitter, for example. These two emotional modes on the spectrum of engagement often work in tandem, and writers, directors and performers are fully aware of how to craft both positive and negative emotions even in the same character, thus inviting intense feelings from audiences who emotionally invest in a story.

Disengagement is often something ignored within media research. There can be an assessment of performative failure: why did viewers ignore a series, or switch off halfway through? But there is little sustained research on how this happens and why it is a routine feature of our media experiences. Disengagement can be sudden, a brusque disconnect with series, or it can happen gradually, an increasing awareness that the presence of a series in your life is gradually becoming an absence. Studying disengagement means interpreting how and why audiences disengage with shows on a regular basis, sometimes due to the simple fact that there isn't enough time in the day and they need to make room for other content, but also due to disaffection and even anger with a brand. In the next section the idea of a spectrum of engagement is explored further within the case study of reality talent shows, in order to highlight the embodied meanings and relationships formed by producers, participants and audiences for live entertainment.

Spectrum of engagement for reality talent shows

In earlier work on reality television I explored this phenomenon in various forms, from competitive talent shows to reality soaps. The book drew on interviews with television producers on the market of reality TV and audience research involving 15,000 participants over 15 years (Hill 2015). A key theme was the way people riff on reality, debating and rejecting reality claims, drawing on notions of performance and authenticity to explore 'reality' relations. To build on this idea of engagement as relationships, this section analyses production and audience research of a live reality talent show to explore the 'reality' relations for popular factual entertainment. We shall see how a spectrum of engagement allows us to consider affective, emotional and critical practices in the processes of engagement.

For example, in terms of audience engagement and 'reality' relations, this genre is mainly based on the moment of viewing, often a live event, as a primary energising force in shaping engagement. Here is a viewer reflecting on themselves in a key moment of *Big Brother* (first season UK): 'I mean it's laughable now but at the time is was Oh my God! I phoned my friend up and I was very upset. I went I've seen someone nearly have a nervous breakdown' (see Hill 2015). Why is this woman distancing herself from this emotional moment? Her inner critic takes over as she knows everybody knows this moment has been so over used it is no longer authentic. Her phrase 'it's laughable now' signals how the engagement she describes at the moment of live viewing is now something illegitimate, it strikes a false note in the spectrum of engagement. John McGrath (2004) uses the idea of performance in *Big Brother* to argue we are 'selves producing selves'. We certainly see multiple selves at work in this viewer's more subjective engagement in the moment and her critical engagement after the event.

Imagine a spectrum of engagement as three emotional notes, positive – I love it – negative – I love to hate it – and disengagement – it's over. Take this young female viewer (aged 12–15 years old) of the British *Big Brother* in 2000 (see Hill 2015):

> I didn't like it at first, ... I was away for a month and I came back and everyone was talking about it. I was like 'What on earth is it?' I didn't know what the big thing was. I put it on and I was like 'this is a joke, this is pathetic!' And then my brother kept having it on, I kept watching and I got so into it! I was addicted! I was mad, I was like 'I love it, I love it, I love it!' So I ended up absolutely loving it and then it stopped and I was crying! I was crying at the end! [laughs] I got so into it I started crying!

Such an example shows how audiences switch back and forth between positive and negative modes of engagement. Indeed, this young viewer went from refusnik ('this is pathetic!') to engaged viewer ('I got so into it!') to fan ('I love it, I love it I love it!'). Such a viewer can just as easily switch to negative engagement or disengagement, depending on their reactions to other series. Indeed, with something like *Big Brother* as a format which returns year on year we find serial engagement, and in this context viewers can be sensitive to any changes made to a returning series that impact on their affective practices which they have built up over time. If the next version of a reality format fails to deliver the same intense feelings during the live moment then audiences start to disengage, breaking their relationship with the series. Audiences form relationships with reality television over time, and these 'reality' relations are something that can be easily lost in the viewing cultures for digital media.

We can see how the dynamics of reality relations work for *Got to Dance*, a reality talent show where children and adults dance in front of a panel of judges and live audience, and the performer with the most votes wins a cash prize. This research draws on empirical data from the fifth and final season of *Got to Dance* (2014, UK). A total of 100 interviews were conducted during the auditions and live shows, including 10 production interviews, 10 performer interviews, 80 audience interviews with individuals and groups of children, young adults and adults, aged 5–65, from all over the UK, and observations at the live venues with crowds of 4,000–6,000 (see Appendices for more information). The focus here is on a spectrum of engagement, looking in detail at the range of positive and negative audience engagement and disengagement with the series.

The ways of crafting audience engagement, including affective practices in the structuring of live events, all starts with the values of the production. Executive Producer Duncan Gray (2014) developed the format with Princess, owned by

Shine at the time, for Sky One, a subscription based service that is part of the Murdoch empire. Gray is an experienced executive producer of talent shows, having overseen the first competitive mentoring talent show *Popstars: The Rivals* (2002, ITV), and ratings juggernaut *The X Factor* (Syco, ITV, 2004–), whilst controller of entertainment at ITV. He wanted to 'make a big show work with the values that were true to the idea of a talent show' (Gray 2014).

Gray called *Got to Dance* an 'authentic talent show'(2014), signalling a move away from the faux participation that had become a feature of shows like *Britain's Got Talent*. The way he articulated these values was through the difference between the production of *Got to Dance* and other talent shows he had worked on in the past, shows he perceived as inauthentic in their focus not on talent, but on the spectacle of amateur performances. Under Gray's leadership the local production company shaped their talent competition around the framing of passion for dance. The very idea for the format emerged from countrywide dance competitions; the show mimicked 'what thousands of kids were doing anyway in dance companies at weekends' (Gray 2014). A number of strategic decisions enhanced the focus of the format as an authentic talent show; there were no celebrity or amateur dancers in the competition, unlike other dance formats such as *Strictly Come Dancing* (BBC, UK, 2004–); performers won a cash prize with no contractual ties to the production company (unlike formats such as *The X Factor*); performers had free choice of style of dance, music and costumes (unlike rival formats such as *So You Think You Can Dance* (Fox, USA, 2005–); and audiences voted for the winners (unlike the voting scandals of other talent formats – see Chapter 8).

The *Got to Dance* brand became passion for dance, youth and optimism, and this brand was imbued in local production values. For example, the casting director worked on all seasons of the show; she noted:

> People who come on our show are used to hard work, training and discipline. They are not a showy type of person. We have to persuade the really talented people who want to be professional dancers and question 'is it right that I go on a TV talent show?'

Thus, the branding of the format as an authentic talent show that was different from others in the format market was underscored by the management of trust between the producers and participants that this reality event was about passion for dance, even though this was set within a commercial context. The casting director noted how she overheard crew members who had worked on other talent shows describing the contestants as punters, and she told them in no uncertain terms that this show was different, and that respect for the dance community was paramount – her crew was forbidden to use the word 'punter'.

The values of authenticity and positive emotional engagement were structured through storytelling for the judges and participants, at home audience interaction through voting and social media, and participation in live events. For example, positive identification with the judges underscored the pro-social brand: 'the judges are not nasty, they make a huge difference, they give them encouragement' (65 year old female viewer). Or 'all the comments from the judges are positive, they are very, very constructive' (30–40 year old male viewer). In particular the series was shaped around positive engagement with one judge, Ashley Banjo. His street crew Diversity won in the same year as Susan Boyle in *Britain's Got Talent*. Boyle's audition and semi-final live performances became the most shared YouTube videos ever – this is reported in the *Guinness Book of World Records*. Producers in reality talent shows called this the 'Susan Boyle effect', a trope where a seemingly ordinary person starts a journey of discovery, rising from their local community to stardom through a reality television competition; in this case a participant's audition sparks a strong emotional reaction from the judges and live crowds, ensuring social media attention. It is a 'moment's moment', showing performance and reaction as a highly mediated and sharable commodity (Hill 2015). The winners of this season three, Diversity, were somewhat eclipsed by the Susan Boyle effect, but Banjo developed his own celebrity brand with the help of the production company Princess. By season five of *Got to Dance* every schoolchild at the event knew the story of Banjo and his street dance crew Diversity: his back story as a street dancer had become a legend for aspiring child dancers. One mum commented: 'Diversity are normal people, not stuck up, just normal kids. They have done well for themselves and you don't begrudge them because they are talented young men.' Another mum said 'Ashley is all for doing things in the community so he can inspire people to dance.' A strong narrative was established in the production, and this was further co-produced by prospective participants who knew to stage their own performance of self to mirror the Banjo legend and pro-social marketing brand. The Banjo legend became part of the affective script between producers and audiences about what made this an authentic talent show.

Another aspect of positive engagement was the affective practices for the dance performers. One contestant was a young freestyle performer from London who made it through to the semi-finals. She was not sure how her style of dance would be interpreted by the judges or audiences: 'I just lay myself out there and do my thing.' Freestyle does not lend itself to the kind of commercial dance that talent shows tend to cast. When one of the judges in the auditions asked her why she came on this talent show, she explained: 'why not, I am 19, my whole life would be nah, not yet, not yet, I just thought why not?' Her performance of selfhood as an ordinary person hoping for their chance to shine was reinforced by Banjo, who noted 'you are really humble and sweet but you have real passion when you dance. I just absolutely loved what you did.' On the day of her semi-final, she reflected in an interview on being in this kind of talent show:

> last night I was so nervous … then when I woke up in the morning I felt calm … and then just before rehearsals, I don't know why, I felt nerves were rushing in … literally I was in tears, even talking about it now upsets me.

Her performance was one that audiences we spoke to emotionally engaged with. For example: 'She really, really moves me. You can tell that she has a backstory, that she was very, very nervous. You can tell from her performance. A lot of pain comes out in her performance' (20–30 year old female viewer). Her performance of self, coupled with the dance performance on stage, worked together as an emotional hub for producers and audiences.

Audiences described being inspired to dance, to express themselves through physical performance. When a ten year old girl was asked at the live venue what she liked about dance she said 'it's a chance to be me'. The performative frame of the talent show and the positive value system of the production became embedded within families, schools, dance companies and local communities across the UK (see Chapter 7). What made the show so positive to viewers?

> The show's message is if you've got talent, pursue it.
>
> *(30–40 year old male viewer)*

> It shows anybody, no matter what their age and background, people love to dance.
>
> *(20–30 year old female viewer)*

> This show allows people to have their chance.
>
> *(16–20 year old male viewer)*

Got to Dance was a family show that, as one dance mum noted, 'kids can look up to'. Time and again parents pointed out that of all the talent shows this was the one they wanted their aspiring kids to participate in. One viewer explained:

> I don't like *The X Factor* anymore, this one is better. The judges make a big difference. Their hearts are in it. People go in it to be like them. The judges get really excited. I like it when they get emotional, then you know they really care.
>
> *(40–50 year old female viewer)*

Another viewer said: 'It encourages kids from different backgrounds that through dance you can still do very well. Out of all the shows I think it has the most positive attitude. It makes me very happy' (20–30 year old female viewer).

With regard to situated affective practice and engagement in the moment, one example at a live event illustrates the mixing of positive and negative engagement for reality talent shows. The filming took place at Earl's Court in London to full capacity crowds of 5,000–6,000 people. There were lots of fans, families, children, dancers, and dance mums and dads in the crowd. It was the semi-finals and whilst waiting for the next act to perform, I overheard a teenager say to their friends 'I love them already and I haven't even seen them dance.' After the performance, the judges and live audience were divided: one gold star and two red stars lit up the stage. Half the audience roared into life, and booing was heard around the auditorium. The other half murmured amongst themselves about this act and others they liked more. The teenager turned to her friends and immediately started plotting how to thwart the judges and support their favourite dancer through strategic interactive voting. What we witnessed was something about this dancer, her skills, style of dance, choice of music, that connected and disconnected with different audience members. It shows how talent shows rely on positive and negative engagement as something that is powerful because it is in the moment, part of the experience at a live event.

And yet for all this positive engagement, the series was axed after its fifth season due to poor ratings. This outcome is worth unpacking in more detail in relation to understanding tensions within television production and the meaning of engagement. For the ill fated season five, there were tensions within the cultural values of the brand as an authentic talent show, something that had been built up over four years, and the economic values of a format that needed a broad appeal to entertainment audiences. From a casting perspective, the show had worked hard from its inception to build trust in the dance community. In fact so successful were the production team in engaging with the dance community that they had to work extra hard to find a balance of highly trained dancers with the characters normally associated with talent shows, those happy amateurs waiting for their moment in the spotlight. By series four there was some criticism that perhaps the focus was too much on professional skill at the expense of reaching a broader entertainment audience.

Series five included a range of performers, ballet dancers, contemporary solo artists, youth street crews and experimental street performers; it also included some dancers who had already appeared on other talent shows. In particular, a double act of a young boy dancer and adult partner offered a popular performance that eventually ensured they were crowned winners of the final season. Both dancers had been in talent shows as solo artists and their strategic co-performance paid off for this competition. Duplic8 had a bone breaking dance style, creating a spectacle of talent on stage, and memorable 'did-you-see-that moments' for social media. They mobilised online voting, carrying over fans from previous performances, gathering new fans, and ensuring vocal crowds at the live event. For the finale at Earl's Court, crowds were cheering 'Duplic8, Duplic8!' and stamping their feet. When one of the judges did not award a gold star for their performance, the crowd shouted back. The social media performance metrics show just how this strategic engagement with viewers outside of the loyal *Got to Dance* community paid off: the top Facebook posts (1,300 posts, 7,000 likes), top Snapchat posts (2,200 likes), and top posts for Twitter (130,000 followers) were all congratulations to Duplic8. This act were not necessarily the best or most original of dancers, but they were certainly the most aware of the strategic use of mediated performance, young fans and online voting.

After the show was over, one producer muttered under their breath that Duplic8 were more like winners of *Got Talent* than *Got to Dance*. This negative comment was echoed by other viewers interviewed at a dance school:

other acts were amazing, complex choreography … I have to watch many, many, many times and that excites me, from a dancer's point of view … and you can learn from them as opposed to be entertained by them … Duplic8 had entertainment value, calling attention from everyone. The votes obviously took them in the position of winning.

For *Got to Dance*, the internal processes that led to the winners of series five signified a wider problem that the series had lost touch with its core audience, the kind who positively engaged with dancers who appeared different from the more strategic talent show performer.

The series was axed after its fifth season due to poor ratings. According to the BARB (Broadcaster Audience Research Board) figures, viewers disengaged with the series, dropping from 646,000 at the start of the auditions to 486,000 for the live finale, losing a percentage point in the share of audiences watching television at that time (from 3.4 to 2.2). Priority was placed on younger viewers and social media buzz in the here and now of ratings, at the expense of loyal audiences who had lived with the series as embedded in their everyday lives. These at-home audiences saw the show as counter to a negative trend in reality talent formats, as one woman explained: '*Got Talent*, if someone goes on and tries to blow bubbles out of a dog's bum, it ain't talent! Whereas dancing is a proper talent. I think *Got to Dance* is good.' By the end of season five these at-home audiences felt sidelined; their sense of engagement as cultural resonance was largely ignored by the industry's focus on engagement as performance metrics and social media attention. And audiences voiced their disaffection with the show by disengaging from it, effectively closing down the show by not watching or voting. The performance failure of this talent show signals how the cultural values of passion for dance, which had been built up over four years, became subsumed within the economic values of a format that needed a broad appeal to entertainment audiences. To go from such a positive emotional engagement to disengagement in one month during the live shows highlights how engagement as a relationship between producers and audiences can be hard won but easily lost in digital media environments.

Reflections on a spectrum

The play on rhymes for engagement (arrangement, enragement, estrangement) is suggestive of the different affective practices within media engagement. One woman described her engagement as similar to a musical composition: 'a cycle of excitement, anticipation, different characters and what they will do, the culmination of winning and losing – these are cycles that are built into music, intended for you to have a specific response, building so you will come back' (61 year old Alaskan female linguist). She is describing the arrangement of a cultural artefact as a mutual understanding between creator and audience. This audience definition of engagement encapsulates the complex interplay between media industries, aesthetic form, and affective practices.

Audience researchers cannot shy away from the difficulties of situating affect in media experiences. There are contemporary registers in popular culture that mark ordinary affects, just as the above quotation illustrates. It is possible to find, through multi-site and multi-method research, what Stewart (2007: 4) calls 'the intensities and banalities of common experiences'. This is when you look at people up close and personally, and combine this with a more collective social analysis of affective patterns in a given context. Wetherell (2012: 79) comments: 'situated affective activity requires formative background conditions that are social, material and spatial, as well as physiological and phenomenological; it demands collectivities who recognise, endorse and pass on affective practice.'

In terms of audience engagement with different kinds of reality TV, the empirical research shows how we riff on reality at this historical juncture in time. After 15 years of dominance as an entertainment genre, there has been a shift towards the dark side of engagement. Say 'reality TV' and first reactions are often negative. Critics have predicted its negative impact on modern culture, protesters have railed against its existence, participants have sued producers for exploitation, and viewers have called it car crash TV. In a previous work I referred to the novel *Dexter Is Delicious* by Jeff Lindsay (Hill 2015: 137), in which the character of a teenage girl comments on her secret desire to be eaten by cannibals. She asks Dexter, a serial killer who stalks other killers: 'don't you have some kind of secret that, you know ... you can't help it, but it makes you kind of ashamed?' 'Sure' Dexter replies, 'I watched a whole season of *American Idol*' (Lindsay 2010: 279). One of the challenges to understanding reality television is to both acknowledge this negative critique of the market of 'reality' in a commercial culture and also see the multiple ways audiences engage with 'reality' relations.

If we return to the scarecrow festival mentioned at the start of this chapter, this kind of event is part of the situated affective activities of audiences and their spectrum of engagement with popular culture. The scarecrows highlight embodied meaning making; the one about Simon Cowell is a direct invitation to express how you feel about his talent shows and the genre's market in negative emotions. When you visit this scarecrow it is situated outside someone's home, next to the plant pots and the British bunting, suggesting an everyday affective action where there is a shared practice of feeling. The satire on another reality dance show (Figure 4.4) also connects with the affective scripts of the 'Britain's Got Egg Talent' scarecrow. In 'Strictly Crow Dancing' the four judges from *Strictly Come Dancing* display their scores, reflecting the typically low scoring and negative comments from one judge, and the high scoring and over-the-top reactions from another judge. The crows as dancers are a fun reference to the job of scarecrows on farms; we might also play with the American colloquial expression of 'eat crow', which is an odd phrase that refers to admitting saying you were wrong and knowing this is emotionally hard to swallow. Visitors strolling around the streets can talk about these scarecrows, voicing a collective understanding of these affective displays; throwing things at the judges, talking back to them, expressing unruly emotions in a humorous way. These affective practices are brought to fruition in the moment of engagement

FIGURE 4.4 'Strictly Crow Dancing', Heather Scarecrow Festival
Source: Photograph Ian Calcutt.

when the scarecrows are burned, signifying the ability of audiences to mark the moment and move on, to disengage and re-engage, making time and space for other artefacts. Here, then we see a spectrum of engagement as suggestive of the processes of being made and remade, as opportunities for renewal.

Roger Silverstone, writing in a reissue of Williams' classic book *Television* ([1974] 2003: x) points out the power of television to offer 'new opportunities, momentarily outside the sway of transnational capital or the grasp of media moguls, for new forms of self-expression'. The example of the scarecrow festival highlights how popular cultural forms can become a physical embodiment of collective expression. The transgressive practices of humour and ritual burning at the festival allow us to glimpse new opportunities for embodied meaning making, such as a critical engagement with talent shows, a knowing take on commercial culture, or recognition of the performance of self in everyday life. The semantics of engagement that I have outlined here is one means of exploring Williams' 'fundamental belief in the effectiveness of human agency' as transformative and transgressive (Silverstone in Williams 2003: xi). We see how people create and shape storytelling through popular culture, and above all, we see how people complicate and outpace the media industries.

Conclusion

Engagement is integral to transformations in the media industries. A term that usually means audience attention is changing currency, combining ratings and social media trends with cultural resonance. New research on engagement as economic and socio-cultural value can open up the meaning of the term, contributing to an understanding of engagement as relationships, where a dialogue between producers and audiences can generate engagement as cultural resonance.

John Corner's work on stages of engagement shows how engagement varies in intensity, from live viewers to brand loyalty, and involves the cognitive and affective work of audiences in how they think and feel about content. The idea of a spectrum of engagement extends this understanding of the term and contributes to new languages and currencies for media engagement. A spectrum of engagement captures the core meaning of engagement as relationships, and at the same time shows the myriad ways people engage and how this differs from person to person, across varying cultures of viewing. There is a dynamic interplay between producers and audiences about the value and meaning of media, something played out in the contexts of media institutions and everyday routines.

The case of the reality talent show *Got to Dance* was used to think through this idea of a spectrum of engagement. Production and audience research, combining interviews, participant observations, ratings and social media, highlighted the tensions within television institutions about the meaning of engagement as economic and cultural value. This was a talent show for a commercial channel that had pro-social values, an 'authentic talent show' that championed people's passion for dance. One woman described *Got to Dance* as like a stick of rock sweet you buy at the seaside with words embedded in it so they can be continually read as you eat it: 'it's positive all the way through.' With such brand loyalty how did the show fail? It is an example of how quickly positive engagement can switch to negative engagement by audiences and fans angry at changes to the series. In the short view, if a pro-social brand like *Got to Dance* is cancelled audiences lose their relationship with a favourite show, but in the long view broadcasters risk breaking trust with their audiences. Such a move is indicative of the fragile relations between television and audiences at a time of fast and furious changes in the entertainment industry. It signals how broadcasters calculate the economic and cultural values of content, weighing revenues for a series with sinking ratings against the socio-cultural value of content that resonates with loyal viewers and fans – in this case a short-to-medium term economic gain can lead to disaffection with a brand and subscription service. And it highlights the risks of disrupting an all important dialogue between creative producers and audiences at a time when power is slipping from the constitution of television as a key social agency to disparate sites of media content and dispersed audiences for digital environments.

5

THE COOL HEART OF NORDIC NOIR

There are no colourful sunsets.

(61 year old Danish male clerk)

The Bridge is the cool heart of Nordic noir. The metaphor captures the cognitive and emotional dissonance of the drama: a cool tone to the visual and soundscapes and the emotional pull of multi-layered crime drama. When asked to describe *Bron/Broen* Scandinavian audiences called it bittersweet: 'It's wet, chilly, cold and there is this sense of the bittersweet nature of life ... in all this cold gloominess here are all these people trying to get by and sometimes there are little glimpses of light' (26 year old Swedish female sales assistant). Another viewer said:

> There is something Nordic to it. There's the darkness and then it goes bright and then dark again, but all the time this gloomy, dramatic feeling ... I think in the North we are so sound and safe, situated in a welfare society but still something is dangerous.
>
> *(40 year old Danish female blogger)*

In particular, the cool heart of Nordic noir is associated with the character of Saga Norén, a female detective who struggles with the very notion of emotion in her drive to solve crimes. 'Cool heart' is a metaphor that refers to the cognitive and emotional dissonance of the characterisation, sonic and visual elements, as it relates to the narrative and setting for this drama; the idea derives from the production research where this cool heart is expressed through a vocabulary of small gestures and silence to invite character engagement and emotional connection, and as such a 'cool heart; connects with Roland Barthes' (1979) notion of the power of cool in crime drama where the intellectual and emotional structures of entertainment allow for a focus on small gestures and silence to remind us of real life.

FIGURE 5.1 Distressed landscapes for *Bron/Broen* season three
Source: Photograph Tina Askanius.

This chapter examines how executive and creative producers, artistic performers and audiences all perform specific practices that in the end come together in a co-production of intense emotional engagement with the cool heart of this crime drama as Nordic noir. The analysis connects with an earlier discussion of roaming audiences for *The Bridge* that addresses the social contexts of the ritual viewing of crime drama. A key issue in this chapter concerns how genre, affect and emotion are interwoven in the fine details of the production of Nordic noir and audience engagement with it. *The Bridge* refers to the international drama format and *Bron/Broen* refers to the original version of the drama located across the border between Sweden and Denmark (*bron* and *broen* mean the bridge in Swedish and Danish respectively); in this chapter the focus is on the original production set in the Öresund region.

Within the production company Filmlance and its Danish partner Nimbus Film, scriptwriters, directors, editors, costume designers, sound designers, and artistic performers craft affective investment and emotional engagement with the character of Saga and her relationships and experiences within the series. From the small details of what sound Saga's footsteps make, to the physical performance of the actress, the editor's focus on silence and small details in characterisation, and the director's understated storytelling, we see the specific practices that make up the overall characterisation and emotional tone associated with the cool heart of Saga. For Filmlance, *Bron/Broen* has become Saga's story across four seasons, a character that symbolises relationship dynamics, moral dilemmas, and political and cultural tensions. The way to tell Saga's story did not emerge fully formed, but was the result of collaborative creative and emotional labour.

This production labour in the crafting of affect and emotional engagement is combined with the work of audiences. Genre work encapsulates the various ways audiences engage with genre as both storytelling and a means of reflecting on the genre itself (Hill 2007). The concept of 'genre work' is useful in helping to analyse Nordic noir from multiple perspectives, taking into account the complex ways in which this genre is a co-creation of industries and audiences (Hill and Turnbull 2017). In the case of *Bron/Broen*, it involves audiences' immersive experience of the drama, for example their reactions to Saga, her work colleagues, her cultural identity, and it involves audiences' reflections on the crime genre and its similarities and differences with other kinds of drama. Many viewers in this study had a love-hate relationship with Saga in the first two seasons because of her lack of empathy. But for season three audiences empathised more with this character's personal struggles, seeing Saga as the emotional hub of the storytelling – the cool heart of the drama; viewers reflected on the details of the script, lighting, performance, and music that affected their character engagement. Thus, the cultural dynamics of genre work highlight a situated understanding of emotional engagement with television crime drama, how it relates to other Nordic noir, and how practices in production contexts co-create and shape cultures of viewing.

Genre work

The study of genre shows its multidimensionality, working across the different areas of production cultures, aesthetics and poetics of storytelling, and cultures of viewing (Mittell 2004, 2015). The term 'genre work' is used to explore how television is co-created by cultural institutions, creative producers and audiences. Genre work as a co-creation draws on structural factors in the cultural industries, using production studies and political economy to understand the context of producer–consumer relations, for example the production and marketing of Nordic noir by Swedish and Danish public service media to transregional publics (Jensen et al. 2016). Genre work also draws on people's voices and practices as audiences and consumers, fans and participants, using audience studies and cultural studies to understand how and why audiences engage or disengage with a genre, for example character identification. The co-creation of genre work might imply equality of labour, but the concept seeks to weigh the structural factors and systemic power issues within the craft and marketing of a genre alongside the significance of audiences' identities, knowledge and reflections on the cultural resonance of a genre within the context of their lives. In this sense, co-creation is not a co-operative endeavour, and whilst genre work can be a rewarding and empowering experience for producers and audiences, it is all too often a 'tense relationship between different groups of people who are engaged in multiple practices' (Hill 2015: 8).

The term genre work is a play on 'dream work', a psychodynamic term that describes the processes involved in gathering psychic material, and recounting and interpreting dreams, in order to better understand the relationship between one's unconscious and conscious self (see Hill 2007). For psychoanalyst Christopher Bollas (2003) dream work is a never ending process where we dream-work ourselves into becoming who we are, thus connecting psychoanalysis and the expression of self experience. Genre work also refers to the psychoanalytic term 'working through', used by television scholar John Ellis to explain the way television processes the material world into narrativised forms (2000). The idea of dream work, as characterised by Bollas, is similar to Ellis' notion of working through, but there are some subtle differences; working through describes the state whereby we worry over and return to experiences in order to make sense of them, whereas dream work implies that we are always working on our psyche and that we never fully make sense of our experiences. It is this constantly ongoing notion of genre work that helps us understand how <u>a genre's meaning and symbolic power is co-created by institutions, producers and audiences</u> (see Hill and Turnbull 2017).

As mentioned in Chapter 4, Stephen Frosh (2011) researches feelings and subjectivity, and he usefully distinguishes human experience as involving both an immersive, in-the-moment experience, and also a reflecting back, or memorialising of this experience. Similarly, the idea of genre work involves immersive and reflexive modes of engagement and experience. Audiences gather generic knowledge prior to a viewing experience; for example 'how does the character of Saga compare across earlier seasons and other crime drama?'; we experience watching, reading or listening to *Bron/Broen* – 'how do we think and feel about this drama in the moment of viewing?' – and at the same time we reflect on this experience – 'how does this drama have value within the context of our lives?' This last part is an intensely subjective aspect of engagement and experience, where audiences see themselves as viewers, consumers or fans and producers: 'that's me watching this drama, what does this say about my identity?' This reflexive element is a significant part of genre work as it intensifies our emotional connection with television drama.

The genre work within Nordic noir as a category is shaped by producers, including marketing and distribution, in the making of this crime genre, and audiences in their engagement with this as a dramatic experience. Creative producers generate expectations in audiences about what kind of crime they will engage with (police procedural or whodunnit) and specifically what kind of local production of Nordic noir they will encounter (Icelandic, Danish, Norwegian, Swedish or Finnish). This involves genre knowledge about crime across novels, films, television, podcasts and so forth, in different regions, so creative producers build expectations about Nordic noir, differentiating it from American hard boiled noir, or French film noir for example, aligning their work with Scandinavian drama and at the same time making their work stand out as different from other rival dramas (see Hill and Turnbull 2017). There is a layering of genre expectations and knowledge which has long been a feature of the crime genre; think of the plot twists in a classic Agatha Christie country house murder mystery with Poirot compared with the melancholy Parisian street crime of the Inspector Maigret novels; both writers feature a character who is instantly recognisable by his clothing, body and mannerisms, and reputation as a brilliant sleuth, but the emotional tone and generic sensibilities of the novels are quite different in style and experience.

We can see genre work in action in the following discussion of *Bron/Broen* as Nordic noir. A Danish viewer compared the series with two well known public service television dramas:

> *Borgen* isn't so dark. It is a bit more toothless in terms of the emotions it stirs. I get so affected by *Broen* in comparison. You really want them to find the killer. I can't feel *Borgen*, it doesn't stay with me that long. Just a simple thing as the song from the introduction in *Broen*, it stays with me all week whereas I can't even remember if there was a song in *The Killing* or in *Borgen*. They have created a strong brand in that sense.
>
> *(27 year old female Danish social worker)*

There is the generic expectation, built right into the opening music and titles, that *Bron/Broen* is different from other Danish drama. In another example, a viewer noted how Nordic noir was more complex than police procedural dramas: 'In other shows and films … it becomes so open-and-shut, so obvious, and it's not good. But they haven't done that in *Bron*. They let the images speak for themselves' (65 year old Swedish male, retired). This reflecting back on other crime series allows the processes of genre work to generate engagement with this particular drama. What makes *Bron/Broen* stand out from its competition? These viewers reflected on what makes the series distinctive, a tender picture of fragile people, built through the dialogue, acting, style and narrative: 'Horrible things and misery, but still with some form of love, some form of respect. And these tired people, they sit there in their police offices, hoping and working, struggling with their personal lives and various goings-on' (51 year old Swedish male designer). They describe this drama as dark and miserable, and vulnerable and touching, a mixture of light and shade that allows audiences to emotionally engage with this drama within the genre of Nordic noir.

As these responses highlight, alongside genre expectation audience knowledge, skills and resources in representation and aesthetics is involved; for example how performance works, or what editing does to the storytelling. The editor draws on audience expectations about tone and style, aesthetics and narrative in the work of making a genre come to life in an immersive viewing experience. The editor of *Bron/Broen*, Patrick Austen, devoted time and energy to what audiences expected of this drama in its emotional tone and storytelling style, and how it connects with other examples of dramatic form. His emphasis is on character engagement, drawing audiences into the crime narrative through emotional connection with the actors and their performances. He explained about the craft of the crime genre for an editor:

The story is so much more than actual plot. A crime story structure and storytelling in general are similar. There are a few different ways of telling a crime story, you can tell who did it at the beginning, and then you can go the other way around that something has happened and you figure out whodunnit. It is pretty similar and audiences know about this. For me, it is all about finding the rhythm and how to find ways of making these characters interesting to audiences.

(Austen 2014)

One particular discussion focused on the film *Twelve Years a Slave* (2013, director Steve McQueen) and the way the camera could hold a moment in time, not cutting to another scene but staying focused on a tableau or character, giving audiences a quiet space for reflection within the narrative: in one of the final scenes there is a long shot of the central character standing by a tree – 'he just stands there. You as an audience can sum up the whole film in this shot where nothing happens. By making the character not do anything you can make the audience connect with that' (Austen 2014). This focus on character, style and emotional tone influenced the editing of *Bron/Broen*, and in turn was significant to audiences who reflected on how the stillness within the drama enhanced their immersive experience: 'It is slow. Normally crime dramas are so quick, swift change of scenes, people running. But I love how they slow down the pace and you can you feel almost part of the images you are watching' (63 year old Danish female clerk).

One of the significant aspects of genre work as a concept is how it highlights the building up of a range of expectations by producers and audiences, and then follows through to the negotiation and realisation of this experience, something that we see in the fine details of the craft of production and the shaping of the dramatic experience. In the next section we look at emotions in television drama in more detail to understand their central role in the genre work of Nordic noir.

Television drama: emotions and genre

According to Robin Nelson (2016: 5) the focus on emotions within television drama is an under-explored area. Much research in cognitive film theory has explored the affective structures within films, analysing the step by step processes in conscious emotional reactions to film texts. When it comes to film theory little attention has been given to emotional engagement by audiences, instead tending to consider the implied audience, or historical and contemporary discourses of audiences in spectators' experiences (see Plantinga 2009). For Nelson, research in television drama has explored moral emotion and characterisation, for example looking at how serial narrative builds 'emotional moments', or how gender and genre impacts on emotions in narrative (2016: 8). In Gunhild Agger's anlaysis of Nordic noir she explored moments of affect and narrative through the use of landscape and cityscapes that are used to evoke the dark and melancholy noir of these Scandinavian television series.

For Sue Thornham and Tony Purvis television drama is a production of stories about contemporary culture, and the meanings of that culture' (2005: 24). They argue that television drama can be theorised as public narratives, 'constructing, mediating and framing our social and individual identities' (2005: 28). If we connect this with theories of affect and emotion, then television drama has affective structures that help to place emotion in the storytelling of the drama and within the everyday lives of audiences (Gorton 2009: 69). Taking a cue from Margaret Wetherell (2012) on affect and emotion, there are affective scripts and practices within television drama that can highlight public narratives of emotions and feelings about ourselves and others in situated contexts. There are 'affective patterns' (Wetherell 2012: 119) which are enacted within television production and situated within cultures of viewing.

Recent work by Jason Mittell (2015: 9) on complex television explores a poetic approach to 'the formal dimensions and cultural practices of contemporary television serial storytelling'. This poetics of television narrative and reception contexts is inspired by Robert C. Allen's 'reader-orientated poetics' (1985) which is a combination of literary reader-response criticism, genre analysis, and reception analysis; Mittell uses contemporary television drama to explore narrative complexity and consumption practices for dedicated fans and intense forms of engagement. In particular, Mittell's discussion of character engagement is significant. He describes how television characters derive from the work of actors and producers, showing how performance is a collaborative process (2015: 119). In this analysis, the collaborative work of actors and producers is connected to that of audiences, not only in the ways in which audiences engage with a character, but in how they imbue a character with values and meanings that are related to their own identities and experiences. This would suggest that the character of Saga is not only performed by Sofia Helin, and the character written, directed and edited by creative producers at Filmlance, but that the character embodies the drama through the co-creative work of audiences as well. Saga is *Bron/Broen* because of the genre work of producers, performers and audiences coming together in the shaping of the character within the public narrative of this crime drama.

We might say that there is a producer–audience oriented poetics that connects creative producers and the formal dimensions of Nordic noir drama with viewers' affective practices for serial storytelling. The producer orientation can be seen in the way the drama is difficult for creatives to pin down as a clearly defined set of values, feelings and cultural practices. When asked what makes *Bron/Broen* the kind of drama it is, producers articulated an instinctive feeling that you know it when you see it. For example Anders Landström, the main producer, reflected on the affective knowledge that is so crucial to genre work: 'Everyone knows the feelings of *Bron*. What is *Bron*? You see it on the screen but it's hard to say what it is. It is your reaction when you see it' (Landström 2014). The audience orientation can be seen in the way the drama stops viewers in their tracks, inviting emotional engagement and reflection on the drama in relation to their lives.

If we focus on emotional engagement we can see how significant this is in the fine details of crafting our experience of Nordic noir. The editor of *Bron/Broen* Patrick Austen (2014) explained how emotion guides his work:

> You can be very intellectual about storytelling, but when you boil it down to the essence, it is about conveying and communicating emotions, both with the characters and the story, but moreover, <u>conveying and communicating emotions to an audience</u>, knowing what is happening to an audience.

In a particular scene at the end of season two, both the editor and director Henrik Georgsson fine tuned this way of communicating emotions to audiences in a powerful moment between the two central characters Saga and her professional partner Martin. In this scene Saga realises Martin has poisoned the person who murdered his son (in season one), a moment where Saga's morally black and white world is set against the grey zone of Martin's revenge; as Martin is the core person who understands her this signifies a fracture in their relationship, one that will see Saga report the crime and thus tragically end her connection with someone she cares for. Austen recalled how he and the director worked on this scene in the editing room:

> Saga confronts Martin in the hotel room about the poison. He asks her do you know it is me, and she says you know I do. If you read the script, it contains a lot of other text, and these lines are placed in a different order of the scene. We worked with the scene where we used shots of Saga where she was a lot more emotional when she delivered her text and reacted to Martin. We both felt that made it very emotional, one of the few times in the series she was able to feel something. We worked with that, and on the last few days we looked for material that made Saga more direct and still, more true to her personality and we found a take that was more direct. It was a question we asked, does the story gain from using a character that shows all emotions, or should we use a shot where the character relies on the script and situation to make the audience feel more? We didn't talk so much in the editing room about this, but looking back at what ended up on the screen, it made the scene even more hurtful, the choice we made was to rely on the audience actually developing these feelings, rather than the character showing it.

Here we see the genre knowledge of emotion within this crime drama, and this specific character, guide the crafting of engagement with the audience, allowing stillness and space for the audience to shape their experience of this scene in the finale.

Thus, producers and audiences shape a poetics for the drama. For example:

> Sometimes I feel it is really poetic. It may sound a bit of a weird description in the middle of all this violence but some of the clips with Saga and Martin, for example the scene on the bridge where they meet by the water, they are

standing there, it is a slow scene, grey and slow. He gives her a hug. He can't help but show his emotions and gratitude and she, despite her character, embraces it. It's poetic.

(63 year old Danish female clerk)

This grey, slow feeling to *Bron/Broen* is about the landscape of this region, the dark winter days and nights, the characters and performances in the series, the lighting, cinematography, and sound design, and it is about human relationships and the articulation of affect and emotion. One viewer explained:

Most people recognise fragments of something in ourselves or in someone we know in a way that affects us A common theme in the Nordic noir stories are people who are somehow a bit lost in their life and don't know how to handle life, it represents people that are really bad at some things in life but really good at others. And that's where it touches us, that's when it becomes real.

(27 year old female Danish social worker)

The question of what is this drama, then, becomes enacted within the affective scripts in the production culture and the affective practices of audiences.

Producing *Bron/Broen*

Research on Nordic noir highlights the values within television scriptwriting and production for public service television (Redvall 2013; Jensen and Waade 2013), for example an attention to lighting design, or storytelling techniques, that utilise both film and television production skills in Denmark and Sweden to create quality television drama (McCabe and Akass 2007). Filmlance International is a production company that makes both feature length films and crime drama. Around a hundred people worked on *Bron/Broen*, and this team also collaborated with Danish production company Nimbus Film; the drama is co-financed by public service media SVT and DR, and German broadcaster ZDF. This drama format highlights what Hansen and Waade (2017) note is the transnational finances and regional development of Nordic noir television drama, making it a combination of a local and transregional production and an international hit with global broadcasters and audiences. Anders Landström (2014) is the producer and he spoke of the challenges of making quality drama for a small market such as Sweden. Filmlance works in a non-hierarchical way with an emphasis on small teams: 'We have a flatter organisation, with not so many layers. It's a different way of working, simpler, everyone works together, talks to each other, everyone takes responsibility for their work.'

Many of the creatives have worked on the drama from the beginning, for example writers Hans Rosendeldt and Camilla Ahlgren, director Henrik Georgsson, cinematographer Carl Sundberg and editor Patrick Austen, composer Johan Söderqvist and costume designer Kerstin Halvorsson, as a well as a host of others.

From this tight team comes an accumulation of sensuous knowledge of how to create the distinctive quality of *Bron/Broen*. Director Henrik Georgsson described this as an instinctive understanding: 'The word we say ... is "Bronish." We are working tight together. We have a universe where we all know something about *Bron*, what Saga is, or how we use the landscape and architecture ... so we have something in common to start with and then we can discuss what directions to take'. Costume designer Kerstin Halvorssen noted how the drama became embedded in her work practice and home life, slipping into her everyday consciousness – shopping with her family, she might see a T-shirt that would suit Saga. She explained how the series had touched her deeply: '*Bron* may end but you cannot take *Bron* out of us.'

The affective structures of the production culture within Filmlance created a closeness that was crucial to the crafting of emotional engagement with the character of Saga. Director Henrik Georgsson (2015) described a key scene in season three where Saga met her mother outside her home. This is a powerful scene containing the hallmarks of *Bron/Broen*, a quiet direction, an understated style of acting that is focused on small details, a modern set design, a muted colour and lighting design, and a focus on cognitive and emotional dissonance (Jensen and Waade 2013). After this unwelcome visit, Saga felt compelled to arrange books neatly on a shelf, an emotional orientation after the trauma of encountering her mother. The director and actress 'discussed different ideas and came up with something very small and very Saga-ish'. He explained:

> In the script from the beginning it was written that she should take her weapon ... we tried to find something that she would do and we came up with this ... she has books in the bookshelves and it is important for her to have her stuff in the way she wants it. This is how we work, when we don't really think that it works one hundred percent we have a dialogue ... there is no prestige really because we all understand that we come up with a better idea. It is a great way to work, it is the way it should be.
>
> *(Georgsson 2015)*

Such a comment highlights emotional labour in a drama production (Hochschild 2003), where the interpretation of a script generates a more subjective knowledge about the value of dialogue and silence, attention to detail and stillness, and trust in each other.

The emotional tone of *Bron/Broen* is one of a cool heart. The phrase arises from the production interviews in the discussions among creatives about the special feeling of *Bron/Broen* that is crafted through contrasts, creating cognitive and emotional dissonance by different kinds of wide shots, and up-close and personal moments, or contrasting colour and soundscapes. The cool heart of *Bron* is an example of situated affective practices within a drama production (Wetherell 2012). Producers spoke of using dissonance across image, sound and colour, helping to craft an affective structure that creates space for feelings of beauty and ugliness, or coldness and humanity.

> We work a lot with the atmosphere in the pictures and then in the sound and the music. I think a lot about how the pictures will work with the music later on, to give space for the music, for feelings and atmosphere in different ways.
>
> (Georgsson 2015)

Editor Patrick Austen (2015) explained how the drama 'has a visual energy that works well with contrasts'. The director reflected on this:

> we do a lot of things with the sound you know, going from the kind of naturalistic sound when you hear traffic and things like that that are on the street and then to change that into some kind of subjective tone that is close to the characters, that the world around them disappears. Especially when you go from one scene to another the way you do it with the sound is you shouldn't think about it, you just feel it. It is also in the details, you know when Saga is closing a door, it could say something about her, if it is a heavy sound or hard sound, or it is a soft sound … every little detail [of] the sound really could say a lot about the characters.
>
> (Georgsson 2015)

Such attention to ordinary affects invites intense engagement with character, atmosphere and sound: 'My friend and I talked about how it's an experience of sound … I think the sound and light create the same atmosphere as Saga, it reflects her dark side' (36 year old Danish female pharmacist).

The process of creating the experience of *Bron* involves an emotional and psychological investment in storytelling. Georgsson (2015) imagined how audiences would react: 'You try to nourish the viewers' own thoughts, give some space for that in the most effective way.' Similarly Austen (2015) talked about an imagined audience during the editing process, the viewer at his back, tapping him on the shoulder, saying 'Hey something is wrong here, or something is very right here.' This is a fine balancing act of editing the story, where the texture and tone of the drama relies on a combination of 'rationally understanding what is going on and being emotionally moved at the same time' (Austen 2015). Such comments highlight the genre work of crime drama where producers and audiences co-create cognitive and emotional engagement with the cool heart of the series.

In his essay on 'Power and "Cool"' Roland Barthes analyses gangster films and the considerable 'vocabulary of "cool" gestures', such as the snap of the fingers as a signal for gunfire, a simple gesture that manifests the presence of fate: 'the residue of a tragic movement which manages to identify gesture and action within the slenderest volume' (1979: 43). For Barthes, the power of cool is in the dissonance: 'the intellectual (and not only) emotive structure of the entertainment' (1979: 44). The power of cool is in the smallest detail and most significantly in the silence, so raising a finger is a gesture that halts action and highlights 'the notion that real life is in silence' (ibid.). The power of the cool heart of this drama signals a considerable sonic and visual vocabulary of small gestures, still moments and silence, where the details and silences carry the audience through to reflection on the intellectual and emotional structures of the drama. As we have seen already, this is a conscious decision by the producers and actors to create space for small gestures that signify larger emotional issues within the narrative and characterisation. The editor Patrick Austen described the power of silence as part of how he shapes the cool heart of the drama, and in the above example from the director we see yet again the way of working within the production team where small gestures and quiet moments invite audiences into the drama and make space for reflection. This cool heart is perhaps most clearly felt in the character of Saga, where the decision to not use the gun allowed the director and actress to highlight the small gesture of Saga silently aligning her books on the shelf. These 'cool' gestures of Saga exemplify the emotional distance of the character and at the same time feel authentic for her character and the trauma of her past, her fate within the series; this is precisely the cool that Barthes refers to where 'real life is in the silence' (ibid.). This cool heart is a pattern within the overall series, a delicate balance between the drama's intellectual structures in particular the narrative and crime plotting, and its affective and emotional structures, in particular the characterisation and sonic and visual style. The next sections explore these mixed elements of the cool heart of *Bron/Broen* in more detail.

Narrative tapestry

One way of creating the distinctive quality of *Bron/Broen* is through complex narrative, which many viewers describe as a rich tapestry with many threads. Camilla Ahlgren (2015) spoke of the writing process as 'working in a very detailed way'. She noted the pressure of writing a third season: 'we thought we had to do something completely different'. Season three started out with several writers, but because of changes to the storyline at a late stage in the process, Hans Rosenfeld and Camilla Ahlgren worked together on many of the scripts, particularly from episode five onwards. She felt this added depth to the writing: 'you can feel it; it's stronger in the scripts. The story has to be original, something extraordinary, it has to be different' (Ahlgren 2015).

For director Henrik Georgsson (2015) 'the script is my best friend and my worst enemy at the same time'. He explained this love-hate relationship:

> I am listening to the script and interpreting the script in a way to make it work. It's a struggle … we have a lot of meetings to look at different versions of the editing. There can be a lot of strong discussions about if we should have this scene or not. This is also fun, we are competing with each other, it's a very strong creative process.

The director and editor have to trust each other in the dynamics of storytelling, all the possibilities that can exist by fine tuning the tempo, or music, contrasting close ups with big expressive shots. There is a depth of understanding about the power of storytelling. Georgsson (2015) explained: 'The audience must think "who did it?", "how this does connect?" We try to keep that suspense all the time ... and we do that from the beginning in the shooting and editing'.

We asked audiences in our sample to describe themselves and they typically used phrases such as loyal, demanding, and hard to please: 'I love to sit and think about what's going on. I really like to think and guess what's going to happen and then find out that I got it all wrong' (30 year old Danish female social worker). We can see the close attention to detail in the production culture, the intuitive feeling that something is 'Bronish', as a crucial feature of the types of intense engagement with the crime narrative in audiences across Sweden and Denmark. Take for example these comments on season two of *Bron/Broen*:

> It's like a tapestry, somehow .... and that's what makes it fun, that's why I sit each time and think I've figured out who it is. People come in, go away to the periphery, and then they'll come back, and I'll think: 'Oh, now he's back again.' That's how it should be. It's like a mystery novel for me. That's how it's supposed to feel.
>
> *(50 year old Swedish female project manager)*

> Now we're all sitting here, wondering what to do with all these threads, and it'll come along in the end. Because that is how it was in the last season, it was all tied together at the end. It's going to be exciting.
>
> *(63 year old Swedish female carer)*

Genre expectations for crime novels and Nordic noir television drama create an attentive viewing experience, where the series 'demands something from the viewer' (58 year old Swedish male, retired). Typical for the history of the crime genre is the ludic qualities of the narrative, solving the mystery, the classic whodunit (see Turnbull 2014). And audiences carry this knowledge into their own genre work. As this viewer reflected:

> You have to be focused. You're participating, somehow, solving the mystery ... Rather than just sitting on the sofa, now you have to apply yourself ... it's a damn good story, so very cryptic, little things all the time. It's woven together.
>
> *(26 year old Swedish female supermarket worker)*

Here are some examples from season three that highlight how audiences carry their genre knowledge of *Bron/Broen* over into the next season, anticipating narrative complexity and giving space for their own co-creative labour in shaping the drama. We can see how Danish viewers responded to the narrative tapestry:

> I love that I can sit and guess who the murderer is. I like being part of the detective work.
>
> *(38 year old Danish male postman)*

> I made a few different guesses but none of them were right. I thought the third season was really great.
>
> *(57 year old Danish male truck driver)*

> The script is just great, it's totally gripping.
>
> *(36 year old Danish female clerk)*

And we find similar pleasures in piecing together the puzzle of the story for Swedish viewers:

> I like shows where you have to think and engage. It feels like you can solve the puzzle and lay out all the pieces.
>
> *(23 year old Swedish male student)*

> You get very satisfied if you manage to figure something out before it happens: 'Oh, I knew it!'
>
> *(23 year old Swedish female student)*

> But the best part is when you think you've figured it out and then they trick you.
>
> *(21 year old Swedish female student)*

The complicated narrative is a key strength of the drama, but it has a tipping point, and some viewers noted how they would reach the limit of what they could handle on a Sunday night, with some taking recourse to repeat viewing, or pausing the digital recorder, so they could fully understand what is going on. These viewers explained:

> My husband thinks it gets too complex. That why he keeps asking: 'Who's that?' That's all we talk about, me explaining that: 'You know, that's the guy with the boat'. I don't have any trouble keeping up, but he obviously has, so I suppose it's possible. But not me, no, I don't think it gets too complex. Rather, the complexity is the show's strength.
>
> *(63 year old Danish female clerk)*

> We have this digital box, and every time we watch we can pause it, and talk about it – 'What was this? Was that the person who was in the first episode?' It's right on the border of being too hard to follow, which forces you to be active: 'No, that was him. Oh, right.' And we'll discuss until we're caught up. It's needed.
>
> *(41 year old Swedish male entrepreneur)*

The close attention to detail that the editor and producer spoke of when creating *Bron/Broen* is there to see in the attentive viewing experience. Although audiences reflect on how demanding the narrative is, they see this narrative tapestry as a core value of the drama. This same viewer further explained how complex narratives in a crime drama such as this speak to the politics of Nordic society: 'It illustrates the complexity of the world we live in and what could actually happen in this polarized political climate we live in' (63 year old female Danish clerk). The double reference to the fictional world of the drama and the world we live in signals the close relations between narrative complexity and audience engagement: 'when politics are put in play in this subtle manner it becomes relevant to me. We talk about it at work. We don't just watch this alone in each of our different houses. We share it afterwards' (63 year old female Danish clerk). In this way the fictional values of the drama cross over into the real world values and societal fears of audiences in their everyday lives.

Bron/Broen invites a particular kind of intense audience-oriented poetics. Fans watch and re-watch the series in a loop where the fictional narrative becomes woven into the details of their everyday lives. The following example highlights one fan's intense commitment to season three:

> I can't wait until nine o'clock, so I've watched it at eight on Danish TV, with subtitles. And then I switch over to channel one and watch it again. And then I'll watch it several more times during the week … I watch it once or twice with visual interpretation and when you're at a certain point in the season you have to go back and check your theories … I realize how crazy this sounds. This weekend, I watched all the episodes before the finale and took notes and when time began to run out, and I still had a bit of episode eight and nine left, I started skipping ahead because I wanted to solve the murder. When you have the answers to all the other storylines, I want to know who the killer is. So I had two A4 pages of notes … this madness kicks in when I want to solve the murder before they do.
>
> *(33 year old Swedish female teacher)*

This fan uses the border territory of southern Sweden and Denmark to give her an extra edge on an intense engagement with the series; starting out on Danish public service television, migrating to Swedish public service television, she spends her Sunday evening in a first viewing, slowly taking in the drama. She then reserves time in the week for re-watching, taking notes, drawing on other resources, websites, news, other crime novels, films or drama, all so as to solve the murder before the end of the series. Just as Cornell Sandvoss notes (2005), this fan forms an intense psychological attachment to the drama, jokingly calling it a 'madness' that takes hold and will not let go until the series' finale.

Fan commitment also includes performing in the production. One woman gained some local notoriety amongst *Bron/Broen* extras for her role as a dead woman with an apple in one episode of season three: 'If I had an apple in my mouth you would have recognized me! Someone even asked me: "What sort of apple was it?"' One group of fans hired as extras regularly met to socialise and watch the show: 'We play the police. We have been part of this for so long, on set from eight in the morning to midnight' (female extra at launch event). They noted how serious the production team were, mirroring how seriously fans treat the drama: 'There weren't jokes and laughter between the takes, the whole team was like: "This is really serious"'(72 year old Swedish female, retired, extra). For these regular *Bron/Broen* extras, there was a local value to their fan engagement, where they could enjoy close proximity to the production, observing filming near their local supermarket: 'Yesterday, I met the medical examiner at the Co-op ... it adds a certain flair to everyday life' (46 year old Swedish female communications officer).

Character engagement: Saga is *Bron/Broen*

The female character of detective Saga Norén has become the core identity of the drama. But it didn't start out this way for the creative producers, performers or audiences. The actress Sofia Helin described at first feeling unsure about the character, having to jump in and 'see what happens' (2015). The creative process was all about trust and listening to the writer and director who were 'interested in my thoughts, my process, how to embody a character. It's amazing to

FIGURE 5.2 Stand-in Saga: at the production offices of Filmlance
Source: Photograph Tina Askanius.

experience that. It's a matter of trust and a willingness to be open, no prestige, to have one goal – what is best for *Bron*' (Helin 2015). The director also discussed this creative process: 'it is not crystal clear from the beginning. You have a picture of it, of course, but when you start working with the details, costume, actress, props, that is what's really fun about it' (Georgsson 2015). Writer Camilla Ahlgren (2015) spoke of crafting the character of Saga so that 'you can recognise yourself in her situations, to feel for her, that is very important'. Thus, the writers, directors and actors shape the character of Saga together in an iterative process, building up emotional identification with her character and its cool heart, with an emphasis on her emotional distance, small gestural movements, and silent moments in the series.

Identification with Saga did not come easily to audiences. One fan, a crime drama blogger, commented:

> There has been a trend that they [female characters] all have a medical condition. First we have Lisbeth Salander, then there is Claire Danes from *Homeland* and then there is Sara Lund from *The Killing* who is also … yeah. I don't know if I am thinking of this because I have a son with autism but I really know the feeling when everyone is saying 'Oh they must be so horrible to be around.' We know what that is like, the distance, how they take everything literally, you can't small talk … These female types we see so much are not normal. Saga has Asperger's for sure and some features characteristic of autism … I am still not tired of watching these female types yet. I know some people are. They can't take any more of these women with abnormalities and ask, why can't we just see normal women?
>
> *(40 year old Danish female blogger)*

The genre knowledge of 'female types' who are 'not normal' in crime drama was both a draw for audiences and also a problem, leading to reflections on the genre and gender identification, the autism spectrum, and the decision to commit to engage with this drama or not.

From the first season, Saga was both a distinctive feature of the series, something that singled *Bron/Broen* out from other crime drama, and also a challenge to viewers as to how to relate to her personality and the way the actress played her:

> She's growing on me … it's taken me so long to begin to like her. My mother, she saw an episode from the second season and said: 'Oh, I can't watch this. What is wrong with her?' because she hadn't seen it from the beginning, she doesn't understand that she has Asperger's.
>
> *(26 year old Swedish female supermarket worker)*

It was a common experience amongst audiences in Sweden and Denmark to describe how they grew to understand the character, just as the actress and production team also grew in confidence in how to portray Saga and engage audiences in her way of experiencing life. This is done partly through the script and Sofia Helin's performance:

> In the first episodes I didn't really like her and a lot of people whom I've spoken to felt the same way. I thought the acting wasn't that good. But then you realised that she was really like that and it must be so hard to play a character that's like that.
>
> *(23 year old Swedish female webmaster)*

– and partly through audiences learning how to engage with Saga through emotional identification with her personality: 'At first I thought she was just completely annoying but she's grown on me. Saga is totally unpredictable, I can't figure her out. I like her incredibly direct way' (38 year old Danish female journalist).

The phrase 'she's growing on me' recurred across audience reflections in seasons one and two, where her difficult personality and relationship with Martin, her Danish detective partner, was part of a hot-and-cold emotional arc to the storytelling. For the earlier seasons viewers related to Saga through Martin: 'she thinks that she's in total control, because she reads the texts, she reads the books, and he gets to tell her how it works in the real world, on the social plane which she doesn't understand at all' (63 year old Swedish female carer).

> It took a while for him to understand just who she was. But he's one of the few who understands her; other characters 'run head-first into a wall' whenever they meet her, and Martin enabled viewers to see the world through Saga's eyes.
>
> *(63 year old Swedish female carer)*

This viewer reflected on the relationship between Martin and Saga in one scene in season two:

> When they were standing by the water next to the bridge and he thanked her, it was nicely put together – because she didn't understand his thank you. She was just doing her job. But she accepted it. It showed how she had developed.
>
> *(61 year old Danish male clerk)*

The moments of silence in scenes such as this underscore the 'cool' power of the character of Saga and her relationship with others, a symbolic power that flows through the drama to the ways audiences engage with its intellectual and emotional elements: 'Without words the scene defines their relationship. That fascinates me and it does something to me. That's what grabs me' (63 year old Danish female clerk).

For season three, returning audiences knew in advance that the character of Martin was not part of the storyline, so this genre knowledge contributed to their serial engagement with the brand. Fans worried about how Saga would react without the friendship of Martin, but soon they realised how the new character of

Henrik added another dimension to the drama. The dark side of the character, his loneliness, drew viewers in: 'he has a lot to wrestle with which makes you feel for him. You get a good feeling of them being two wounded animals who need each other. There is a beautiful symbolism in that' (27 year old Danish female advertising worker). Audiences committed to Saga, in some ways taking on the role of Martin in understanding her character:

> I hated Saga in the beginning. I couldn't stand her because I had watched *Homeland* before and it's similar. The way the actress acted was so unusual; it was annoying at first: 'She can't act like that!' But now I'm on Team Saga all the way. I'm really upset that her mother came along and ruined things: 'Leave her alone!' That's how I feel. It's really been a journey with Saga, you understand her better … You really empathise with her.
>
> *(23 year old Swedish male law student)*

The decision to make Saga central to season three was a creative risk that paid off with audiences who, through the process of serial engagement, became Saga's main supporters: 'Come on, Saga, stand up for yourself! Ignore that bitch!' (22 year old Swedish female student).

For season three of *Bron/Broen* there was an emotional rollercoaster for the character of Saga, mixing crime with melodrama. Helin (2015) could 'never relax, never feel comfortable and safe':

> We put Saga in situations where she could not rely on her usual way of being. She goes to a dark place, and that interests me as an actress. I had to dig deep inside myself and dig deep into Saga's world. I know her well and yet I didn't know how she would react under so much pressure. I just had to experience that.

Audiences reacted strongly to this vulnerability: 'Saga's shield has been dismantled' (46 year old Swedish female communications officer). Another noted: 'I feel she becomes more and more humane. She now does things that you couldn't imagine in the first episode' (47 year old Danish male support worker). Fans felt protective of Saga, some even worrying that the script had gone too far in pushing the character to the brink: 'I really felt like a big sister and I wanted to defend Saga against the script: "Leave her alone. Can't she just be allowed to have this time?"' (35 year old Swedish female psychologist). How viewers reacted to Saga said something about themselves as well as the technicality of the performance: 'We've talked about how there should be more room for different types of people in our society … we should look a little further before we judge people' (37 year old Danish female accountant).

Viewers found the final episodes especially powerful in terms of character development. This was something the production team worked hard to achieve. Georgsson (2015) commented on seeing the freshly edited final episodes: 'That is one of those moments that really are so fantastic, a feeling from shooting it to what it could be. That is hard to do. It is like finding gold in the river.' Audiences looked for these nuggets of gold:

> She even cried! And it's certainly difficult for her, she has such an extreme need for control. They have filmed it very well, from such a strange angle that you couldn't really understand the face … It was just a collection of random facial features. Eyes, mouth, you didn't understand how they all fit together. It was ugly. Not that she was ugly, but it was an image of ugliness.
>
> *(46 year old Swedish female communications worker)*

Saga's story, then, became a story of vulnerability (her 'shield has been dismantled'), one that was shaped by the creative producers and actors, and in turn reshaped by audiences in their serial engagement with the drama.

Human constellations

Bron/Broen has a dual identity of crime drama and melodrama. For Lars Blomgren (2015), this dual identity is a strength of Swedish crime drama that is 'a family drama on steroids. The centre of our universe is the family. The worst problems you see here are family problems, so basically all the crime stories are about entering people's home where there is a tragedy or distress.' Such a comment is echoed by the writers – 'every story is something to do with the family; we have worked hard to find different stories about the family and society from a new angle' (Camilla Ahlgren 2015). And the director: 'it is very much about close family relations; it could be seen as a critique of society. A key theme is how you claim responsibility for creating life' (Henrik Georgsson 2015).

Viewers noted the critique of social norms and issues of inclusion and exclusion in the drama: 'There's a lot of exclusion in society, for example, in this season they've shown rich people, foster families, and people who fall through the cracks' (29 year old Swedish female dance teacher). 'It has to do with the picture of the family. It's a commentary to how we live our life' (41 year old Danish female copy editor). Some viewers noted a specific Scandinavian social critique: 'Nordic societies, I see it as very individualized which is very bad because people get used to being alone and they don't seek help' (27 year old Swedish-Egyptian female dancer).

Season three featured a complex killer, not easily recognisable as a psychopath and therefore not identifiable as one to most audiences. The director explained:

> The actor is very fragile, that is a special quality to him. I tried to make him as three-dimensional as possible. He is killing people, but he is shy, and so you can feel for him. 'I shouldn't have been born' is a line of his.
>
> *(Georgsson 2015)*

The actor Adam Pålsson (2015) reflected on playing the role of Emil:

You have so many images of what a psychopath looks like and you have to resist that cliché. You have to tune into something else. As Emil I don't have to scream. The only way I express emotions is when I lose control. My style of acting is different, I wanted to create the character through improvisation, through bigger emotions. Henrik is more technical, and we had a good balance between his focus on smaller details and my expressive style.

The production designer lovingly created the killer's dolls' house with miniature crime scenes to reflect the loneliness and horror of Emil's world. He recalled: 'I found the dolls' house left at the back of a film set, nobody wanted it. The dolls' house is horrible.' The attention to detail in the crafting of Emil and his macabre art was appreciated by viewers, offering reflections on 'sick ways to handle loneliness' (23 year old Swedish female student). People responded to the message that although 'revenge was the motive for the murders' this wasn't a straightforward portrayal of a psychopath; he acted 'to prevent other people from living the horrible life he had lived' (42 year old Danish male photographer).

In the following comments focus group participants reflected on the moral landscape:

> Everybody is weighed down from the start, and you know that everybody will be weighed down when it ends too. It sounds weird but that's what draws me in, there's something about the hopelessness that I like.
> *(23 year old Swedish female student)*

> Right. The more depressing something is the better it is ... if everyone was happy and everything was going well ... it's a bit stupid, a bit naïve. You can tell how well made it is, the gloomier and more serious it is.
> *(24 year old Swedish female student)*

> It always feels like it's all really hopeless: 'Oh no, everything is going to hell.' And then something happens that makes you feel a tiny bit of hope. They always trigger that sense of hope: 'Oh, it might work out.' And then: 'No, it won't.' And then: 'Well, it might.' I suppose that's where the suspense comes from. Things are always on the brink of destruction.
> *(23 year old Swedish female student)*

This feeling of being weighed down, the vulnerability of human relations, was a powerful and compelling part of the genre work of this crime drama. In such a way, we see the crafting of affect and emotional engagement in television drama production and how audiences engage with the crime genre as both storytelling and a means of reflecting on the genre itself.

Conclusion

The creative and viewing experience of this drama is an example of genre work, where creative and emotional labour help to shape audience engagement with this drama and the genre of Nordic noir. Genre work involves the labour of making, marketing and distributing a genre, and it involves the way audiences engage in watching a genre, including processes of reflecting on this experience. The empirical production and audience research suggests a social contract where producers and audiences emotionally and intellectually invest in the product. We can describe this drama as the cool heart of Nordic noir, a phrase that emerged from the interviews with creatives and their affective practices for dissonance, using cognitive and emotional contrasts across the storytelling, landscape, characterisation, soundscape, editing and cinematography. Roland Barthes (1979) commented on the power of cool as signifying the intellectual and emotional structures of entertainment, and we see the cognitive and affective work of Nordic noir in this shaping of a 'cool heart' within the production process and the cultures of viewing. In particular, the attention to silence, the quiet stillness of a camera staying focused on a character, and the small details and vocabulary of 'cool' gestures for the main character of Saga, help to shape the affective climate of the drama and invite cognitive and affective engagement.

Saga's story also demonstrates the symbolic power of serial engagement. Viewers described a process of learning to love her. Typically, conversations would start with 'in the beginning I didn't like Saga' and then viewers would reflect on their journey with her through the seasons and how they have come to love Saga. Her directness and difference was highly valued: 'Saga has no filter and just tells it as it is' (37 year old Danish female accountant). Sofia Helin's performance was singled out and audiences reflected on themselves and their reactions to watching the drama, feeling protective of Saga and their experience of the series as 'a story of vulnerability' (35 year old Swedish female librarian). This intensely subjective mode of engagement signals the symbolic power of genre work; it is an iterative and situated process, almost like a call and response where producers and actors communicate to an imagined regional audience and in turn viewers react to, engage with and reflect on the meaning of the drama in their lives. This combination of emotional engagement with the affective structures of the drama, and reflexive mode of engagement with Nordic noir, is a significant part of genre work because when producers and audiences enter into a social contract where they talk about, share, reflect and produce their own experience of Nordic noir, together they are transforming the genre into something far more powerful than its original elements by giving it cultural resonance. As this viewer said: '*Bron* is part of you. So I'm very loyal. I get emotionally involved; it's like you enter that world and you live in it' (39 year old Swedish female communications officer).

6

ILLEGAL AUDIENCES

Utopia

> It treated me like an intelligent audience member of the story.
>
> *(28 year old female American musician)*

Audiences are an absent presence in media industries' research on piracy and distribution. This chapter introduces audiences into piracy debates, not as pirates, but as people who use formal and informal routes to media content in their everyday lives. Whilst this may seem a simple point to make, the absence of audience research on illegal viewing, listening and reading points to a significant lack of understanding of what people actually do beyond the point of illegal access. Indeed, the very labelling of piracy is designed to frame audiences in commercial and legal terms, according to the specific transactional norms established by media industries. If illegal viewers are given this label then they are positioned as thieves, locked into market and legal discourses. The person behind the piracy label is an absent presence. By focusing on audiences and fans we move beyond law and order and commercial and industrial labels of piracy to understand their practices and pleasures, and the relations between creative producers and audiences in shaping intensive engagement and experiences with television drama.

There are particular kinds of audiences and fans who articulate 'rights talk' within the broader sense of roaming audiences discussed in Chapter 3. A 'right to roam' builds on the meaning of roaming in nature and the environment, where the landscape is a worldly place, open to all, and we as citizens have a right to roam across borders and enclosed, or commercial, spaces (Macfarlane 2012). This right to roam is articulated through 'rights talk' regarding economic, temporal and geographical freedom to watch content without restrictions, free from commercial culture, geo-blocking and time delay. A right to roam can be used to understand cultures of viewing for informal media economies (Lobato and Thomas 2015).

The audiences and fans for cult conspiracy drama *Utopia* (Channel 4, Kudos, 2012–14) offer a rich site of analysis regarding their sense of legitimacy, their feeling of a right to

Illegal audiences: *Utopia* 95

FIGURE 6.1 Cult drama *Utopia*, on the wall at Kudos
Source: Photograph Annette Hill.

roam across dispersed sites of production, distribution and reception. *Utopia* is described as an 'unnerving global conspiracy thriller' by its makers; in short 'when five online strangers are drawn together by the legendary manuscript of a cult graphic novel, they find themselves pursued by a secret and deadly organisation known only as The Network' (Kudos website).[1] The drama attracted audiences and fans from diverse political, regional and cultural backgrounds. In particular, the drama's questioning of a false social imaginary (Taylor 2004: 143), constructed by powerful elites in shadow democracies, is especially appropriate for an analysis of how the alternative world of the drama is carried beyond the television form into cultures of viewing. *Utopia*'s audiences and fans frequently questioned the concentration of wealth and power in the media industries and other business organisations and political parties, feeling that the fictional narrative of a false social imaginary shone a spotlight on the ruling ideas of elites, rather than the needs of citizens. Audiences related the narrative to their own experiences of life in Chile, for example, or of watching this drama during a media panic about the Ebola virus. These audiences and fans had a strong feeling that much of what was shown in *Utopia* was happening in real life. There are global political powers that are destroying the planet, and the drama connects with pessimism about the tender fate of humanity, the dark answer to the ultimate question of *Utopia* – are we worth saving?

Piracy and audiences

The majority of research on piracy comes from the media industries, including industry research on the economic and legal impact of piracy on content creation and the future of media industries in a changing landscape. These reports paint an economic and geographical picture of piracy, with an emphasis on numbers of sites, downloads, and illegal users for film, television or sport, and a tracking of piracy in different 'pirate states' such as the Ukraine, and regions such as Asia (McDonald 2018). These reports address piracy as theft and propose ways to control it, including watermarking content, enforcement of copyright law and trade sanctions. According to Karaganis (2011: 3) there is an industry 'organization and practice of enforcement – from street raids, to partnerships between industry and government, to industry reporting and policy lobbying'. Heavyweight players in the protection of intellectual copyright, such as Hollywood and the film industry (see the Motion Picture Association of America), or trade policy (see the Anti-Counterfeiting Trade Agreement) have lobbied to enforce tougher legislation and penalise 'pirate states' that are said to allow such black markets to flourish.

Industry research tends to paint a pessimistic picture of piracy as spiralling out of control. For example, the BBC claimed that more than 60 million viewers were accessing the iPlayer service from abroad; the service is funded by licence fee payers, but transnational audiences found workarounds with proxy servers or virtual private networks that enabled them to access BBC content – *Sherlock* (2010–) was a particular favourite with Chinese viewers (38 million) (Revoir 2015). The report came at the same time in 2015 when the BBC cancelled their pilot service of a globally accessible iPlayer. Also in 2015, a report from Google indicated it received over 2.2 million piracy takedown requests every day (Price 2015); for 2017 the numbers are much higher and the transparency reports for the removal of copyrighted content show nearly 1.8 million top level domains from which URLs were requested to be removed.[2] In 2016, a report stated that a quarter of EU citizens were found to have accessed illegal content online, in a survey of 28 EU member states focusing on citizens aged 15–24 (Mann 2016b). A BBC survey in 2017 showed that over a third of football fans were illegally accessing Premier League matches online, a cause for concern for Sky and BT Sport who held the live rights to show the matches in Britain (BBC 2017). Further reports can be found from various industry bodies, anti-piracy lobby groups and IP rights groups, using economic impact studies that are based on an assumption about the cost of piracy to paid consumption, to convey the message that piracy is something that needs to be controlled. What we find is that piracy is framed as a pathology, a symptom of a moral problem, as Brian Larkin noted in his research on the informal production and distribution of Nigerian video (2004). This pervasive discourse means 'piracy has thus incited an economic, legal, and moral panic' in the media and film industries, ensuring pirated content appears as 'monstrous transgressions of copyright laws' (Klinger 2010: 107).

There is some evidence to show that people who access content via informal distribution also pay for content as well. For example in Australia, a report in 2016 by Essential Research indicated that although 66 per cent of Australians download film, TV and music from piracy sites they also subscribe to Netflix, Foxtel and other streaming services (Mann 2016a). Amidst reports by TorrentFreak in 2015 that 14 million illegal viewers watched the finale of season five of *Game of Thrones*, other studies indicated legal television viewing was still popular with audiences, for example 15 million people watched an episode of *The Walking Dead* through its broadcaster AMC, compared to nearly 7 million watching through informal routes (McCormick 2015). This less catastrophic discourse would suggest that piracy is part of the formal and informal distribution of screen culture and print media that has existed for over a century or more. As Lobato (2012: 1) highlights, 'unmeasured, unregulated and extra-legal audiovisual commerce' intersects with formal distribution, so that local video clubs, pop up screenings, street markets and grey internet sites co-exist with cinemas, Netflix accounts and family television.

In the academic research on informal media economies, piracy and distribution there tends to be a playoff between the pirate as thief and the pirate as resistance fighter, positioning a law-and-order frame against a more romantic view of the radical activist. Lobato (2012: 72–85) analyses what he calls the six faces of piracy: these include piracy as theft, a framing of the issue within legal and industry practice; piracy as free enterprise, which positions piracy as a critique of the market forces in the media industries; and piracy as free speech which offers a critique of copyright law. These political economic and industry faces of piracy are compared with a more cultural approach: this includes piracy as authorship, using postmodern and post-structuralist critiques of the relationship between author and text; piracy as resistance, a reaction against copyright as a hegemonic institution where piracy is perceived as a subversive strategy against capitalism; and piracy as access, drawing on postcolonial and critical legal studies that consider the transformative potential of piracy to disseminate information and culture in countries where content is controlled or censored.

In all of these faces of piracy there is little empirical research of pirates themselves and their everyday lives, a missing aspect of the processes of engagement and experiences of piracy. Lobato addresses this issue through his own work on the everyday ethics of being a pirate, running an informal media store on the streets of Mexico City, for example. Interviews with an informal distributor show just how normal piracy can be in this region. Lobato explains:

> while media industries paint piracy as a sin and the neo-hacker generation enjoys the kicks it provides, the piracy-as-access perspective asks us to remember that piracy is often an everyday act ... rarely self-consciously a resistant act, especially in contexts where legal alternatives do not exist.
> *(Lobato 2012: 85)*

To understand piracy as access, and as an everyday experience, challenges the dominant ways of framing piracy within political economic contexts, protection of copyright, and the information systems that attempt to capture the unmeasured audience. Everyday access to illegal content is a fairly common experience for transnational audiences (Athique 2016). Patrick Vonderau's work on piracy in Sweden used industry research, internal reports and surveys of Swedish viewers and their online activities to look beyond the metaphor of piracy and highlight the shadow economies of digital media; he notes how the Swedish Pirate Bay used this metaphor in response to anti-piracy groups and the success of the first instalment of the Hollywood franchise *Pirates of the Caribbean* (2003, director Gore Verbinski), not a counterculture phenomenon then, but 'an out-of-the-box solution that would benefit viewers of commercial entertainment' (Vonderau 2014: 115). Indeed, for Vonderau (2014: 115): 'The Pirate Bay's significance thus goes far beyond the exchange practices it facilitates – it greatly contributes to normalising the idea of copyright infringement as being fair use, or indeed a social norm.' This would suggest that claims regarding digital pirates and cord cutting practices as at the margins of screen culture may overstate the piracy and resistance frame at the expense of the rather ubiquitous experience of mixed modes of illegal and legal viewing of streaming and broadcast television (Strangelove 2015). For example, industry reports show that people accessing football games illegally are unaware that watching this content is a crime, assuming it is the black market distributors who are the target of legal action (BBC 2017); crackdowns on viewers who watch a film or football game seem to miss the point that informal media economies are so much a feature of our daily lives that we rarely question it.

These everyday aspects of piracy highlight the shifting boundaries between legal consumption and piracy, a grey zone where we can rethink industry structures and ways of both allowing as well as enforcing informal media economies (Karaganis (2011). Everyday piracy does not efface the legal, ethical and political economic issues within shadow economies of television, music, sports and streaming services. In current research on Spotify by a team of researchers in Sweden (Eriksson et al. 2018), they argue that the early practices of illicit music listeners related to the Pirate Bay and Swedish file sharing communities has transformed into a powerful industry in need of regulation. Spotify is not the answer to illicit downloading, as the company claims, instead it is a commercial enterprise that like other platform economies such as Google, Facebook or YouTube, is in need of careful scrutiny regarding legal and ethical frameworks in the digital economy. Empirical studies of Spotify and music listeners, using a combination of ethnographic, political-economic, historical or industry-based research can only enhance our understanding of piracy in situated contexts.

For example, *GeoBlocking and Global Video Culture* (Lobato and Meese 2016) is a collection of essays that explore online blocking and circumvention in an historical and theoretical context, and across countries, using situated case studies such as Turkey and political activism in the use of Twitter's Periscope live streaming, Brazilian Netflix subscribers, pirates and fan subbers, Iran and official and unofficial geo(un)blocking, or American circumvention of BBC iPlayer services. These different types of research question the tools people use to access restricted content in different geographical regions, thus emphasising the significance of place and time in an analysis of the changing media landscape of screen culture. The authors offer a nuanced analysis of the political-economic contexts to geoblocking and circumvention activities, indicating the territorial grabs made by commercial and public service broadcasting and streaming services, and piracy services, and offering a more macro perspective on audiences and users, including discourses of audiences, reports and consumer habits. In one case of Brazilian circumvention practices we learn about the political-economic and distribution issues for Netflix in this region and get a glimpse of bloggers and online discussions debating the issues surrounding subscription and illegal viewing. One of the issues that arises in the various case studies is the political-economic framing of the discourses surrounding piracy and audiences; for example geoblocking tells us about distribution and flow, where we see the usual way of looking at global flow of content masking 'the experience of blockage as a foundational logic of the internet' (Lobato and Meese 2016: 12). Another issue is the over-emphasis on geoblocking circumvention practices as political resistance and social activism; the case studies illuminate the often mundane activities of people getting around borders and censorship to watch their favourite television drama, thus highlighting 'the relationship between political censorship and pleasurable consumption' (ibid.). To extend this way of looking at piracy to audience studies where the everyday is taken seriously, where piracy is unpacked to show the embedding of illegal content into everyday routines and social rituals, is a step forward in understanding the faces and voices of piracy in practice. What might we find if we put audiences at the beginning of an investigation into the people behind piracy?

Academic research on the sociological, cultural and historical aspects of piracy is a significant means of tracing the history of piracy through film, videos, music and books, and the diverse geographical spread of piracy – in India, for example, or Nigeria (Larkin 2004). There is also research on piracy and film distribution (Crisp 2015) which considers the informal distributors, local markets and underground film networks that are part of screen culture and commerce. Amongst this growing body of research on piracy and distribution there are some studies of illegal film reception (Klinger 2010), transnational fandom and illegal content (Hu 2005), and piracy distributors and fan producers of remixed content, such as fan subbing (Lascia 2005).

In research on fandom and piracy, there has been a focus on the blurring of the boundaries between legitimate and illegitimate practices. Work by Matt Hills (2002), Henry Jenkins (2006) and Paul McDonald (2007), amongst others, has focused on the way fans of film and television, for example, become pirates, and how piracy can be fuelled by fan practices. These relations between piracy and fandom occupy what Denison (2011) calls a liminal zone, where there is an unclear distinction between copyright infringement and fan practices as producers of content, fan subbing, and fan remixes. Who is in control of the text? Who is the author? are questions that dominate these debates, linking fan studies with work on piracy and informal media economies, especially in relation to piracy as authorship, and piracy as resistance. Abigail De Kosnick's (2016) research on digital archives and repertoires for fan fiction writing highlights the performative aspects of this work and the ongoing dialogue between readers, writers, producers and cosplayers. In her research on fan subbers, Denison (2011) notes how fan subtitling and fan networks helped distribute Japanese anime in the 1990s, indicating a range of fan practices in anime production, subtitling and sharing (see also Leonard 2004 on Japanese anime fandom); however, the popularity of anime within Asian and American markets, and the rise of digital fan subbing (digisubs), has meant fan practices are being curtailed by the industry in their crackdown on piracy (Denison 2011: 450). Fan subtitlers transgress the boundaries between fan community practices and piracy, offering a hybridised model of fandom and piracy (Denison 2011: 465).

Research on piracy and fandom can also highlight unequal access and the power dynamics within popular culture. The geographic disparities of Netflix, for example, can be circumvented if you know how, and have the right skills and devices, to unlock these services. Lobato points out that the idea of a 'spatialised experience of abundance' (Lotz 2014) is promoted by Netflix and other content providers, and by the more organised piracy and semi-legal services such as Encodi or FilmOn, but the reality is that only some people have the resources to enjoy this experience of abundance. He notes in his analysis of Netflix that there are 'different degrees of mobility on the part of viewers, with a small number able to easily cross digital borders and access programming meant for viewers in other territories, and a much larger number remaining effectively immobile' (Lobato 2017: 181). Kaufmann (2002) uses the term 'motility' to refer to the unequal distribution of skills and resources among mobile audiences for digital content, a category that can be expanded to include the technical skills of converting content to be shared in release groups, the time allocated to finding and watching content, and the economic resources to maintain media devices and subscriptions to unblocking services. The motility of mobile audiences highlights the economic, geographical and temporal strictures to being an illegal viewer, user and consumer.

This is where the idea of roaming audiences comes into play within research on piracy. The idea makes two interventions into research on media industries. First it introduces the audience into the piracy debates, not as pirates but as people who use formal and informal routes to media content in their everyday lives.[3] This way of describing audiences and users avoids the language of legality or illegality, situating their practices within broader ways of engaging with media content. If illegal viewers are labelled as pirates then they are positioned as thieves, locked into the piracy-as-theft discourse. If illegal viewers are positioned as entrepreneurs within free enterprise and free speech contexts, they are still locked into market and legal discourses. Even the more cultural approaches to piracy as authorship, resistance or access, use the framework of piracy to argue for critique of legal and political economic matters. The person behind the piracy label is still an absent presence.

The second point of using the metaphor of roaming audiences is to explore the right to roam in practice, using a concrete example of what it means to engage with television drama through formal and informal routes. Empirical research on transnational audiences and fans in different regions, with varied media systems, shows just how multifaceted the practices of roaming audiences can be. If you roam around storytelling in a country with public service and commercial television, for example, you will have options for content with and without advertising breaks, thus allowing you the freedom to immerse yourself in narratives that are not continually interrupted by commercial culture. If you roam across the grey internet in a country such as Russia, then you can compare censored content with alternative content; for example *RuPaul's Drag Race* (2009–, Logo, VH1, Netflix) is available in Russia but because trans is illegal, this series has a subversive element in its values of inclusion and cultural citizenship for LGBTI rights, including freedom of expression for lesbian, gay, bisexual, transgender and intersex people. These are just a few examples that highlight the multiplicity of the meaning of illegally accessed content for audiences themselves, not the meanings we might ascribe the unmeasured audience as an aggregate mass. Audience research has a role to play in exploring informal media engagement. Of course, not all roaming audiences access content in informal ways, nor are they interested in subversive tactics; and not all informal media engagement is wide ranging, rather there are localised habits and preferences for content: we cannot claim a broad trend of audiences and fans transgressing the norms and rules of dominant media systems. However, by conducting empirical audience research for a specific case study, we find the pleasures and practices of audiences and fans unmeasured by the broadcaster, but nevertheless offering powerful examples of informal media engagement.

Indeed, in terms of the rights talk of roaming audiences, illegal fans are the most vocal about their communicative rights. They are by default critical of certain models of distribution premised on scarcity, or restricted access, both in European countries like Britain and in countries such as Chile that have a fan base for *Utopia*. Andrew Calabrese's work on communicative rights argues that there are modes of narration for political will formation and radical mobilisation (Calabrese 2017: 100). He explains:

> Today, in the midst of a global crisis in the media industries due to a confluence of factors – including the failures of big media to adapt to digital disruption – the subject of public communication as a human need is more important than ever.
>
> *(Calabrese 2017: 122)*

A similar tendency is evident in audience engagement with *Utopia*. As we shall see, for some passionate fans of *Utopia* the drama was a resource for radical mobilisation, choosing to live off-grid, protest against human rights abuse, and become involved in environmental activism. Their informal engagement with the drama led to intensive affective, emotional and cognitive investment in broader political and moral debates, questioning the rights claims of citizens compared with corporate persons, believing that 'the needs of capital (including media capital) have so thoroughly eclipsed the "needs of the people"' (Calabrese 2017: 122). What we shall see in the rest of this chapter is this rights talk articulated through the imaginary world of *Utopia* that made a real impact on people's lived experiences.

Researching *Utopia*

The research on *Utopia* combined production studies and audience studies in order to explore the meaning of the drama in people's everyday lives. The production research was conducted by myself and Julie Donovan; the audience research was conducted by Jose Luis Urueta, with help from Koko Kondo for the UK interviews. At first we had some difficulty gaining access to the production team, who had been informed of the cancellation of the series after its second season and had moved on to other work. After some exploratory interviews with the executive producer and marketing manager, together with Douglas Wood at Endemol Shine, we were able to gain access to the team. Once inside the door, we were overwhelmed by the willingness of the creative producers to talk with us; the show's production company Kudos made available a room where we conducted interviews over several days in April 2015 with the executive producer, producer, editor, director, writer, cinematographer, sound designer, marketing manager, costume designer, set designer, location manager, casting director, actors, assistants, and more. In total, 21 production interviews took place with executive and creative producers and actors; there were 8 female and 13 male interviewees.

People came to share their experience of making *Utopia* and to reflect on what it meant to them, the themes and issues the drama raised and their creative practice in this production culture. The type of interview for this production research resembled the elite interview (Bruhn 2015), where a topic guide was constructed, and then much space given in each interview for questions and reflections on the creative skills of the individual persons. For example, when interviewing Marc Munden, director of *Utopia*, preparation was done on his previous work and specific questions were asked about the craft of making this drama, the collaboration with other people in the production culture, and sources of inspiration for the style of drama. Indeed, the open and flexible nature of this interview led to a free flowing conversation about the cultural dynamics of television drama as a potential art form, and a further interview was done to follow up on some of these issues, for example constructing archival news footage for the retro *Utopia* episode in season two. A group interview with the script writer, executive producer and producer had the feeling of a more informal roundtable discussion than a formal interview, with reflections on making television drama, collective creative energy, or the use of negative space in television aesthetics, for example. What became apparent from the production interviews was that flexible and critically reflexive interviews worked well for this kind of production team with esoteric interests in music, film, photography, literature, theatre and art, and socio-political issues.

After the producer interviews we then encountered difficulties in recruiting audiences and fans; at first we thought this was a general problem of lack of time or lack of relevance – the drama wasn't trending anymore in public discussions in the summer of 2015. We then tried putting a call out for participants through official social media, done in a playful way and using conspiracy as a frame. And we received lots of responses. It was at this point we realised *Utopia* was more popular abroad than at home, and that it was especially popular with fans watching the show in informal ways. But further problems arose when we started to pin down times for interviews, ask for written consent forms, or request permission to record the interviews. Audiences from Europe, Russia, America, Central and South America, Canada, and Australia started acting strangely, disconnecting calls, or not wanting to be registered with the research. Their responses went from 'I love *Utopia*' to '*Utopia*? never heard of it.' This happened with around 50 potential participants in the study. They felt that even to be recorded for an interview might put them at risk, either through a digital record of their thoughts and viewing activities, or as a critical reflection on the themes within the dramatic narrative and its cultural resonance with political regimes in their home countries. Looking back it seems so obvious now. A cult conspiracy drama about the fate of humanity, corruption and shadow democracies, would be very likely to attract shadow audiences who distrust the media industry and its measurement systems. We had stumbled into a study of audiences who wanted to live off-grid.

This shock of recognition (Williams 1979: 164) had an impact on our research. When faced with *Utopia's* specific type of viewer and social group we had to adapt the research methods in order to reach out to them. Alongside the official *Utopia* social media, and snowballing through friends of friends, we discovered the sites and fan forums where *Utopia* was talked about. The ethical sensitivity of the topic meant that we had to place greater emphasis on their choice – to participate or not, to be recorded or not. We changed the signed consent to a verbal consent and started the interview with a ten minute talk about how their identity would be made anonymous. Email exchanges became a common part of the process of getting audiences to participate and we adapted the language of the emails with knowledge of the show, such as jokes and conspiracy lingo. Swear words were particularly apt: *Utopia*'s script has creative use of swearing (see fan remixes of Becky – 'what the fucking fuck is going on?') and fans took to swearing in homage to the show. In such a way, we slowly established trust in order to find a place in the social structure of the *Utopia* audiences and fans.

For the audience research, 56 audiences and fans participated in individual and group interviews (2–3 persons). When we recruited participants to the study, people were asked to define themselves as viewers and fans of the drama, with some people self -defining as intensively engaged audiences, and others as passionate fans, which connects with the discussion on the spectrum of engagement in Chapter 3. Throughout the analysis the terms 'audiences', 'viewers' and 'fans' are used to reflect the way participants perceived themselves. The fieldwork time frame was June 2015 to April 2016, a long period with which to patiently recruit audiences for a cancelled series. The recruitment method involved snowball sampling, primarily through social media and friends of friends. After the project was flagged on the official *Utopia* social media we received 4,000 views and 1,000 likes; this led to 170 fans emailing and Skyping about the project. Many dropped out after learning that we would audio record the interview. Although we guaranteed anonymity, audio recordings made *Utopia* fans nervous, due to their illegal viewing, and conspiracy theories regarding the cancellation of the television series. For every interview, the researchers needed to patiently build trust with these audiences and fans, conducting most interviews in the middle of the night due to time differences. For the overall sample of 56 participants there were 15 females and 41 males, aged 16 to 38, reflecting a younger audience and more male profile for this drama; this kind of ultra violent conspiracy thriller tended to attract more males than females, with similar tastes as fans of the cyber thriller *Mr Robot* or the satire *Black Mirror*. There was a range of occupations represented, including students, unemployed, artists, activists, musicians, charity workers, graphic designers, teachers, a translator and a spacecraft operator. Audiences and fans were from the UK, Sweden, Denmark, France, Germany, Italy, Greece, Spain, Slovenia, Russia, America, Canada, Colombia, Argentina, Chile, Australia and New Zealand. Interviews were conducted in English and Spanish. Each interview lasted between 40 and 60 minutes and took place via Skype and telephone, or in homes and public places.

There was a tension between the non-commercial objectives of the project – based at Lund University, with academic publications and so forth – and the commercial partnership with Kudos, the company that produced the drama. Audiences and fans wanted their voices heard. They had specific messages for the makers – 'Bring *Utopia* back, dammit!' being the most popular refrain. But they also wanted to share their concerns about why the show was cancelled. Was it their fault, or the fault of 'The Network'? They had ideas for the third season, offering to crowdsource the drama, and yet they also wanted to be sure that we were not a marketing research firm, mining their experiences for commercial exploitation. It helped that the show was over, so in essence we were reflecting on its creative value and impact rather than commercial value.

We made the report available for free on our website to share the research, with comments from the production team on the value of listening to audiences and fans voices. For example the show's writer, Dennis Kelly (2015), noted:

> how an intelligent audience interacts with a show, broadens it and helps it live way beyond it's original broadcast. It succinctly captures the making, the viewing and the discussing of *Utopia* and perhaps gives a glimpse into why a show this odd and fucked up couldn't really survive in our existence for very long.

The show's director Marc Munden (2015) described the research as 'epic and detailed, mixing technical and creative views with the voices of audiences and their views of *Utopia*'. Its composer Cristobal Tapia de Veer (2015) said 'it feels as if *Utopia* and its audience have a relationship close to a band with its fans. It's not disposable and forgettable like most shit on TV.' As noted in Chapter 3, Alistair Petrie (2015), who played a despicable politician in the series, commented:

> *Utopia* invites its audiences to look hard at themselves and the world around them; and they do this in a way that is curious, sometimes surreal, often emotional but also with humour. The fans have taken ownership of it in the best way,

embracing the drama and continuing its legacy. Perhaps its greatest payoff is that people talk of *Utopia* in the present tense when they discuss it. Fans say '*Utopia* is this or that' not 'was this or that'. On it lives as well as the questions it asks.

And fans responded by saying 'We will share the fuck out of this.'

The rise of *Utopia*

The commissioning editor for *Utopia*, Piers Wenger, read the first script one weekend, while in the bath. Still in the tub, he excitedly texted his colleague. 'I wanted to green light it because the script felt like it had a bright light shining through it.' His enthusiasm was connected to an original story: 'I just thought that the idea was so sophisticated that an audience would really connect with and appreciate it' (Wenger 2015). Alex Wells (2015), who was director of marketing for *Utopia*, said after reading the script: 'This is incredible, I really want to work on this.' The combination of the writer Dennis Kelly, director Marc Munden, and Kudos' reputation for original drama ensured creatives scrambled to work on the project. Alistair Petrie (2015) said he would walk over hot coals to work with such a team.

For Alex Wells this was a huge story, full of esoteric influences on sound and image, lots of dirty shots, and lots and lots of graphic violence. On set, Wells would pore over the scripts and early footage, struggling to create a coherent marketing campaign for an unruly artwork:

> I just felt like one of the dementors in *Harry Potter*. I was in a fun place and I was the only one saying 'right I have gone through the scripts for episode three and someone gets shot in the head in this page, there is a person in this page that gets stabbed; and some of those things are really problematic from a press perspective so can we have a conversation about this?' To Dennis that was tantamount to 'You are killing my creative vision.'
>
> *(Wells 2015)*

She wondered how to promote this original drama: 'there were so many ideas in the script … how are we going to present this in a way which is true to the heart of the series but equally gives it a broad appeal?' (Wells 2015). Wells created a viral marketing scheme using tailor made content on YouTube and Twitter that alluded to The Network as digital surveillance. Danny Layton (2015) at Shine worked on a marketing campaign that brought out the soundtrack on eye catching yellow vinyl and Soundcloud, and encouraged fans to make their own sounds in a participatory project. On the day of transmission of the first season the viral marketing campaign led to 24,000 tweets mentioning *Utopia* (14,000 during the broadcast window), and 1.1 million viewers, skewed to a younger, cult, male audience (internal report, Endemol Shine).

And then *Utopia's* cult status became a problem. Producer Karen Wilson (2015) noted: 'people stacked *Utopia*. They were so excited about the second season that

106 Illegal audiences: *Utopia*

FIGURE 6.2 The Network is watching: *Utopia* on the wall at Kudos
Source: Photograph Annette Hill.

they wanted to binge watch. And yet the industry and press reports do not reflect that. What I get in my inbox is the overnights and +7s.' Channel 4 did look carefully at catch up viewers. The commissioner noted: '*Utopia* was a show that was watched mainly on catch up' and this was valuable to the channel 'because when you watch on demand you have to watch the adverts once you log into that platform'. But, even with the catch up option *Utopia* did not reach the ratings the channel was looking for to justify public-commercial funding and the drama was cancelled after two seasons.

What caused the death of *Utopia*? The most common answer within the industry is that '*Utopia* was ahead of its time.' Such a comment is a compliment to the producers – 'this is visionary stuff'; and it implies audiences are just not ready for this kind of thing – 'people want to be entertained'. One fan who watched via the Channel 4 streaming services echoed this common perception of the cancellation of *Utopia*: 'it's a show that requires a lot of effort from the viewer and it's difficult to hook them' (23 year old British male student). But this view that viewers caused the death of *Utopia* is really not the full picture. *Utopia* was not ahead of its time, it was a television drama of its time, attracting roaming audiences and fans who accessed the show through informal byways.

The voices of piracy

There were several reasons why *Utopia* appealed to a transnational audience watching predominantly via informal routes. Perhaps the most significant is that the drama was intended as a dialogue about global matters. The writer Dennis Kelly (2015) explicitly said he wanted to create 'not a national conversation, but a broader geopolitical conversation'. *Utopia* fans certainly represented a broad geopolitical community, and these people were finding *Utopia* in informal, advert-free, hard to measure ways, from online streaming and cloud sharing, to friendly passwords and personal exchange of discs and sticks. Even British viewers, who could access the drama legally and for free, live on television and also via catch up services, often chose to watch in their own way. This was due to the summer scheduling slot and the advert loop of the formal streaming service. Many chose the ad-free route to *Utopia*. For example, on the piracy streaming site One Channel, through Kodi, *Utopia* has stayed in the top ten spot since 2014 as a highly rated show. In relation to fan discussions and campaigns, over 11,000 people signed the change.org petition for a third season, the goal was 15,000; Reddit has around 3,000 threads on the drama.

Here are some typical ways audiences and fans found *Utopia*:

> I torrented it and had a *Utopia* marathon.
>
> *(21 year old Chilean male student)*

> The first scene was on the TV sub Reddit. I watched that and was immediately hooked. Right now I use Reddit to find out about new shows and all the best things I have ever seen on television come from there. I have to pirate it to watch because it's not available legally in the US … all I use are illegal sharing sites.
>
> *(19 year old American male student)*

> My friend came over with a flash drive and he had the soundtrack. I streamed it in some random sites … and binge watched the whole thing.
>
> *(29 year old Russian male, unemployed)*

Such encounters with *Utopia* highlight the common experience of watching this kind of drama when and how you want it.

Another reason *Utopia* generated a global conversation was the geopolitical issues and subversive tactics of the characters. Like director Marc Munden (2015), viewers are 'drawn by things which are counter culture and subversive'. For example: '*Utopia* is probably the best thing I've ever seen on the television. The storyline of abusive power was very relevant to current times' (26 year old British male musician). Or, 'I saw some tweets about it and how excited people were. I knew that there was a lot of controversy and I watched it on a Russian website. I still can't forget about this show' (19 year old Russian student). Many noted how the drama uncannily echoed headline news, from the school shootings at the time of the first season's transmission, to the Ebola virus of the second season, and more recently the Zika virus. For some fans, *Utopia* articulated their own concerns about global capitalism and an imbalance of power: 'My friend and I were talking of how the world is going down the drain and *Utopia* is one way of researching that … I downloaded it and I binge viewed it' (35 year old Slovenian female translator).

A third reason why *Utopia* appealed to illegal audiences is the way it addressed viewers as intelligent members of the story. The producers created a drama that gave viewers space to think and reflect on big issues. Marc Munden (2015) explained:

> People are often challenged on TV with ideas and stories, for example about politics or morality, but they are very rarely challenged with tone, or visual grammar. You want to challenge the audience to draw their own conclusions about tone and morality. I want to make content that is a demanding experience.

One American fan spoke about this dialogue between creative producers and audiences:

> I seek stuff out so I found *Utopia* on the web. I am a very intelligent viewer, and so for me this story was one of those that 'got me'. I was trying to figure shit out and being surprised and rewarded and devastated. I was just like 'man this is so good!'
>
> *(28 year old female American musician)*

Drawing on Lobato's (2012) work on shadow economies of cinema and the faces of piracy discussed earlier, the research suggests there are four kinds of illegal fans for this drama. There are fans as self-informing media citizens, the kinds of users and viewers who gather information from the press, other fans, and television news websites to assess which drama to illegally access, share, watch and talk about with others. There are also consumer choice advocates, the kinds of users and viewers who like to be able to choose content anytime, anywhere, and will find various ways around distribution that blocks access to television they want to watch. Then, there are decentralised media sharers, a type of user and viewer who prefers to watch their favourite content outside of the main broadcaster, network, or official catch up service, usually as a means to avoid advertising loops and/or to avoid being counted through the ratings and algorithms that are part of the monitoring systems for the official sites of distribution. There are also fans as activists, campaigning for a specific show, leading discussions online and offline, and, if a show is cancelled, organising letters and petitions to the producers, or attempting to crowdsource the return of a favourite drama. In relation to the faces of piracy these fans tend to move between piracy as access, including the everyday experience of illegal viewing, and piracy as resistance, which takes into account a political motivation that is connected to both the media industries and global capitalism, and more generally to political corruption, conspiracy theories of deep states, and environmental destruction. To borrow from Virginia Crisp's work on constructions of the deviant pirate (2014), this empirical research on *Utopia* deconstructs piracy, offering a more nuanced picture of illegal fandom.

For example, this self-informing media citizen saw herself as an underground news feed for Italian audiences:

I am a TV series addict and *Utopia* was one of the greatest discoveries that I made ... I am the one who spread the news about *Utopia* because it was just new when I discovered it, so I watched it every week after it was aired, and in the meantime I told everybody about the show.

(30 year old Italian female translator)

Another viewer was a consumer choice advocate:

I just ran into it by chance. I downloaded it ... right now I have twenty-five different series running during the week ... I have so many series waiting in line right now. When shows get released I have a pop up that says 'hey, today is season one from this show'. I have some friends writing blogs and I see if I get a feeling I would like something.

(24 year old French male student)

Typical for *Utopia* was the anti-industry audience, favouring decentralised media sharing in order to watch television in spaces free from advertising:

No commercials. I do binge view, I'm terrible, if it takes two days I probably won't do anything for two days ... the nature of how we watch things and how we get our entertainment is different. It does always seem like the best TV shows get cancelled.

(35 year old British male, unemployed)

And this fan was a media activist, signing petitions, contacting Netflix:

If they measure ratings on shows like *Utopia* from a TV channel, well you are doomed to fail because the numbers are not going to be true or realistic. *Utopia* is a show that you watch in your space, up close and personal, on your own terms.

(24 year old Chilean male student)

There is a paradox of being both a de-centralised media sharer and activist; the two go hand in hand when TV shows get cancelled because of low ratings.

There was a mixing of formal and informal media economies for fans of the drama. Some first saw *Utopia* on Pirate Bay in its top 100 list: 'I downloaded it and then as soon as the DVD was available to buy I bought the DVD because I thought that those guys deserved to get paid for their work' (38 year old German male spacecraft operator). Here we see a viewer checking out the show through informal routes and then buying the DVD in order to watch the rest of it in formal ways. He describes piracy as access, a pragmatic means to watch the drama without geoblocking or advertising. As this fan explained, streaming without commercial breaks is just a normal experience:

I followed the Reddit threads and it seems to be a very stupid rating system, I say stupid because of how it ruins our lives. So, they should really get with the times and look up what this Internet thing is and utilise it.

(30 year old Swedish male record producer)

These fans avoid legal language associated with production rights for a commercial format. *Utopia* is a drama format, but it is seen as a creative piece of art rather than a commercial product for different territories and media platforms. Nor is there a discussion of the intellectual property rights of producers, or performance rights of musicians and actors. There is critical appreciation of these professionals, a following of their work on social media, or in the form of fan videos about the show; there are some fans who create their own artistic contributions, music for example, published on Soundcloud, or made for a competition as part of the promotion for the drama. For these fans, their sense of ownership is similar to their role as co-creators and supporters, as part of this drama, not consumers who are extra to it.

What this research highlights is that pirate activities are part of wider socio-cultural processes. In Crisp's work on piracy and film distribution she argues for seeing distribution as a gatekeeper to culture, suggesting that distribution is both about global and regional flow of content, technological infrastructures and commercial relationships, and also about cultural power and control. We can see how audiences and fans push back against the infrastructures of national television and geo-blocking in Britain: they use alternative online technologies and distribution flows. Some fans become the national gatekeeper, an 'autonomous distributor' of the drama, adding fan subtitles, and making it available to a particular file sharing community (Crisp 2015). Most of the fans in this study fit the category that Crisp uses of intermediary distribution; this is when a drama is part of a first release group and then other fans act as the intermediary to wider forums and sites for watching the show. Indeed, fans themselves reiterated a point made by Crisp that mixing formal and informal distribution is the norm for television audiences, not the exception. As this fan said: 'Just make *Utopia* available where its audience is, so you are not forced to sit there at a specific time. I mean, it's a no-brainer!' (30 year old Swedish male record producer).

The glitchy palette of *Utopia*

How do audiences articulate their experience of this cult drama? In the following analysis I want to suggest that their articulation of the experience of *Utopia* reveals a glitchy palette. This term is taken from one of the fans describing the feeling of the drama as a 'glitchy palette'. It is a phrase suggestive of the odd mix of political and social critique and dark beauty of the *Utopia* experience. The glitch is a reference to the unexpected tone of the drama, the faultlines exposed in the narrative of environmental crisis and population control, and the unexpected power of the drama in addressing these issues; the palette refers to the range and composition of emotional colours, the mixture of soundscape and landscape, direction and design of the drama. This glitchy palette creates a 'whimsical, wondrous, playful quality to a really heavy theme' (28 year old female American musician). We can extend the tone of the drama to the experiences of audiences, when new and experimental work produces a shock of recognition. Because the drama is set in an imagined present that offers a frightening future of environmental disaster, audiences offer their own interpretation of how the narrative speaks to their lived realities, able to place themselves in the dark drama at this historical juncture in time. Their articulation of this experience tells us something about their identities (as viewers and citizens), observation of world events (the Ebola virus, or school massacres), and what it is like to live within these circumstances (global capitalism, big pharma, big media, and so forth). The experience of *Utopia* expresses the affective and political climate of the drama as it stutters and improvises with audiences and fans.

Let us start by asking *what* is Utopia? For one actor (2015) *Utopia* is a series of feelings: 'terrifying, beautiful, ugly and harrowing'. A production assistant called it 'so bright and beautiful and yet horrific'. When director Marc Munden (2015) read the script:

> The first thing that struck me was the politics of it. It felt like there was no one talking about the politics of population control. Secondly, I really liked that it was funny, it's not an obvious humour. Then alongside those things, I thought the characterisation and the storytelling were just brilliant. *Utopia* is so distinct, it's really never been done before.

One fan made a YouTube video imploring people to watch the series. He described in an interview how tricky it was to capture the drama in short form:

> To answer what is *Utopia* is difficult because there are different elements coming together. I would say it is a dark comedy, conspiracy thriller that deals with large ethical problems in a visually stylistic way. That is the reason why it is so good because it's not easy to classify. It is something new and original.
>
> *(23 year old British male student)*

He worried the show was too different, calling it the drama 'everyone was talking about and not watching' in his video. But the fact that *Utopia* is so hard to pin down is part of its international appeal. Fans from America, Denmark and Argentina explained:

> I actually have no way to describe it and that is one of the reasons that I like it so much. It's a conspiracy thriller but there is some comedy in there. It just flows seamlessly, that's why I'm unable to put it in one type of genre. Mostly *Utopia* is the cinematography and the music, every little frame, those shots of fields.
>
> *(19 year old American male student)*

> *Utopia* is fantasy and it's science fiction, but then it's also critical-political cinema.
>
> *(33 year old Danish female teacher and educational activist)*

> *Utopia* is a great TV show with excellent artistic direction, a great soundtrack and it's a great audiovisual experience.
>
> *(27 year old Argentinean male student)*

As their comments highlight, there is not one identity for the series – it's a multi-faceted audio-visual experience. One fan tried to describe this:

> I had an insane experience watching the show. The uncompromising nature of the show was great, and the visuals, the narrative, the characters, the little nuances of the show will stay with me. It really felt like poetry, the bright colours and those crazy in your face moments. I never had a show that meant so much to me, so powerful, so vivid. It felt like this was happening right now, not some world elsewhere.
>
> *(24 year old American male cable contractor)*

He sees through *Utopia* to the possibilities of television pushing the boundaries of popular culture.

Influences for *Utopia* include the Swedish director Roy Andersson, or the Finnish director Aki Kaurismäki: 'their films are so dark and funny, and feel totally unique. Roy Andersson's work exists in a space which is non-naturalistic' (Munden 2015). The director talked about 'going to places where television normally doesn't take you', such as 'the camera not moving very much, staying wide on a tableau' or the use of negative space, the empty spaces in the frame that give room for audiences to reflect on the narrative. Another visual influence was Martin Parr and John Hinde's photographs of Butlin's holiday camps of the 1970s, offering a distinctly British tone to the camerawork, colour palette and framing. Other esoteric influences include the sound of bones symbolising death rituals, or the sound of frogs mating, taken from sound archives. These sounds could be seen as disruptive noise, shaping an affective structure where we hear this acoustic presence as percussion accompanying the moral themes in the narrative. This is the kind of affective quality of noise and sound that Thompson (2017) describes as the transgressive poetics of noise music. The sound of frogs mating is an ironic reflection on the population crisis that the story tackles, breaking the silence through sound, manifesting an affective and political engagement with this moral issue.

The Early Bird Joe scene is a good example of experimentation in the production culture. Munden (2015) reflected on this scene and the influence of abstract aesthetics:

> Dennis' writing always takes you to the edge. For example, in season two, episode three, there is the scene when Lee comes in and kills Early Bird Joe.

The way that the scene was written was pretty grotesque, this choreographed violence. The actor that played Joe was so brilliant, using physical movement, bouncing off the desks. You have to work out how to make it less grotesque. That is a good example of trying to keep the camera still and just observing what happens within the frame.

Working with sound designer Tim Barker, the dark humour came through the collage of sounds as much as the actor's physical performance, alluding to French comedian and filmmaker Jacques Tati in comic tone:

> the squeak of Joe's bicycle as he traverses across the landscape, the squeak then turns into Lee on the computer screen, it is a super accentuated squeaky squeak. There is also this exaggeration of all the actions, the slicing, the sound of the telephone as it falls, the sound of dripping blood, then the slopping of his hands when he bangs against the glass door adds a glass squeak. To me this was a perfect scene.
>
> (Barker 2015)

Viewers spoke of how they first knew about the drama through watching this scene as a YouTube video: it's a memorable moment for fans around the world, capturing the glitchy palette of the *Utopia* experience.

'Sticky sound': music and sound engagement

One of the most influential aspects of *Utopia* is the music and sound design. The production designer said the music stuck in his mind, a background hum to everything he did on set: 'That soundtrack was so important in creating the rhythm of the whole text. The score is always in your brain.' For Danny Layton (2015), who promoted the soundtrack, 'the music has a life of its own'. He explained:

> When you asked me could I describe the music?, this strange music vocabulary reflects the fantastical nightmare of *Utopia*. This is a really good example of why music has such an impact. It is something intangible that works on so many levels; you may not be able to articulate this with words but this is a different way of expressing feeling and emotion.
>
> (Layton 2015)

It was Marc Munden who asked the composer Cristobal Tapia de Veer to collaborate. For him:

> sound is about idiosyncrasies, what sound can do when it is taken out of context. In *Utopia* there are a lot of sounds that are not to do with the picture, it's the opposite. The visual element is not at all dark, or sinister, so the feel of darkness is in the sound.
>
> (Munden 2015)

He and Tapia de Veer listened to drones, working with the sound designer on unusual folio sounds. Not much in *Utopia* is sound as sound, most of it is enhanced, such as the sound of frogs mating in a series about population control.

Tapia de Veer created a soundtrack that took inspiration from cinema, and from artists like Miles Davis, whose style is renewable, 'always pushing towards the future' (Tapia de Veer 2015) He described the collaborative process, where Munden gave him permission to try out new and weird things, to make mistakes. For example, there are Latin rhythms in the theme to *Utopia*, where did they come from? In a memorable scene of torture, Wilson grabs a gun and tries to shoot Lee, although he cannot see:

> Both of them are moving in a dance form, so I started to do something with percussion and the director saw that and he almost started dancing; he had this big smile and he said 'that's it, that is what we must do. This is perfect!'
>
> *(Tapia de Veer 2015)*

This surreal combination of graphic violence and dark comedy summed up *Utopia*. Even then, Tapia de Veer (2015) thought this would be too eccentric – 'I thought it was going to be a catastrophe' – he just didn't believe 'people actually like this?'

Fans described *Utopia* as a sticky sound: once you heard it you were caught in its web. 'It is the best music I have ever heard' (30 year old Swedish male record producer). Another fan explained: 'I listen to the soundtrack a lot more than I watch the show ... what I like about it is the strange sounds done in such a catchy and listenable way' (23 year old British male student). Like the production team, audiences found themselves caught in the soundtrack, listening to it at home or walking around the city, music that expressed engagement on a deeper level:

> I have the whole soundtrack on my phone and I walk through the city and listen to that and it just sounds so cool when you are just walking and you picture yourself in a scene from *Utopia*. It is reality enhancing, it is the best way to put it.
>
> *(19 year old American male college student)*

What he is describing is an example of Thompson's (2017) affective theory of noise and sound; she argues that sounds weave together with acoustic ecology, geopolitics and sonic art practices to create an affective practice for listeners. Manifestations of sound in *Utopia* produce this sticky affective encounter; it becomes a powerful force that is part of our composition of realities (2017: 175).

Reality round the corner

The narrative of *Utopia* addresses a politics of silence on the environment and human–animal relations; it counters this silence by exposing a dystopian world for us to see and hear. In Charles Taylor's work on the social imaginary we can see how the drama's narrative tells of an 'all pervasive order' (2004: 183), the pervasive power of hetero-normative relationships and families for example, or the pervasive power of social inequalities. In his analysis of a social imaginary across economics, public spheres, a polity ruled by the people, and the articulation of rights, Taylor resists a romanticised view of a social imaginary, acknowledging that an imaginary can be false, 'meaning that it distorts or covers over certain crucial realities' (2004: 183). He explains:

> Take our sense of ourselves as equal citizens in a democratic state; to the extent that we not only understand this as a legitimating principle but actually imagine it as integrally realised, we will be engaging in a cover up, averting our gaze from the various excluded and disempowered groups or imagining that their exclusion is their doing.
>
> *(2004: 183)*

This false social imaginary challenges our reality: 'like all forms of human imagination, the social imagination can be full of self-serving fiction and suppression, but it also is an essential constituent of the real. It cannot be reduced to an insubstantial dream' (2004: 183).

This false social imaginary in the fictional world of *Utopia* is a means of provocatively engaging audiences with another reality that is concerned with cover-ups, exclusion and disempowered groups. The production designer noted, 'there are two worlds of *Utopia*, the world you live in, and the world you are making' (2015). For audiences the drama really felt uncomfortably close to home: 'It really changes the way you look at the world. The world in the show is brought into your life, it's like an alternate reality. It makes you feel like an outsider in your own home' (18 year old British male student). It is the clash of the dramatic world of *Utopia* and the reality of violence and abuse of power that gives audiences pause for thought: 'What if this is my reality?' (22 year old German male student).

Dennis Kelly (2015) created a world that mixes fact and fiction, 'just around the corner from reality'. Producer Karen Wilson (2015) explained: 'it had to feel that this could be a real thing, that it could happen'. This partly explains why *Utopia* seems to uncannily connect with news events. First the school massacre in season one, where the drama was criticised for showing graphic violence at the same time as the Sandy Hook shootings in the US; then there was the second season docudrama episode that mixed factual and fictional footage from the late 1970s, in which the Network was involved in the death of the real politician Airey Neave and the rise to power of the conservative political leader Margaret Thatcher. The production team even made news footage that looked like 1970s footage of the so-called 'winter of discontent' in Britain (where, for example, strikes by public service workers led to rubbish piles on the streets), and Neave's assassination.

Alex Wells (2015) commented: 'Dennis is asking the audience a question that he doesn't have the answer to. I had so many moral conversations with the team about how to convey the message.' Audiences also engaged in moral conversations, circling around the fate of humanity:

> I really didn't know where to stand on this and that is the thing that got me trapped in the story, especially because I wanted to have an answer to it and at the same time I didn't want to. Sometimes I would be more on the side of Jessica Hyde and there were times where I stood next to Milner and said 'yes the world needs to be restarted.'
>
> *(24 year old Italian male student)*

> There is a part to the story where the moral compass is on one side and then it flips, that is why I think it's good because it's thought provoking. It's a great show.
>
> *(18 year old New Zealand male student)*

The drama leaves audiences to decide: 'that was one of the things that cemented my love for the show, when you try to humanise everyone so no point of view is dismissed, all opinions are given human faces' (23 year old British male student).

The editor spoke of the 'amoral tone' within the mix of dark comedy and conspiracy. He recalls: 'I remember reading the script and being very worried about the spoon. Are we really going to show this?' Producers felt the drama had to earn the violence, and it did this through the moral heart of the narrative. Audiences repeatedly said that when the violence occurred it was justified within the storytelling. Sometimes they might look away, but nevertheless they felt the show earned their respect for never making the morality black and white. For example, on the iconic spoon scene: 'the violence in *Utopia* is quite different, like the chilli, then the sand, then the bleach and then the spoon … actually really normal things but very menacing, a very personal torture' (36 year old British male charity worker). Here, the spoon serves the purpose of the narrative, never gratuitous, but nevertheless very disturbing: 'The torture scene has burned itself into my mind' (24 year old American male student).

There were audiences who did take a moral stand, either picking the side of the resistance or the Network. For example, one viewer made a YouTube video arguing against moral identification with the Network. She explained why she made the video:

> I think it's the product of a broken system in which you believe that not everybody can be taken care of. This is brain washing bullshit that has been going on through capitalism and is simply not acceptable in the twenty-first century where we have space rockets and mobile phones and we are a technologically advanced species. For us to believe that many of us have to die for others to live a decent life is just complete and utter bullshit.
>
> *(35 year old Slovenian female translator)*

Another viewer reflected on the global political landscape and environmental crises:

> We are humans and we are selfish in nature. There is no solution and that's why such moral ambiguity in the show just makes it real … That is what's so brilliant about the show, it's not directing anyone towards either side, it's leaving it up to the viewer to make the ultimate decision, to pull the trigger or not … Although, I understand the romantic vision of the resistance, it's unsustainable in the long run if we just continue like this. So, I'm on the Network's side.
> *(31 year old Colombian female, unemployed)*

There were fans in our study who believed *Utopia* did represent a reflection of their fears about the environment:

> *Utopia* is going to happen naturally anyway. I feel pessimistic saying this but there is going to be either a natural disaster that wipes everything out, or there is going to be some pathogen that mutates and knocks out half the population.
> *(36 year old British male charity worker)*

> *Utopia* is not only plausible, it is in some ways happening right now. We have come to an apocalyptic moment. I think a day will come where either we will all kill each other with atomic bombs or we look for solutions like the one presented in the show.
> *(31 year old Colombian female, unemployed)*

One fan from Chile felt that *Utopia* spoke to him personally, as if the writer knew his innermost thoughts:

> For me *Utopia* has been the only series that actually has represented the stuff I believed in since I was young, that there is an unmeasured abuse of power, that there is no real value to life, that we are lied to in order to get stuff from us, everything because of this hunger for power … Here in Chile there is way too much corruption, injustice, social differences and control of information by Chilean elites. To see this happening in a TV series was spectacular, it felt like meeting a missing twin brother.
> *(21 year old Chilean male student)*

He lived on his own farm, grew vegetables and kept chickens, living off-grid because he was concerned about consumer culture and its impact on environmental catastrophe:

> I know that [over-] consumption will make us become extinct, and I know the world cannot handle more people … The world is running out of

resources, and Chile has a lot of resources we do not use so we are going to be on the map … I'm 21 years old and I am going to be extinct; even if you have a chance to have a child why would you? Global warming is real.

(21 year old Chilean male student)

For this fan the drama enabled him to engage with a false social imaginary that conceals power elites and geopolitics; this catastrophic future would 'usher in new liberal economic orders', a form of 'disaster capitalism' (Thompson 2017: 178). His experience of the drama connects with his own disaster planning for a macro-disruptive event that he feels is imminent, a fearful reality just around the corner in his lifetime.

To return to the discussion of a right to roam, and Calabrese's (2017) argument about the urgency of public communication in a time of global crisis, fans questioned why *Utopia* was cancelled, with some critically reflecting on the needs of global capitalism superseding the needs of citizens:

I think it was so strange how season three got dropped right when the Ebola virus was happening. I was like 'what the fuck, what the actual fuck!' I really think that had a lot to do with season three not coming back. I just felt like the climate of news and the climate of the environment really didn't lend itself to *Utopia* continuing.

(28 year old female American musician)

This overworld of *Utopia* has led to speculation about the cancellation of the drama. 'Perhaps the government has got something to do with the cancellation' (24 year old French male student).

The Chilean fan base was clear on why *Utopia* was cancelled:

We here in Chile are under the impression that there are outside pressures, some people are not interested in keeping this series going because it touches on quite delicate matters that are real. They are not false, it is a combination of things that are happening all over the world.

(21 year old Chilean male student)

These fans want to crowdsource the next season, sending a strong message to the makers: '*Utopia* can be insanely famous. It can help to bring awareness and change to the issues it presents. We are in Chile, at the end of the world, and we know about *Utopia*! We just love it' (23 year old Chilean male student). And, these fans gave a positive message to research that includes audiences in the conversations around *Utopia*:

Well I think it's amazing that a TV series develops this kind of connection with the fans. Usually we just sit here and watch and perhaps become a number in the ratings, but we also want to have a voice. I feel that I have a voice through this interview, you get to know us, you get to know who we are behind the ratings and what we think.

(21 year old Chilean male student)

Utopia made a symbolic and emotional impact on audiences:

> Thank you for making something so amazing, but fuck you for making me think so much. I really feel like Wilson, you know? I've been thinking about this all the time and I've not been able to do other stuff, as I'm still just trying to grasp it.
>
> *(22 year old Chilean male student)*

It also inscribed itself into people's bodies, a literal example of affective practice as embodied meaning making (Wetherell 2012):

> I showed it to a friend and he watched five minutes and then he went straight to the tattoo parlour and tattooed 'Where is Jessica Hyde' across his neck … The show has also made such an impact on a couple of my friends that they went and sterilized themselves. I would do it too if I didn't have a principle 'no knives around that area'.
>
> *(30 year old Swedish male record producer)*

Utopia goes beyond audience engagement, giving fans so much to enjoy, and worry over, and reflect on, leaving a little chip of itself in everyone who encounters it.

In a short postscript, an adaptation of the drama format has been in the pipeline for some time, first at HBO and more recently with Amazon and its premium subscription video on demand service. So, *Utopia* lives on in an adaptation for Amazon, with the producer and show runner Gillian Flyn (author of *Gone Girl* 2012 amongst other novels) making a nine-episode first season with global distribution to over 200 countries (Bakare 2018). According to one journalist, the influence of the drama spreads across television, including the colourscape and violence of *Preacher* (AMC, 2016–), the paranoia of *Mr Robot* (USA Network, 2015–), and the language of *Black Mirror* (Channel 4 and Netflix, 2011–) (Bakare 2018). This adaptation may return *Utopia* to television but it remains to be seen if it can hit home in the same way the original managed to do with such dynamic energy and poetic sensibility.

Conclusion

Utopia is a cult conspiracy drama that attracted illegal audiences and fans. In an odd way, it became too cult precisely because of its challenging style and tone, and geo-cultural conversation about the environment and population control. In listening to people from Sweden or Chile who accessed the drama through informal routes, there was distrust of the media industry, academic institutions and global capitalism. This distrust related to their feeling of being a problem to the industry, a collection of statistics for the negative economic impact of piracy on creative content. This economic and legal framework does not capture their passionate engagement with the drama and the real value of it in their everyday lives.

The empirical production and audience research highlights how *Utopia* hit home, daring to address moral and philosophical issues and asking audiences to consider the big question about the fate of humanity. Their media experiences tell us how the imaginary world within the storytelling became a creative space for audiences to critically reflect on what Taylor calls 'an all pervasive order' (2004: 143), that is to say the how we imagine and question power and inequality in social life. The aesthetics of *Utopia*, experimentation in image, colour and sound, all contribute to a unique audio-visual experience. This experience had a profound impact on audiences and fans, as they engaged with multi-faceted storytelling about power and morality. The drama speaks to them directly about current affairs, global capitalism and political regimes. Although *Utopia* is over, the drama lives on, whether through online fan discussions, in people's dreams, or in media and political activism. When you look at the people labelled as pirates for a drama like *Utopia* what you see are intensely engaged fans and viewers who use the drama as a narrative resource to make sense of frightening times.

Notes

1 *Utopia* synopsis, official website of Kudos, www.kudos.co.uk/productions/moredetail/utopia/30
2 See website https://transparencyreport.google.com/?hl=en
3 My thanks to Ramon Lobato for his insightful comments on this chapter.

7

EMBEDDED ENGAGEMENT

Reality talent shows

> I'm missing my TV time. I want to watch them for longer, not sit down and 'oh, it's over already.'
>
> *(20–30 year old female viewer)*

'Embedded engagement' refers to the kind of long lasting relationship we form with media content during the course of our lives. The notion of roaming audiences explored earlier in Chapter 3 highlights the spatial and temporal relations of audiences in media landscapes; as audiences roam pathways they inevitably engage with media in fleeting ways, involving a short term engagement with particular content, paratexts and ephemeral media, and they can also engage in a more sustained way with media, involving practices of placemaking. This way of seeing audiences suggests that there are deeper connections with a particular drama or entertainment that involve embedding particular media experiences in the spaces and places of regular routines, family rituals and cultural memories. A key element of this relationship is time. When we embed media in our lives, time becomes enfolded in our everyday media practices over weeks, months and years. This chapter considers embedded engagement, where people form relationships with entertainment over time, in the context of their everyday lives.

We might think of examples of embedded time in the context of fandom; an intense attachment to a celebrity, a drama series, or a sporting team can mean making time for your object of fandom, and staying loyal over the course of changing seasons (see Sandvoss 2005 amongst others). Sometimes we grow out of our fandom, disengaging from our attachment to a particular person or drama, looking back with a sense of nostalgia for that time when our fandom was entangled in our daily life. At other times we form a durable relationship with a media personality, artefact or event that stays with us, indeed it might be something we pass on to younger generations. For example, there are loyal fans of the Eurovision

FIGURE 7.1 Auditions for *Got to Dance*
Source: Photograph Tina Askanius.

Song Contest who plan fan dinner parties, book tickets and travel to the annual show, making an affective and temporal investment in this media event which is likely to weather changes to the event itself and in their own lives. Embedded time encapsulates our strong relationship with media, including the live experience that we make time for, the moments of reflection after the experience, and times devoted to remembering past experiences.

We form a relationship with time and the media that operates across several zones, including social structures and media institutions, daily life, and our everyday lives year on year (see Scannell 1996). Media institutions include broadcast time in the daily and weekly schedules for channels; there is an on demand time built into the subscription streaming services that allow us to access content when we want across geographical time zones; and there are media archives that hold content for retrieval and re-purposing, including formal archives held by museums, and informal ones such as those collected by amateurs. Another time zone is that of our daily routinised experience of time, from when we wake up to the radio and drink that first cup of coffee, so our sense of this daily time is intricately bound up with media – that early morning text message is just one of many media devices you will access during a normal day. A third time zone is that of our everyday life as it is experienced season by season, over the years. These different temporal relations can intersect with each other, for example a live media event usually entails people organising their daily life around broadcast time, whereas a catch up service like the

BBC iPlayer means people make their own personalised schedule of media content when it suits their daily routine. For Sarah Sharma (2015: 3) there is an 'entangled and uneven politics of temporality'. Our relationships with time and the media signal power dynamics across varieties of human experience of time that is 'enabled and performed through the structures and practices' of live or pre-recorded media (Frosh and Pinchevski 2018).

The case of reality talent shows is used to explore the value and meaning of the live event as a temporary experience, and the more enduring collective-social experience of the series. We will see how media industries strategically privilege the temporary over the durable experience of live reality events, in the form of performance metrics such as ratings and social media. The performance metrics for live television signal the primacy of the now; this flow of power to the live shows and the constitution of television obscures the sense of community and viewer agency that is built up over time through the embedding of these series in everyday routines. There is a 'power chronography' (Sharma 2015) at work in the temporal relations between television itself, the production of live television events, and the practices of audiences. In the case of the talent show *Got to Dance*, producers and audiences created a form of embedded engagement over five seasons, but the broadcaster treated audiences as disposable, only of value in the moment of the live show. In the short term, viewers lose their relationship with a favourite show as embedded in their everyday lives, but in the longer term broadcasters are breaking trust with audiences at a time when power is slipping from the constitution of television to disparate sites of media content across multi-platform environments.

Power of time

In order to understand embedded engagement within the empirical case of reality talent shows we first want to examine the temporal relationships we form with media. Our 'TV time' with talent shows arises from a broader sense of the meaning of time as a shared imaginary; time to work and perform, time to relax and share, are all ideas of time that are constructed within political and socio-cultural contexts. The language of time and temporality often involves common phrases such as 'time passes', or 'in the nick of time', and in these phrases time is a thief that steals our ability to maximise human experience, to have a good life. To spend time implies it is a commodity, and this means that there are temporal dimensions to labour, especially the labour of others, that enable us to spend time with work or leisure activities. The time we spend with media, for example, is at the expense of others; first there is the factor of the creative labour involved in the making of media, where other people such as producers, below-the-line workers and participants have come together through their paid and unpaid labour to shape a text or event; and then there is the socio-cultural context to these texts, so that if we spend time with our favourite drama, this means we choose to engage with this over other content available, and we choose to spend time with a screen rather than with our family, say, or with friends on a nature walk. In order to watch drama, the labour of others has helped to generate this TV time.

In her book *In the Meantime: Temporality and Cultural Politics*, Sara Sharma (2014) develops the concept of power chronography. She explains how we have a shared imaginary of time that constructs it as 9–5, a Monday to Friday working week. She conducted ethnographic research of people whose job it is to make time for those of us caught in the imaginary of the 9–5, from taxi drivers to yoga instructors, or frequent flyers in business class. In these studies she found people worried about time, there was not enough time in their week, and they felt the need to speed up and slow down time, depending on their professional labour. Some of these people, such as nannies or cleaners, provided time for more middle- and upper-class workers, affording time for these affluent lifestyles through their labour. Sharma found there were 'differential relationships to time' and these relationships 'organize and perpetuate inequalities' (2014: 137). When researching taxi drivers in an American city, for example, she discovered differential time relationships, and in her critical analysis of this labour she noted 'gendered, raced, and classed itineraries of temporal worth within a heteronormative patriarchal global capital' (2014: 148).

Sharma argues that we need a radical politics of time and space. She draws on Doreen Massey's argument of power geometry which sought to highlight the existing differential relationships between people and space, arguing for a sense of space that can accommodate the differentiated mobility of people in global contexts (Massey 1994). Sharma explains how a power chronography 'provides a politicization of time that dispels individualistic accounts of time and allows the social and relational contours of power in its temporal forms to emerge' (2014: 14). For Sharma, media and communication do not flatten out time but instead contribute to uneven temporalities that make us vulnerable to power over us as publics and citizens. Sharma advocates temporal pluralism, urging researchers to focus not only on a critique of time in global capitalism and neoliberalism, but to see how time management affects different groups of people and to recognise the mutual benefits of time for ourselves and others.

The contours of power in its temporal forms can be a starting point for understanding embedded engagement within the media and audiences' everyday lives. With institutional or broadcast time, there is less of a 9–5 imaginary and more focus on peaktime, or primetime, which varies from region to region but is usually associated with the period after the evening meal in a household when families are relaxing, or when people have finished work; for example in Northern Europe peaktime usually runs from 7 p.m. to 10 p.m., and in Southern Europe from 9 p.m. to midnight. This kind of media institutional time is shaped by our daily experience of time, and in this case the 9–5 working week is used for daytime television, or after school television, which builds to the peaktime schedules for national audiences. This institutional time is significant because several ways of assessing the performance of a programme will be tied to advertising revenues, ratings data and social media analytics during peaktime. In Sharma's terms the temporal form of broadcasting, including public service and commercial television channels, relies on the daily management of time that ensures leisure activities during the evenings. The audience information systems prioritise daily time, with overnight ratings and social media chatter; there are windows for consolidated viewing which also measure catch up viewers over a week or month but these are less of a priority than the overnights. We get a sense of the power chronography of media institutions as connected to the fleeting time of daily access to media content, the here and now is given priority over a more longitudinal perspective of temporal relations.

Alongside this more traditional view of broadcasting, there is the digital content available to users whenever they want it, including television on demand, daily social media feeds, the sharing of content on YouTube, or smartwear and Fitbits which allows you to manage time efficiently for sports and other leisure activities. Much digital content circumvents a media-institutional management of time; the broadcast schedule is dispensed with in favour of personalised content schedules. Here, the priority is on the daily management of time for users; they control what content to access and when, what to share, and what to give weight to in their juggling of time in any given day. According to Arvidsson and Bonini (2015), media companies that operate across digital content, including platform players, are more focused on the value of audiences in relation to their affective investment, their passion for products, rather than the ability to measure audience attention at a given time and place.

There are two different imaginaries for time within the media industries and discourses of audiences. One is a more traditional valuation of audiences and their attention, which places emphasis on time as a commodity. Criticism of this model in terms of labour has focused on audiences' immaterial labour exploited by global capitalism; in this imaginary the work of audiences, their attention, time, and production of content, is used to generate economic value. The other valuation of audiences recognises the shift from analogue to digital media and places more value on affect and emotion, an economics of passion. Arvidsson and Bonini (2015: 177) explain: 'what is commoditized is increasingly not the ability of audiences to produce content, but their ability to form the kinds of affective bonds that make up publics'. This means 'the value of passion is not measured according to some external fixed point – like time spent in front of the screen – but rather according to the strength and make up of the internal affective ties that make up a particular – however temporary – public' (ibid.).

The power chronography of digital platforms is related to the dominance of certain companies and their proprietary software, and their synchronisation of social media with the everyday life of users. For example, the power of algorithms is one such way in which differential relationships to time may be understood as unequal and in some cases having a negative impact on people's lives – think of the targeted social media posts for undecided voters in the Brexit referendum and subsequent scandal over political use of personal data by right wing parties to persuade these voters, as reported in the British newspapers in March 2018. We should note that although it appears as if users have more control over the management of time, there is still priority given to the 'now' of social media and the value accorded to audiences within a passion economy for their fleeting affective and temporal relationships with media content and brands.

To connect engagement with a power chronography, from an industry perspective media engagement priorities the here and now of audience experiences; it is the moment of engagement that is given value, whether this is in the form of attention or affective investment. Short form engagement is, of course, a regular part of people's daily routines, such as watching a live sports event, or tweeting about a reality show whilst watching it. Returning audiences, the loyal consumers of a brand, are also valued in the media industries and commercial culture; and performance metrics for returning series will assess the ratings and social media for a current season compared to last season, or the one before that. Similar to sports teams who play every season, performance metrics for a programme accumulate into a more longitudinal picture of a production company that creates content that appeals to audiences. This is one of the crucial factors in determining success for local production companies and their performance in digital television (Doyle 2018). Note how we accumulate a picture of the performance of a company and programme based on metrics, where the programme is effectively in competition with itself: how did it perform this year compared to last year? How many people voted for the winner this time compared to the previous series?

This point will connect with our case study later in this chapter, as measuring the value of audience attention and affective investment is a snapshot, and what is missing is a more nuanced understanding of media engagement within everyday life. The notion of embedded engagement goes beyond performance indicators to look at the contours of power and its temporal forms in everyday life. This will involve more focus on embodied meaning making for popular culture, daily routines of organising media and time in the home, and in particular, how families embed specific examples of popular culture in their lives because it is meaningful to them and their lifestyle and identities. What follows is an analysis of media events and time within live television as a context for understanding the case study in this chapter, where we consider how embedded engagement works in practice and assess the value of reality talent shows for media industries and in everyday family routines.

Media and entertainment events

In a commentary on the classic book *Media Events* (1992) by Daniel Dayan and Elihu Katz, Frosh and Pinchevski (2018) focus on time in the management of a media event. They argue that we have moved from a more traditional sense of a media event, such as a royal wedding, or a news event, interrupting daily routines and acting as a marker point in the live broadcasting of history, to a 'networked configuration of media events' (2018: 136), such as eye witness news for citizen journalism or human rights activism. They claim there are new formations of 'event-temporalities' and they map this across two areas of analysis, that of 'eventfulness' and 'eventness' (ibid.). Eventfulness is when an event is given status through the media; a contemporary event has a 'thickness of real-time' (2018: 137), and audiences travel together through the duration of the event, seeing time enfold itself in the present moment of engagement. Eventness is when there is an assemblage of media devices, networks, representations and persons that interconnect around an event, or several events. There is no stable perspective of an event in this interpretation, rather there is a dynamic fluctuating eventness 'spreading and disseminating feeds, streams, posts, tweets and images' (2018: 138) by citizens and publics.

This interpretation of the human experience of time for media events captures the dynamics of time as it is organised in different ways in the structures and practices of broadcast and digital media. Eventfulness is an experience more in tune with broadcast media and its organisation of time, although it incorporates users and their engagement with social media during an event, helping to endow an event with status alongside the work of producers and marketing teams. Eventness is related to a durational and aggregated experience of time, where there is an assemblage of affective, temporal and mediated practices that shape and are shaped by the events themselves. For Frosh and Pinchevski there are hierarchies of power in media witnessing, so that even for a networked configuration of events, media institutions and digital platforms often occupy privileged positions of power. Nevertheless they see media witnessing in the form of eventfulness and eventness as a bottom-up rather than top-down orchestration of media events, where citizen engagement can flourish in digital media environments.

The issue with regard to entertainment events and our case study in this chapter is that the idea of witnessing is less significant when considering this kind of popular culture. The presence of audiences and crowds at reality events is important to cultural participation and having a good time. The management of time by a production company for a live reality event is geared towards eventfulness, giving people an intensive experience, both in the venue and for audiences at home; the producers, participants and audiences at the venue endow the event with status, and audiences at home add further status through watching, voting and interacting with social media, thus all contributing to a thickening of the real time of the event. This is a primary way we can understand time within entertainment events for live digital television. However, there are interconnected points of agency before and after the live events that extend the moment of the live experience, offering a more extended notion of time that is part of the dynamics of engagement.

For example, participants in a reality talent show prepare their performances for auditions well in advance of filming, involving an invisible labour of training within the profession of dance, and the invisible labour of family and friends who help make the performance we see at an event and on screen happen; after the performance itself, there will be a forensic analysis of videos of this performance, the sharing of memorable photos from the live events, and the maintenance of social media created by dancers and dance schools in the afterlife of a series. This work by reality television participants and their supporters for a dance talent show is bottom-up in the sense that their labour and passion is self-managed and part of their developing career as a dancer; but they would not choose to devote their time to this talent competition without the orchestration of broadcasting to endow the live performances with event status. What we see is a primary focus on time and eventfulness for this kind of entertainment event, but there is a secondary focus on the assemblage of affective and temporal practices for what a live event might become both during and after the moment of engagement. In the next section the power of time for a media event such as a live reality talent show will be explored in more detail across media producers, participants and audiences.

Researching live reality talent shows

Got to Dance (Sky One, Princess, 2010–2014), is a reality talent competition showcasing adult and child dancers, with a series of live events, public voting, and integrated online content. The format's flagship series ran for five seasons in the UK, with other versions in America, Germany, France, Finland, Poland, Romania and Vietnam. The format uses a familiar narrative of talent competitions where participants first perform in regional auditions filmed in mobile domes, and if selected by the judges go on to perform at semi-finals and finals, with interactive voting by the public during the live events. The empirical data in this section draws on production and audience research for the fifth and final series of *Got to Dance*

FIGURE 7.2 Researching *Got to Dance*
Source: Photograph Tina Askanius.

(2014). The case study featured in Chapter 4 in relation to a spectrum of engagement and modes of disengagement within the series; here the emphasis is on the embedding of the series in people's everyday lives, including participants and their supporters, and audiences at home.

To reflect on the design, this case study took a flexible, pragmatic approach to production and audience research. For the production research, there were interviews and observations of the auditions, semi-finals and finals for *Got to Dance*, from May to August 2014. A team of four, comprising creative content consultant Julie Donovan, Annette Hill, Tina Askanius and Koko Kondo, conducted the research, sharing the work across the different sites of data collection; 10 production interviews took place with executive and creative producers; 30 interviews were conducted with performers at the auditions and 10 interviews at the semi-finals and finals, including family and friends there to support dancers. The production study also included a cultural analysis of the structural factors underlying the reality format *Got to Dance* in terms of financing, the statistical performance indicators for the series in the UK television market, and the creative practices of reality television production. The social media analysis includes industry reports on the digital performance of season five, and the ratings data include performance metrics for all five seasons (see Hill 2017).

Observations took place front- and backstage at the Roundhouse, London, and Earl's Court, London during a two-week period, resulting in audio recordings, visual and aural data, and fieldnotes. The team discussed the participant observations during several periods of reflection during and after each production day. This continual reflection and analysis of the ongoing fieldwork allowed for flexibility in the data design, as each day the participant observations would be attuned to the production environment and the different kinds of participants at the venues. For example, in relation to the live shows, participant observations involved shifting attention to the backstage rehearsal space for the dance groups alongside the spaces for friends and family which were semi-backstage, and the main venue for audiences. Production practices for the participants, family supporters, and crowd management worked across these production and reception zones. Such observations supported the theory-building and analysis of embedded engagement within the production of a live reality event.

For the audience research, 50 individual and group (1–5 persons) interviews were conducted with live crowds at the semi-finals and finals, in the queues, coffee shops and on the street, outside and inside the venue. Each interview lasted from 5 to 20 minutes. Recruitment was focused on a range of participants and audiences, including professional dancers, individuals and dance troupes, dance teachers, family groups, people at the live show who received tickets as Sky subscribers, and people who were there to experience the filming of a reality talent show. Interviews were conducted individually and in groups in order to ensure both one-to-one and group interactions. The interviews were designed with a topic guide, including social contexts related to the routines involved in attending the live show, or watching the series at home, and theoretically informed themes such as

130 Embedded engagement: reality talent shows

emotional and critical engagement with the series. Further follow-up interviews were conducted with dance schools and at-home audiences, in order to explore issues raised by the fieldwork in August with regard to the final outcome of the series and its cancellation by the broadcaster. Participant observations of the live shows, where the venue was filled with crowds of 4,000–6,000 each day of filming, followed the same pattern of flexible and pragmatic design, with notes, diaries, and visual and aural recordings building a nuanced picture of the experience of live reality television. The interviews and observations served as valuable sources of knowledge construction for the significance of time within live entertainment events

Embedding engagement within live reality TV

As live reality television, *Got to Dance* exemplifies what Elizabeth Evans (2011: 156) calls the 'hyper-ephemeral', where a mediated experience privileges 'engagement with a particular moment that can never be replicated' and underscores the value of 'being there' (Evans 2011: 168). A live experience can also become embedded within everyday life, part of the memories of individuals and communities, a marker point in the routines of existence. Live reality television can offer an infrastructure for the moment-to-moment of the event itself, and also the hourly, daily, monthly preparations and routines that come before, during and after an event. This is especially relevant if reality television is a returning feature of a

FIGURE 7.3 At the *Got to Dance* venue
Source: Photograph Tina Askanius.

broadcaster's seasonal schedule, similar to football seasons for example. Live spectaculars matter in the moment of a unique experience, that particular performer, the crowd's reactions at that venue, the way the voting worked for that winner. But reality entertainment spectaculars are usually replicated, due to the format market and the economic model of broadcast television that recoups start up costs for an original production by reproducing the same show with less risk and more return on investment. A returning talent show brings with it the power of the live, and the expectation of this live experience being constitutive of the everyday lives of audiences and performers year on year.

This means that an interpretation of live talent show spectaculars as the 'ultimate fulfilment of reality TV's aesthetic of immediacy' (Deery 2015: 40) ought to be set alongside the return appeal of a talent show, especially for the targeted younger generation of reality participants and audiences. Holmes (2004) noted early on in the development of talent shows the marketing of live entertainment and the feeling of being there in a performance space; it is the sense of participation in the process of identifying talent, the stage shows, voting and interactive elements that suggest audiences can make a difference to the outcome of who wins. These interconnected points of agency can become unstuck in voting scandals, or a perceived commercialisation of the talent on offer. Dance talent shows have an added complication in that a dance performance is perceived by audiences as a powerful expression of selfhood, and yet the performance space is that of commercial entertainment which creates tensions for how audiences make meaning from this commercial type of dance (Heller 2012: 39–41).

As discussed in Chapter 4, *Got to Dance* attempted to overcome these tensions by developing a strategic emphasis on passion for dance, and by encouraging dedicated performers from the dance community to audition for the series. One of the ways producers and casting directors reached out to the dance community was to go beyond London, the centre of the dance industry, to make contact with local communities, schools and audiences to create a regional event that could be integrated into the dance school season. Up until season five, *Got to Dance* was scheduled for the winter months of January to March. There were domes – temporary sites that travelled across the United Kingdom for the auditions which were lit up so the show symbolised light during the winter months. To audition for *Got to Dance* meant a lot of preparation – dance school teachers spoke of planning routines once children were back at school in the autumn. Schools gave permission for children to go to the auditions while teachers and friends supported their participation, voting and organising parties back home during the live events. Parents and friends booked time off work, helped with logistics and attended the auditions and live shows. As the series gathered momentum season on season, it established a temporal and affective relationship with its cross-regional participants and audiences.

At the live event for season five, buses arrived full of schoolchildren, with teachers taking their pupils to learn what they described as the *Got to Dance* values of positive role models and a can-do attitude to life. One teacher explained how they replicated the style of this talent show in school performances, using gold stars and constructive criticism to highlight how dedication and hard work can lead to opportunities in life. Legions of young children watched the show so they could learn about dance. One family we interviewed in the queue for a semi-final commented:

MUM: We share our views, what we like and what we don't like, the more we watch the series, the more we become dance critics, we give our own opinions before the judges do [laughs] … so we are judges in our living room.
INTERVIEWER: So, when you are watching the show, do you dance together?
MUM: [to boy] I do notice that you try to copy some of the moves.
INTERVIEWER: [to boy] So what is your style of dance?
BOY: More street style. I take street dancing because I am pretty young.
INTERVIEWER: How old are you?
BOY: Six.
INTERVIEWER: [to mother] Do you dance as well?
MUM: I'm just watching. I'm a very embarrassing mum dancing.

This six year old was taking street dance lessons, participating in the live shows, watching and learning about dance and the reality talent format; and this exemplifies their embedded engagement with this event built up over time.

Parents spoke of organising their everyday lives around the twin interests of their children in dance and this television show. Thus for every live performance, there was a support network of mums and aunts and best friends who sewed the sequins on costumes, prepared hair, took a day off work, all to hold the hands and support the energy of those practising for their big moment. Alongside the crew and participants, this invisible workforce got up early and hired the bus to make sure the dance troupe arrived on time for rehearsals. The production company made sure to invite large groups of friends and family to auditions and the live shows, giving away free tickets, understanding that the support network for dancers is significant to the level of practice and training it takes to pull off a live dance performance.

In one interview with a family (teenage sister and mother and father, 27 August 2014) just before the semi-finals were to go live, they explained the support for their teenage daughter from Unity Academy, a dance school run by two former participants in *Got to Dance*. There were over 100 supporters from Unity wearing specially made T-shirts: 'We are here to make a lot of noise.' Their daughter started dancing at the age of four, and after she saw Unity perform in a previous series she joined their academy. She regularly travelled three hours each way for training. The family were there to help her with travel, competitions, training and live performances. Not only were they part of the Unity crowd, shouting, sharing on social media and voting, but at least 20 members of their extended family and friends were squeezed into their living room to watch it live on subscription channel Sky One and vote for their daughter. There was recognition that it was a tough challenge to get this far in a dance competition; her sister said 'you have to really want it' to succeed as a dancer. Her parents added:

you have to have your parents behind you, for the travel and training. She has been down here every day, hours and hours and hours of training. You can forget your social life, there is no social life. It's all about dance.

There are several points of analysis here. There is a cyclical process to the embedded engagement with this series, audiences transforming into reality talent show participants, and reality participants becoming actors in commercial culture (see Deery 2015). What we also see is the organisation of time by families and supporters of reality talent performers. They travel to the auditions, training studios and live venues; they organise supporters at the live event, wearing branded T-shirts, providing vocal support to the performers on stage and backstage support in the form of doing the makeup, and transportation to and from the venue. They mobilise people at home, co-ordinating live viewing and voting in a strategic move to combine access to this subscription channel for the all important votes from the public. This type of entertainment event highlights the considerable resources of time, money and emotion that are needed for each individual to make it as a reality show participant in a dance competition.

What was apparent in the build up to season five of the series was a recognition by the production company that family viewers, and dedicated dancers as participants, contributed significantly to the eventfulness of the live experience. Audiences and participants travelled together with the producers for the duration of the event, including the long build up to the event itself, and the time after the event when a process of reflection and archiving of performances and memories took place, before the start of a new round of training in preparation for the next season. For these child audiences and participants, their passion for dance drove them to engage with the talent show; family and friends provided support and helped to embed this engagement in everyday life and local communities. Although the production company ultimately managed the time of the event, and the broadcaster managed the scheduling on television, they relied on bottom-up time management by children, and their parents and friends, dance teachers and school heads, to be in readiness for the dance performances that made a success of such a reality spectacular.

During 2014, *Got to Dance* experienced major problems in its fifth season. The first season had started with over a million viewers, but by seasons three and four the numbers were declining. Sky's strategy was to extend the live shows whilst at the same time reducing total screen time. The budget was halved, from around £13 million to £7 million, the number of programmes was cut, in particular auditions, and all the weight was placed on the live events, squeezing the show into a few weeks during a new scheduling slot of 9–29 August 2014. This slot was supposed to attract family audiences during the summer holidays, and to have a short transmission window just before the autumn broadcast schedule for the two rival talent shows on BBC and ITV. Another strategy was to give more attention to social media. For example the production company hired a YouTube star; it integrated social media reactions into the live event by the use of a large screen on stage; it included digital hosts who were former winners of the series in Facebook live studio interviews. Overall, the broadcaster's strategic decisions led to a major overhaul of the series, including a change in the annual schedule, significant cuts in budget and transmission time, and a digital marketing campaign aimed mainly at social media users rather than broadcast audiences. For local producers these changes signalled an uncertain future; one producer described the broadcaster as sabotaging the brand through the summer scheduling slot; another crew member working on casting felt that the reduced number of audition shows lessened the audience's emotional engagement with the participants during the live events – how would viewers know who to vote for if they hadn't had a chance to follow the performers from auditions through rehearsals to the live finale?

Compared with around a million viewers for the first three seasons, the ratings performance for the final season showed a sharp decline. According to the BARB (Broadcaster Audience Research Board) figures, viewers disengaged with the series, dropping from 646,000 at the start of the auditions to 486,000 for the live finale, losing a percentage point in the share of audiences watching television at that time (from 3.4 to 2.2). The share drop was especially shown amongst children (from 9.5 to 4.6), and the share halved for women, adults aged 16–55, and housewives (for example housewives went from a 2.5 to a 1.6 share). If we analyse the ratings for children, there is a stark picture of younger audiences disengaging with the show. In season one, 230,000 children watched *Got to Dance*, but by season five at the auditions 160,000 were watching, and only 80,000 remained for the live finale. In terms of mums, recorded in BARB as housewives, the ratings dropped from around half a million viewers for season one to 200,000 for the live finale of season five. The ratings show that the strategic decision to focus on the live shows backfired with core audiences (children and parents) for the series.

Indeed, the switch in seasons was devastating for the series. In the past, families watching at home established a routine for the series. One mum explained how she made a ritual of the show, dinner and a bath before watching the auditions and live events: 'it is one we can all sit around and watch as a family. My husband doesn't care about *The X Factor* whereas he will sit and watch this. It's family time.' For the final season, gone was the school and weekend routine and families now had to make special time for the compressed live shows during the summer holidays. In the queues for the live events audiences expressed their frustration with the broadcaster and changes it had made to the show. A brand based on passion for dance seemed oddly lacking in dance content due to the compression in the programme time:

INTERVIEWER: So what do you think of this new format?
MOTHER: I just don't like it. We don't see much dance.
INTERVIEWER: Do you dance?
MOTHER: Yes, I used to do line dancing and Latin samba.
DAUGHTER: Yes, it's a family thing [laughs].

In another encounter, two sisters and their children were waiting to enter the venue for the semi-finals. They had no idea about the acts as they had been on holiday during its transmission:

I must admit that I haven't watched this one. I never missed any series but we have been away on holiday. We love dance ... the previous series were shown in January and they changed it' (30–40 year old female viewer). If viewers missed the auditions 'then when it comes to the semi-finals they won't know what the acts are – 'Who are these people?'

(40–50 year old male viewer)

One fan explained how she felt the broadcaster cut her 'TV time': 'I was looking forward to ten weeks of the show and feeling like you get to know the acts, whereas with the time and space I feel like I don't know them as well.' An embedded engagement, so hard to create and something to nurture and value in a seasonal event such as this, slipped away with the broadcaster's decision to change the timeslot and cut the running time. In such a way the broadcaster dismantled the temporal and affective relationship with audiences. As this fan noted, their sense of time – the season, time to watch and share with others – was changed for the worse: 'I like the fact that it used to be week in, week out. It has been compressed. I feel like my enjoyment is going to be a lot shorter.' What she is describing is a differential experience of time, her experience as 'TV time', which is time to enjoy the event as part of her everyday life, and the compressed time of the live events, which is the orchestration of time by media institutions.

To reflect on time and entertainment events within this talent show, the producers and audiences created an eventfulness (Frosh and Pinchevski 2018) for this entertainment experience, one that followed an event's journey across England, Scotland, Wales and Northern Ireland and across the winter months of the television broadcast season when the show originally aired. The production company understood the embedding of the brand with local communities year on year through the build up of the regional auditions and the *Got to Dance* dome, spread across several months that culminated in the live semi-finals and finals. Change the location to London only, and the sense of local communities engaging with the show starts to fall away as they travel to the capital and the hub of commercial dance, rather than the show travelling to them, seeking out ordinary people in regional cities where dance is embedded in local communities, including schools, families, youth groups and volunteers. Change the transmission to the summer season and the sense of embedded time also starts to fall away as families are forced by the broadcaster to change their routines established over several years to accommodate commercial interests, routines that have contributed to the status of the show as eventful. These changes to the brand shifted the power dynamic so what previously felt like a travelling and dynamic show much loved by regional participants and audiences became stuck in one place and at the wrong time.

The sense of eventness for reality entertainment may be less obvious than for news events, which from the bottom up can generate an assemblage of eyewitness videos and social media commentary that can extend for a period of time. However, the contributions of the dancers and their supporters in the long build up to the talent show ought not to be forgotten in the practices of participants as they prepare for training, compete, and review their performances. Their participation is not always filmed and circulated on social media, but their practices are integral to the event taking place, a physical and emotional labour that builds over time into an assemblage of affective practices and embodied meaning making that is visible in the screen time of the event and is still there afterwards; in the iteration of each season these reality participants and their supporters help to generate an ongoing eventness to a long running talent show.

The physical and emotional labour within a reality talent show such as this helps to illuminate the power chronography (Sharma 2016) at work in this entertainment event. The dancers as participants, and their family and friends, offer their time freely to the production company. They perceive this as a trade-off between their physical and emotional labour as dancers and the opportunity for this labour to be made visible in screen time, with the bonus of a cash prize if crowned the winner. As one mother lamented, their young daughter spent 'hours and hours and hours' training before and during *Got to Dance*'s fifth season; her parents sacrificed their social life to support her, effectively offering their time as well as free labour to the production. There are different labour relations scattered across this event journey, relations which are routinely accepted as part of what it takes to participate in a reality talent show and to take pleasure from this as an audience. For the most part the dancers, their supporters, the producers and audiences came together in the endeavour to co-produce an entertainment experience. The people in this study were clear in what they offered the show and what the show offered them.

It is the economic driver of the changes to the series that tipped participants and audiences over into a critical position. The broadcaster's management of time highlighted their inability or unwillingness to value the embedded time of participants, supporters and audiences. This failure of time management affected these different groups in negative ways; there was not enough time to train, not enough time to engage with the show, to care about the dancers and vote for them. Here, then the broadcaster showed an inability to recognise the mutual benefits of time management for the programme makers, participants and audiences. Family viewers, and in particular aspiring young dancers, made time for the series, integrating it into their schedules for dance competitions and everyday life. However, the broadcaster occupied a position of power where it could change the time of the show in detrimental ways, ending people's engagement with the event. This lack of recognition of an audience's investment in time as part of their long term engagement with the brand made a significant contribution to the failure of the series overall.

Conclusion

Reality talent shows place emphasis on the immediacy of live events. The feeling of being there in a performative space, watching and interacting with participants, being part of a live experience, is essential to talent shows that draw audiences to a particular channel at a certain time and place. The talent show offers digital television an entertainment brand that results in ticket sales, voting, ratings and social media metrics that show how broadcasting relies on the 'now' of live entertainment spectaculars to attract audiences to spend time with a live event. We can see from the empirical research reviewed in this chapter that there are temporal and affective investments in the individual and collective feeling of being there. Indeed, the broadcasting organisation concerned becomes visible to participants and audiences of a talent show, where there is an understanding of how media time intersects with the time of audiences and their everyday lives.

In the case of *Got to Dance* the live event became fraught with difficulties. There was a play off between the value and meaning of the live events as a temporary experience, and the more enduring collective-social experience of the series. The strategic privileging of the temporary over the durable experience of live reality events led to a breakdown in the temporal and affective relations with audiences for the brand. The performance metrics for live television signal the primacy of the now; this flow of power to the live shows and the constitution of television obscures the sense of community and viewer agency that is built up over time through the embedding of cultural values in everyday routines. This woman spoke of her disaffection with *Got to Dance*: 'I'm missing my TV time. I want to watch them for longer, not sit down and "oh, it's over already"' (20–30 year old female viewer). This meaning of a live entertainment event, built on the relationship between television producers and audiences, is lost when a broadcaster treats audiences as disposable, only of value in the moment of the live show.

8

AUTHENTIC REALITY TV

The case of *MasterChef*

> *MasterChef* put people in a positive light. They don't make a fool of anyone.
>
> *(48 year old Danish male IT consultant)*

Is there such a thing as authentic reality TV? The 'real' in reality television has always been tricky; for some critics the real signals a deception and for others a staging of reality that plays with the boundaries of fact and drama (Kilborn 2003). Claims to authenticity in reality television are a significant site of analysis if we want to understand how audiences value the genre. To try to produce authenticity is no easy feat. If scholars are sceptical of authentic reality television, audiences are equally, if not more, critical of this genre as 'just entertainment'. Audiences have grown up with reality television, watching and reflecting on the use of factuality in entertainment and becoming tough judges over time, for example critiquing contestants in *The X Factor*, or the management of celebrity brands in the *Real Housewives* franchise. Back in the early 2000s it was clear that viewers of *Big Brother* season two approached it rather like computer game players, expecting a reboot of the original and bringing their genre skills acquired in the first season to play the game of reality. In a genre that audiences often treat as trash entertainment to consume and throw away, a programme that feels authentic is something that goes against the grain of the usual value judgements about reality television.

In this chapter I want to analyse audience engagement with a specific kind of reality food talent format: *MasterChef*. Talent shows are not obvious examples to use if we wish to understand audience engagement with authentic reality television. They are entertainment formats, which means that the creative idea is formatted so the series can be remade, with minor variations, in regions and countries around the world (Oren and Shahaf 2011). *MasterChef* is made in fifty territories (Endemol Shine). This status as a format might suggest that audiences take 'authentic' to mean a certified copy of an original, for example *MasterChef Sverige* is

Authentic reality TV: *MasterChef* 139

FIGURE 8.1 *MasterChef* participants
Source: Photograph Tina Askanius.

an official version of the original. But this is not what viewers and contestants mean when they claim these shows are authentic; they are talking about emotional truth, where these series are meaningful to people's lives. Thus, when audiences engage with what they perceive to be authentic reality television they are signalling a culture of viewing that embraces positive values, the pro-social side of television as enriching their lives somehow. And when audiences engage in such a way they are doing so against what they see as a market in predominantly negative emotions within reality television; what people commonly call 'emotional porn' which they describe as high drama, scripted emotional moments, and a manipulation of reactions through casting, editing or performances. Engaging with authentic reality television is thus a counter-manoeuvre to more negative engagement with the genre overall.

We might see examples of authentic reality talent shows as reflecting television for the public good, and whilst there are elements of this public service ethos in formats (some are broadcast on public service channels), perhaps what is more apparent is the way popular culture connects with audience reflections on living in late modern societies. For Peter Lunt (2014), reality television can play a role in citizens' critical reflections on life politics based on experience. Such a reading of reality television disrupts a common critique of the genre, drawing on the influential work of French theorist Michel Foucault and his ideas regarding power and surveillance by state institutions. In this view of reality television, the 'contours of modernity' are a neo-liberal project and critiques of neo-liberalism and reality television highlight how the media 'construct, constrain and shape conduct' (Lunt 2014: 512–513). A neo-Foucauldian interpretation of the genre sees the individual as involved in competition, caught in an enterprise culture. Work by Palmer (2003) and Andrejevic (2004) amongst others critiques the neo-liberal project in popular culture, calling for resistance to this subtle control over citizens, viewers, consumers and users. Lunt offers an alternative perspective that places more agency with audiences where popular culture can have value in everyday life.

There is a way in which the mediation of authenticity in talent shows can connect with both the production of entertainment, what we can call the entertainment spaces of reality television, and the habits, values, and life politics of people in everyday life, what we can call the real world spaces of reality television. The talent show discussed in this chapter uses the inter-generic space of reality television to balance the construction of entertainment, in this case a talent competition set in a televised studio, with the real world spaces of amateurs and professionals within the world of creative labour. What is crucial in the specific case of *MasterChef* is that this format places emphasis on the practical skills of cooking, which anchors the series in real world practice and invites audiences to connect these skills with their practical, everyday life. *MasterChef* uses the imaginative spaces of storytelling to reflect and engage with food culture, and physical performance, to explore healthy eating, self-identity and professional work ethics. In such a way this reality format has a role to play in inviting audiences to critically engage with claims of authenticity and the broader moral and social issues of living in late modern societies.

Mediated authenticity in talent shows

According to Gunn Enli in *Mediated Authenticity* (2015: 3) 'a common treatment of the term authenticity in academic literature is to position it in opposition to whatever is fake, unreal or false and further to acknowledge it has multiple meanings'. For Enli, there is an essential paradox to mediated authenticity as it is a social construction but at the same time 'traffics in representations of reality' (2015: 1). The word 'traffics' suggests something untrustworthy, trafficking in false merchandise for example. Enli refers to Umberto Eco's (1986) criticism of popular culture where he wrote about people's desire for simulacra, preferring a fake version to an original. In previous research I talked about reality TV as a magic trick, not quite what it appears to be (Hill 2005; 2007), often using misdirection to pull off mediated authenticity (Enli 2015). For some critics of the genre this is an example of Eco's 'counterfeit reality'; a simulacra that we should acknowledge as fake from the outset. Such a criticism could be read as an example of Banet-Weiser's (2013) discussion of authenticity in commercial culture: reality television plays with the notion of authenticity whilst also signalling to savvy consumers that this is a branding strategy. This commercial driver would support Enli's discussion of reality television as trafficking in authenticity.

The mediated authenticity within talent shows is quite distinctive within the genre; talent shows offer an entertainment narrative set within broader production practices in light entertainment as well as reality talent formats, and as such they offer rather minimal claims of reality, compared to docusoaps for example. What is significant for our focus on authenticity is the representation of a real craft and professional skill, such as cooking, where there are quality standards, codes of conduct, and appreciation and criticism; this invites audience engagement where there is a focus on practical skills as they relate to their everyday lives. For celebrity talent shows, programme makers usually cast celebrities with very little experience who are then put through their paces with a professional who wants to win the competition. Behind-the-scenes footage of the celebrities hard at work in training, or interviews where they profess their commitment to the competition, are designed to counteract a critical viewing mode where audiences may think a celebrity is only taking part in order to promote their brand (see Deery 2015).

A pressure point for a talent show can occur in scandals related to casting, the judging panel, or the transparency of the voting process. Minor scandals can occur around repeat performers who audition for several competitions; scroll through the showbiz web pages of British newspapers like the *Daily Mail* and there will be YouTube clips of an amateur in one talent show being revealed as auditioning in a rival series. The social media chatter about celebrity Debbie McGee performing in *Strictly Come Dancing* 2017 (BBC, UK) signposts the gossip that circulates around a reality scandal; McGee's previous experience as a trained dancer dogged her progress through the competition, with questions of fairness being raised by viewers and social commentators concerning casting and the scoring by judges.[1] Enli (2015) calls this an 'authenticity scandal', and this has become so common in talent shows that tabloid media and public discussion tend to promote scandals as part of the entertainment value of reality television. Take this example in Britain's national newspaper the *Daily Telegraph*: '*Britain's Got Talent* is entering its week of live semi-finals. Can we expect scandals, snarl-ups and shrieks of indignation from sofas nationwide? Let's certainly hope so.'[2]

One scandal concerned the case of the 'double dog' in *Britain's Got Talent*. The winner of series nine was a dog trainer and her border collie Matisse; the final performance involved Matisse doing a tight rope walk, and yet after the live event and voting by the public it was revealed that Matisse had a body double. Eight hundred viewers complained to the regulatory body the Office of Communications that they had been misled into voting for a double act when in fact this was a team effort. Twitter feeds were full of the scandal, generating gossip about the winner and what this signified about reality television and the great British public. For example, on the night of the finale, there were around 370,000 tweets (*Kantar Media*, 31 May 2015); after the announcement of the winner people tweeted their congratulations to Jules and Matisse, but others moaned about those who voted (an estimated 4 million), claiming Britain's got crazy viewers, Britain has no talent, even asking for a referendum about 'Britain's membership of Britain'. This dog-gate, as some called it, also led to negative engagement with the voting process, calling it a fix, asking why dogs could enter the competition, why the British public keep voting for f***ing dogs to win, and so forth. All this chatter only added to the buzz of the talent show; the scandal did not stop the series being recommissioned by ITV and as we can see from the newspaper article of 2017, scandal has become part of this brand and its status as a must-see show.

In the next section we look more closely at how talent show formats operate in the entertainment space of the genre, a made for television space that is designed to be an entertainment spectacle; and yet talent shows also draw on the real world space of professional labour, people and everyday life. This is a means for talent shows to produce authenticity within entertainment television and related social media that connects with audiences and their practices in everyday life.

Reality talent shows as inter-generic space

Jonathan Bignell suggests thinking about reality television as 'a nodal point at which different discourses within and outside television culture have temporarily come together in an unstable conjunction' (Bignell 2005: 171). This is a useful position to take for a reality talent show as it resists a single identity, adopting multiple aesthetics and appealing to various audiences living in different regions and cultures. Talent shows are a container for a range of diverse programmes, series, formats and live events in which elements of lifestyle, entertainment, sports, fly-on-the-wall documentary and soap opera, mix together. For Corner (cited in Hill 2015: 9) 'reality television is a new kind of inter-generic space rather than a genre'. In this case, reality talent shows have two distinct spaces that draw on sub-variants of other genres across factuality and entertainment television.

Entertainment space of talent shows

Talent shows primarily take place in the entertainment space of television. Shows like *Got Talent* or *Strictly Come Dancing* are set in specially designed studios, theatre venues or locations. These programmes are often formats and have proven to be very successful business models in the development of reality television for cross-media content. This type of series is usually described as entertainment in order to indicate the reliance on a certain amount of scripting and producer intervention. The inter-generic space of these series and formats set in created-for-television environments usually contains participants as contestants who are both performing as themselves and taking part in a contest; these series also feature professionals and celebrities as judges who are also performing as themselves and as experts who give opinions of and score participants. This is reality television as entertainment spectacle, often imagining what might happen in a real dance competition, or a real restaurant, and then casting, filming and editing so that viewers can see what did happen in this created-for-television show. Although these kinds of talent shows rely on storytelling and entertainment aesthetics, there are usually claims to reality involved in the form of real experts and critics, or the following of real professional practices. As Francis Bonner notes, presenters and judges in reality television perform key roles as cultural intermediaries between the television programme and audiences in the studio and at home (2011). It is common to see an expert in French cooking, for example, teaching contestants how to make an authentic regional dish. Somewhat similar to role play, professionals will perform as if they were actually training apprentices in their kitchen, even though these are amateur cooks involved in a television production.

A long-running example of a talent show is *MasterChef*. It started out in the 1990s as a gameshow and lifestyle series, created by Franc Roddam for the BBC, following a tradition of cookery television where ordinary people would cook a plate of food under time pressure in a studio and be judged on the quality of the food by professional chefs. There was a light touch to the early series, a chatty attitude to viewers at home, a family-friendly gameshow where audiences could cheer for the contestants. The visual brand for the series was a round plaque rather reminiscent of a gold medal with the name of the series and a classic chef's hat in the middle. The action all took place in a studio where presenter Lloyd Grossman would introduce ordinary people as contestants, for example 'This is Brian from Norfolk and he works in accounting…'; there would be a short video of each contestant in their real life – here's Brian at the office …, followed by each amateur chef introducing their three-course menu, typically elaborate dishes such as pot roasted venison in fig wine, to signal that this was a cut above the normal daily meal for the British public. Whilst the contestants got on with preparing their dishes in a quiet and calm fashion, a short instruction video from a professional chef would show viewers how to make a bread sauce, say, and then the very same chef would walk around with Grossman to chat amongst the amateur chefs at their island stations. Friendly introductions by the announcer – 'here is another tasty offering' – and endearing comments from the presenter about the contestants and their dishes – 'we island dwellers do have a genius for pudding' (*MasterChef*, BBC1, April 1992) – all helped to create an invitation to a pleasant and delicious evening out with some good dinner guests.

The original version of the series underwent a major transformation after the wave of competitive reality that dominated the television schedules in the late 1990s. The original British version had followed a typical gameshow format where ordinary people displayed their practical skills, interacting with the presenter, and competing to win the title of *MasterChef*. The premise of the revised reality format is a cooking talent show where amateurs audition and attend bootcamp before being whittled down to a select group who participate in a tough competition judged by professional chefs, where one person is crowned the *MasterChef* winner. The transformation to reality talent show turned the format into a combination of gameshow (the competition), an observational documentary (fly-on-the-wall elements in restaurants), a soap opera (the emotional identification with characters and their interactions with each other) and a media event (the auditions, bootcamp, and semi-finals and finals).

The key moment was the Australian revamp of the format from gameshow to talent show. The broadcaster Network 10 had cancelled *Big Brother* and was looking for a stripped reality series to replace it in the nightly schedules. According to one executive producer 'they totally re-engineered it for six nights a week, turning it into a massive talent show. It became the highest rated show in Australia' (see Donovan 2013). On the back of this success the format was sold to Fox in America; with the Michelin-starred celebrity chef Gordon Ramsey on board the revamped version of the format was a hit on Fox and subsequently the brand spread to other territories. According to the official website (Endemol Shine 2018) the format is 'produced in over 50 territories worldwide and broadcast in over 200 territories', and '*MasterChef* is watched globally by over 250 million viewers and has transformed over 100 amateur chefs into professionals'. It goes on to say 'the success of *MasterChef* is down to its highly adaptable format that taps into a global appetite for watching everyday people fulfil their dreams of achieving something extraordinary' (ibid.). There is the original amateurs version of the format, a celebrity version, a professional version, a spinoff that includes children, and an allstars series of previous winners. To briefly compare the original version and the revamp, the British *MasterChef* retains its own distinctive visual tone, with a more observational style of factual entertainment that fits with the development of public service television in the UK; most other versions of the format follow the Australian/American model with more emphasis on a talent competition, including faster pacing and dramatic storytelling that works for commercial broadcasters and advertising breaks.

The entertainment space of this format is clearly signalled to viewers through the competition. This talent show has all the hallmarks of reality television such as emotional highs and lows, strong identifiable characters, and the pressures of a competition. The emotional hub of this format is people's relationship with food. An executive producer explained: 'one of the key elements is that it is completely relatable for everybody; it evokes an emotional reaction when you watch it and when you think about food' (see Donovan 2013). The entertainment space is also signalled by the acknowledgement that the cooking is being artificially heightened for the show. For example, the time it takes to make a dish is artificially speeded up in the *MasterChef* studio to create dramatic tension and place pressure on the contestants; to choose a high-risk dish means the pressure is on – will their soufflé rise on time? Casting is crucial: 'the most important thing is getting the casting right and telling the stories of the contestants and the food' (see Donovan 2013). Contestants need to care about cooking, to be able to express their passion on a plate in a way that audiences can relate to. The judges are also crucial as they need to be able to perform as professionals, with the right credentials that ensure trust in their expert opinion; the judges lead the journey of the contestants through the competition as we come to root for particular persons in the auditions, semi-finals and finals. Unlike other talent shows that include public voting, the judges stand in for the viewer, tasting and critiquing the food, and ultimately deciding who will be the winner.

There is a *MasterChef* online universe that contains different information and entertainment elements, from recipes and how-to videos, social media promotions, cookbooks, travel and lifestyle, and other consumer products. The local television series is the mothership, but the social media spaces of the *MasterChef* universe are spread far and wide; rather than see this as a problem in knowing what audiences to address and whether to control the brand, producers positively welcome informal media (see Deery 2015; Hill and Askanius 2015). One of the reasons for this is that the global format has various engagement points with audiences as a reality series set within the entertainment spaces of television and social media. For example, viewers will post Instagram photos of delicious dishes they have cooked whilst watching *MasterChef*. Comic photos of bad food, accompanied by a mocking line from the series, are also common, for example a close-up of chunks of pineapple and cheese on a stick and the caption 'Cooking doesn't get tougher than this.' Other informal distribution of entertainment related to the format includes fan mashup videos, GIFs, blogs and fan fiction. Probably one of the best known examples of a mashup video is Swede Mason's 'Buttery Biscuit Base': this started out as a user-generated video and became a commercial success, making it to the Top 40 in the 2011 UK singles chart; the song now has its own fan base, and remixes of the original remix, such as a ten-hour loop dance version.[3] Fan fiction, where fans create their own stories inspired by the format, is a more unusual example of the entertainment spaces of reality television. These are self-produced fictions, fanzines, videos and songs that draw upon characters and settings within the format, for example romance between contestants, or slash fiction based on erotic stories between same sex characters.[4] Thus the entertainment space of this format spreads into the real-world space of food culture, gastronomy, viewers at home in their kitchens, and fan production that remixes the format in other entertainment genres, such as fictional romance, comedy and satire.

World space of talent shows

Although talent shows are defined as entertainment, they connect with the real world of music, dance, theatre, and skills such as cookery. These elements of the format often contain on-scene footage at places of work or rehearsal studios, mixing in observational-style documentary and entertainment news. Although these series and formats are not set in real-world locations for the duration of the season, the participants will go to professional locations; for example *MasterChef* contestants prepare lunches in schools and office buildings or cater for outside events, and in the latter stages of the competition are put to work in high-pressure kitchens in Michelin-starred restaurants. The amateur versions of talent shows usually contain participants who are performing as themselves in recognisable social roles, such as a stay-at-home mum now looking to start up her own restaurant. Talent shows connect the representation of creative performances with related news articles and online content, and with actual chefs, critics, restaurants, recipes and culinary ingredients, or singers, musicians and producers, dancers, choreographers and composers, critics and performance venues. There is a world of human work associated with a reality talent show.

It is the performance of creative labour that enables the producers to build trust in the authenticity of the series. Trust is built across a number of areas; the judges, as mentioned previously, should have accreditation and peer acknowledgement as experts in their profession in order to safeguard quality standards. Bonner notes (2011: 139) how 'the judges perform presenter tasks and lead the show, but hardly ever address viewers directly'. And yet audiences are encouraged to trust the judges, to accept that they are basing their opinions and scores on the quality of the craft, that their comments are not scripted by the producers, or that they are not coerced into decisions for commercial reasons. The contestants ought to be serious about their craft; a certain amount of entertainment can be gleaned from auditions where audiences expect a few people without talent to try their luck, but the journey of each contestant needs to be paramount in the latter stages of the show. Critical appraisal from invited experts currently working in acclaimed dance shows or restaurants, is another authenticity marker, signalling that the skills of a contestant are being acknowledged by professionals outside of the television industry.

And another significant feature of the real-world space of talent shows is the public voting process. Whilst this can be risky, with scandals resulting from unpopular winners or mishandling of votes, most talent shows rely on the public vote to make the show feel very present and real to its viewers. By voting in the semi-finals and finals, viewers can make a difference to the outcome, sometimes overturning the judges' scores and voting for the underdog, or giving a popular vote to a plucky but untalented performer to keep them in the competition. In this way the TV viewer and social media user is invited to participate in the talent show, reviewing performances, playing the role of judge, sharing comments via social media, running online campaigns for favourite contestants. The live event of a talent show with public voting enables audiences to engage with the series in ways that connect the representations of artistic performance with the real life drama of creative competitions.

When the entertainment spaces of reality television connect with real-world spaces there can be tensions. For example, the commercialisation of television and entertainment industries means that some talent shows tie their winners into contracts with the company making the series. *Idols* is one example, where the winners will be contractually bound to produce songs under a certain label and work with a PR company associated with the brand. This commercial packaging of new talent can lead to creative decisions that hinder rather than promote careers; the supposed 'curse' of talent show winners means that sometimes performers booted out of the competition fare better than the winners. The case of Ella Henderson is a good example of the tensions within an authenticity contract; Henderson performed a rendition of 'Believe', a previous hit for Cher, in the 2012 series of *The X Factor* in Britain that had the judges in tears and the crowd on their feet, but was voted out of the competition at a later stage. Fans and former contestants blamed the producers for turning the series into an entertainment spectacle where novelty acts reigned supreme and the public were encouraged to vote for the worst rather than the best talent. At the time the series was struggling with plummeting ratings and losing out in a head-to-head scheduling war with the BBC and its rival Saturday night talent show *Strictly Come Dancing*. For Henderson, the crossover from reality television to the music industry was more important than her journey through the competition. Indeed, James Arthur won this series, sold 1.4 million copies of his debut single, and yet he is still trying to shake off the taint of talent show stardom and be taken seriously as an artist rather than another pop act 'who have done foolish things and run out of career road'.[5]

The issue of labour and contracted work has been criticised in reality television, both in relation to the immaterial labour of participants (Grindstaff 2013), the production labour of workers in a reality programme (Mayer 2011), and the representation of class and labour (see Biressi and Nunn 2013). Deery notes that reality television is considered to be an entry level job and most professionals hope to graduate from this kind of programme to something with higher status in the industry (2015: 76). She writes that 'investigations are just beginning into the labour status of RTV participants and the extent to which they might be subject to the same legal rights, protections, and compensation as other workers' (2015: 78). She refers to Hearn's work on immaterial labour in an American reality series (2010) as one example of the exploitation of participants who 'must obey explicit and tacit conventions', who are expected to commodify their personal life experience for the benefit of entertainment (Deery 2015: 79). Talent show participants can find themselves locked into contracts during the production of the live event and in the valuable period post-transmission where further product placements, advertising deals and live performances can boost revenues. Although some manage their labour and contracts with television, music and PR agencies to their advantage, others find themselves locked into a career route.

In her research on *MasterChef Australia* and the legal ramifications of contestants and labour conditions in reality formats, Bowrey (2012) criticises the 'commercial dynamics' of the format, where the 'authenticity of the human drama' activates 'commodity relations', supporting corporate control over the 'extended narrative of the enterprise' across the series, its paratexts, live events and social media (2012: 74). She argues that contestants provide access to not only texts and images but their whole person, seeing *MasterChef* participants as 'forced' into overtly competitive social relations, effectively locked into a 'contract of servitude or voluntary enslavement' (2012: 81). This critical legal position sees contestants caught in the 'logic of the reality TV game format' and that these conditions of confinement contribute to 'feeding participant delusion about the nature and extent of the postgame opportunity on offer' (ibid.). Bowry perceives not only this format but much reality television as supporting the production of global capitalism and consumption, and the commodification of affective labour.

In another critique of reality food television, Tasha Oren (2013) argues there has been a shift in food television from cookery competition to formats gone wild, what she playfully describes as culinary S&M. By this she is referring to the stress tests, the emotional highs and lows, and the critique of food within these shows. She argues that competitive food formats have shifted emphasis from teaching audiences how to cook to being critical of food culture. The food format 'encourages audiences' investment in their own expertise as critics, diners, foodies, and even wanna-be professional chefs'. Food TV, in turn, feeds back into a web-powered, gastro-culture and critique-economy where 'appraisal outranks delight' (2013: 33). Oren's comments are useful for a critical analysis of food formats and social media, where the judgement of others becomes a major feature of the genre and its reception contexts. It connects with Skeggs and Wood's (2012) research on audience criticism and the competitive appraisal of participants in reality series. Some talent formats invite harsh criticism from viewers and users who situate their negative engagement within a 'moral evaluation' of the entertainment spaces of reality television (Gray 2008: 5). For Oren, competitive food formats have stripped away the competition and learning about food and become reality entertainment that is primarily concerned with offering a critique of food culture.

The empirical research in this chapter on production and audience practices for *MasterChef* offers an alternative perspective to these criticisms of the affective labour of participants and audiences of talent shows, and the overtly critical reception of food talent formats. *MasterChef Australia* is a significant but not the only version of the format, and the public service and commercial settings for the local variations of the format tell us that *MasterChef* has its own distinctive production and reception contexts. It is also a rather distinctive form of a talent show, with its history in public service media and focus on practical skills in cookery that embed the show in the everyday lives of audiences, alongside commercial culture. Let us not forget there are talent shows for sewing, singing in community choirs, playing in a brass band, and watercolour painting, amongst others, developed on public service and commercial television which are not only about consumption and global corporations but also about pro-social values that are woven into the fabric of our lives. What we shall see in the interviews and observations of participants in three versions of the format in Northern Europe is more of an entrepreneurial labour relation for contestants in the local productions and a strong feeling of care and respect for participants in these regional versions of the format, running through the production, from casting to the judges, and experience of contestants, to the value of fair treatment of contestants by audiences. This all suggests that a critical appraisal of *MasterChef* as commercial culture, or a sense of food reality television as contributing to critical food culture, can be challenged by an empirically led approach to production and audience engagement that recognises the inter-generic space of this format and its regional variations.

Audience engagement with *MasterChef*

If we now turn to a case study of the production and reception of *MasterChef* it is possible to see how contestants and audiences perceive this distinctive food talent format as authentic reality entertainment in the context of certain production environments and cultures of viewing. The research draws on qualitative interviews and participant observations for the *MasterChef* format in Britain, Denmark and

Authentic reality TV: *MasterChef* 149

FIGURE 8.2 Behind the scenes at *MasterChef*
Source: Photograph Tina Askanius.

Sweden. Briefly, the research began with a pilot study in Britain, conducted from March to May 2014. The data included three interviews with Shine producers, production observations of *Celebrity MasterChef UK*, ten audience interviews with individuals and groups of adults aged 21–55, and website analysis of the official and unofficial *MasterChef* universe. From this pilot research two projects were developed for Denmark and Sweden, working with the local production companies on the amateur series.

A total of 60 interviews with producers, participants, and audiences were conducted during the auditions and semi-finals of season five of the amateur series *MasterChef Denmark* from September 2014 to August 2015. The data included 13 production interviews, 27 contestant interviews, and 20 audience interviews with individuals and groups of children, young adults and adults aged 6–65+ from western and eastern Denmark, and observations at the auditions and semi-finals. For *Masterchef Sweden*, a total of 48 interviews with producers, participants, and audiences were conducted during the production and post production of season five of the amateur series, from November 2014 to June 2015. The data included 12 production interviews, 6 contestant interviews, and 30 audience interviews with individuals and groups of adults, aged 18–50, from Lund, Malmö and Gothenburg in Sweden, with observations during week eight of filming and during the middle stage of post production. A team of researchers (Tina Askanius for Denmark and Sweden, Koko Kondo and Julie Donovan for Britain) helped conduct the research, including translations of interviews (see Appendix for full information about the production research, the interview questions, sampling and the social demographics for audiences).

In this chapter, the empirical material is primarily focused on audiences in order to explore the mediated authenticity in a food talent show. The voices of audiences are paramount, as they reflect on what is authentic or not in the inter-generic space of reality television. The interview data have been analysed using descriptive and analytical coding, going back and forth with the original transcripts, and using a flexible coding process that helped to generate theoretical coding related to the social context of viewing, the reality genre and its scheduling contexts, the look and feel of the series, performance and authenticity, personalities, formats and food culture (see Bazely 2013). The production interviews and observations are used in a light touch way to illuminate this analysis of audience engagement. Elsewhere in this book, and in other articles (see Hill 2017), the production research takes more of a centre stage. Thus, the reflections by audiences on the production processes, and participants in a reality series, is given the main attention in this chapter in order to show how authenticity works in this specific talent show.

A brief note on the comparative research: in terms of production, the British series is by far the largest of the three cases, with an established production company (Shine) and a range of experienced producers, editors and sound designers to draw on, many of whom have experience in documentary production rather than entertainment; the two other programme makers, Metronome in Denmark, and Meter in Sweden, work with a smaller production crew in smaller nations when it comes to the television market; producers working on this series will also have worked on similar live event television, light entertainment, and factual entertainment. In addition, the series in Britain is shown on a public service broadcaster, BBC2; in Sweden it is shown on a hybrid public service and commercial broadcaster, TV4; and in Denmark a commercial broadcaster, TV3. These three broadcasters are quite different in terms of their values and strategies, and the influence of television itself on the local productions and audience engagement can be seen in the research. The countries also have intra-regional audiences for the Scandinavian series, a national audience for the British series, and transnational audiences for the various versions of the global format, such as the American or Australian series, also shown in Scandinavia and Britain. What we see in action is the geo-cultural paradox that Moran and Aveyard (2014: 19) note is so distinctive to formats: 'On the one hand television formats are highly transferable, and on the other hand these formats possess specific qualities that appeal to particular audiences.' The research in this chapter shows how food talent formats can have a go-anywhere quality and create a sense of locality and regional specificity for authentic food cultures.

In short, the findings highlight how, against the grain of much talent show gossip and scandal, this format invites people to positively engage with its prosocial values. It does this through authentic storytelling, where careful selection of judges and contestants places a primary focus on their passion for food, expressed through professional labour. Another means for producers to construct authenticity is through inclusivity, where diverse people participate in the format. This inclusivity generates a positive engagement with the format as addressing gender equality or ethnic diversity in the wider context of television and its public address (see Corner 1995). Such a finding is in keeping with what both Bonner (2011) and Peterson (2005) refer to as the work of authenticity within entertainment, which can be achieved through cultural and ethnic identity in a presenter-judge-participant performance, for example. A third way in which authenticity is constructed is through a dialogue with audiences about food culture in their reception context. The cultures of viewing for *MasterChef* highlight social ritual, eating whilst watching the series, and being inspired to cook by it. Here, then, we see the entertainment spaces of reality television, the storytelling, emotional engagement and the competition, connecting strongly with the world spaces of audiences and food culture in their everyday lives.

Authentic storytelling: 'you feel their happiness and their heartbreak'

As a talent format, the series balances different storytelling elements, from the setting in the studio to the narratives of the contestant's journey through the competition. For regular viewers, the building blocks to the entertainment space of this reality television are familiar; they have an expectation of the format's elements, from auditions, to bootcamp, pressure tests, semi-finals and finals, and they align these expectations within their genre knowledge of reality talent shows and food

FIGURE 8.3 Backstage at *MasterChef*
Source: Photograph Tina Askanius.

television more generally. One viewer explained: 'MasterChef is addictive ... building the show so you will come back' (60 year old Alaskan female teacher). Starting with the studio, the setting is a core identity of the show: 'It kind of signifies the atmosphere of the competition, that it's serious' (46 year old British female public health consultant). The judges are essential as a quality and authenticity marker: 'this is what *MasterChef* is, this is what you buy into when you watch an episode' (34 year old British male charity worker). The moment of tasting the food creates 'a real sense of anticipation, nervousness and excitement and just hoping that they enjoy it' (22 year old British female customer services worker). Clever editing builds excitement and anticipation: 'I like the way they edit, it's always really exciting and you have to sit there and watch it. Chop, chop, chop. Show us the clock. Intense music. Chop, chop chop. Aw, someone's dropped something' (34 year old New Zealand female art director). And the invitation to an event shifts emotional tone during the series overall: 'In the beginning the entertainment is at the expense of other people's misfortune. At the end it's because you are rooting for whoever you want to win' (34 year old British male charity worker).

Here, audiences describe the affective structures of the format and their engagement, these cycles of emotional highs and lows created through editing, narrative, and performance. Although this is a construction, viewers expect authentic storytelling through the narrative of contestants as talented amateur cooks. This supports research on the affective work of participants in reality television (see Deery 2015: 79), in this case suggesting their affective work and immaterial labour helps to shape audience engagement. The combination of passion for food and emotional engagement go hand-in-hand: 'I get a positive, happy feeling. I like to cook, and I can see happy individuals who are passionate about a certain subject. It's contagious' (49 year old Swedish female nurse).

In the *MasterChef* shows for Sweden and Denmark, the producers were working with a long established series in the local context of their production companies. Whilst some crew came and went, there were line producers, costume designers, make up artists, production managers and executive producers who had been working with the format for several years. One Danish producer had made over 400 episodes of *MasterChef*. They described a typical day, not in a way that suggested over-familiarity, but rather a family atmosphere:

> I ensure everything flows smoothly, including the schedule for the day, technical tests have been done, that everything is thought through: how do the participants enter? How are they cared for? Is food prepared for everyone? How do we ensure they feel taken care of? How do they leave us again? I want them to leave with a smile on their face feeling it's been a great day despite the fact that they've been here for many hours on the trot.
>
> *(Hill and Askanius 2015)*

The fact that so many experienced producers work on this format, for several years, shows how in the Danish context this kind of reality television is not considered to be an entry level job that they would quickly graduate from in order to gain a better position in a more high status television series (Deery 2015: 76).

The labour practices in reality television may be precarious, but in these production contexts the feeling of doing a good job, and treating each other, including participants, with respect, helps to generate a more visible affective structure for audiences. A casting producer said 'it's great when everything is going well and everyone is happy and then it gets tough and its tears and goodbyes. It can really take its toll' (Hill and Askanius 2015). The contestants spoke of the emotional rollercoaster of their experience. One Swedish female contestant described the intensity of emotions as 'you're hurled between hope and despair'. A judge noted how they were proud to be part of the show because it represented 'normal people with a dream, and they try to make this dream come true by cooking' (Hill and Askanius 2015). The authenticity of their dream was crucial for this judge: it would kill the programme if contestants were perceived as inauthentic. This emphasis on authentic emotions was something contestants were aware of: 'we cry real tears when somebody has to leave. It's not just TV' (Swedish female participant), or 'you wear your heart on your sleeve. There's no facade anymore. I now understand why people cry on TV' (Swedish male participant). 'It's not just TV' highlights the awareness of contestants that audiences may be critical of emotional highs and lows in reality entertainment. And whilst the authenticity of the series is paramount to viewers, they are sceptical of big tears and emotions. 'You get annoyed with some of them, because they cry a lot and go all in. And it's the same with the auditions, lots of emotions, and you understand that they become really happy, but the crying?' (44 year old Swedish female nurse).

This balance between what is perceived to be authentic storytelling versus an emotionally manipulative staging of reality is a continual problem for producers, participants and audiences of reality television. Audiences look for honest emotions in contestants, and yet are alert to a fake reality in a contestant's presentation of self (Goffman 1959). For example:

> I like when people are open about themselves. But I don't like it when they use this to garner sympathy: 'This is so hard for me, because this and that happened.' When you use it as a defence it's like 'I'm supposed to feel sorry for you, you deserve to win.' I like it when people put themselves out there and you feel like you're getting to know a person through television.
>
> *(22 year old Swedish female student)*

Viewers are resistant to talent show contestants using emotional storytelling in clichéd ways to 'garner sympathy'. It has become a trope for contestants to make an emotional connection as a means to manipulate viewer voting. This viewer resisted by focusing on what they perceived as an authentic performance of self, in Goffman's terms a 'backstage self', where they felt a connection with a real person through the mediated spaces of entertainment television.

Audiences are not only critical of contestants' performance of self but also pay close attention to production techniques:

> I'm tired of the type of dramatic storytelling. They drag it out and add some music.
> *(50 year old Swedish male high school teacher)*

> It's just that when you've watched a lot of reality shows, you know how they work. They put a lot of focus on those who do well, and on those who don't do well. Then there are a bunch of people in the middle who are overlooked. You can figure that out.
> *(33 year old Swedish female pre-school teacher)*

> It sort of follows the same format as all the other reality shows. It bothers me that I can tell when it does. And when you notice that, it becomes so obvious … Like in the trailers before the breaks. You hear something, and you see something negative, and the production wants to connect that to a certain event. But it never turns out to be like that.
> *(32-year old Swedish male biologist)*

Such criticisms focus on the details of storytelling, from overly dramatic editing linked to commercial breaks, or the use of music to cue emotional reactions. Audiences' genre knowledge of reality television is put to good use in their critical reflection on this food format.

The playoff between the entertainment- and real-world spaces of *MasterChef* can be problematic, summed up by one viewer as 'the people feel real. The format maybe feels a bit contrived' (35 year old British female project manager). Here, they are signalling an awareness of the commercialisation of reality formats. This can be noted through critiques of editing: 'Is he going to get his pot to boil in time, is he, is he? There is always going to be some fake drama in there' (34 year old New Zealand female art director). Or critique of the melodramatic moments so common to talent formats: 'this one woman was crying all the time and I grew really tired of that. In the end I came close to stopping watching' (32 year old Danish female unemployed). Criticism can also be directed at variations of the format, in particular *Celebrity MasterChef*. For example in Denmark, viewers noted how refreshing it was to see the amateur version after many seasons of the celebrity format. They had developed format fatigue with the celebrity version of *MasterChef* on TV3: 'we have seen enough of the celebs now, we are running out of celebrities really' (32 year old Danish female shop assistant). Another viewer noted: 'The celebrities are so phony, It is almost as if they are acting, playing the role of whatever they've become famous for. I don't like that' (45 year old Danish female secretary).

This genre knowledge influences how audiences engage with variations of the format on commercial and public service media. In the case of Sweden, *MasterChef* is shown on TV4, a hybrid public service/commercial broadcaster. These young adults commented on what they termed a 'TV 4 cliché':

> You get tired of the drama. Everything has to be such a show, that a bunch of things have to happen. It feels like TV4 always has to make a big thing out of everything.
>
> *(21 year old Swedish female student)*

> They ask certain questions in the interviews, you can tell what they're trying to get at. They want you to talk shit about each other. They want you to be annoyed with the other contestants because that's good TV. And I think it becomes the opposite, it becomes cliché instead. It's so typical of TV4 to do certain things. I'd like to see more spontaneity.
>
> *(22-year old Swedish female student)*

These viewers noted how they are developing format fatigue, associating the melodrama with a more commercial model that relies on emotional porn – 'lots of everything, be it happiness or sadness' (26-year old Swedish female PR consultant).

In Denmark the format is broadcast on the commercial channel TV3. Similar criticism was directed at commercial spaces saturated with reality entertainment: 'this genre is so well known to us all by now. It is on all the time' (33 year old Danish female teacher). One viewer noted about TV3: 'there are so many programmes where people fight ... this negativity is what counts as entertainment and to me that is a bit sad' (42 year old Danish female actress). There's a fine line between constructing authenticity that feels fresh and spontaneous and a fake reality that trades in emotions; the line can be crossed when audiences feel contestants or judges are 'playing with emotions' (30 year old Danish male musician). These viewers are all too aware of an emotional economy that drives commercial entertainment.

Inclusivity: 'a chance to see ordinary people shine'

One of the core elements of this format that audiences consider authentic is the 'concept of amateurs cooking good food' (22 year old Swedish female student). What makes the amateur series distinct is the emphasis on ordinary people from different backgrounds who come together in their passion for food: 'food is something that anyone can do. And you can develop your own skills quite easily at home. You don't have to take classes or become a star chef. It concerns everyone' (28 year old Swedish female nurse). This pro-social value of inclusivity is crucial to casting; contestants channel their passion into their affective work: a 'shared bliss when it comes to food' (male contestant) (ibid.).

Swedish viewers reflected on various aspects of the amateur series that made it inclusive, including the diversity of contestants and judges, a sense of humility amongst the contestants, and warmth of atmosphere in the studio. Gender equality on the judging panel was a positive value: 'Honestly, I've associated the show with men in the jury. It was fun that they brought in a woman' (26 year old Swedish female PR consultant). They saw the appointment of a woman as a positive step: 'we don't live in the middle ages! I thought it was really great that they brought in a woman' (26 year old Swedish female student). The diversity of contestants is another pro-social value: 'they're tall, short, fat, thin. They work in all sorts of fields, and they have this as a hobby. That's cool, it's nice to follow these people' (45 year old Swedish female nurse). For Swedish viewers it was important that contestants conveyed their passion for food through a camaraderie in the cooking process, rather than through competitive aggression. Such humility was perceived as different from the bullying tone of other international versions of the brand. These viewers tuned into TV4 specifically for this regional version of the brand that evoked a 'certain Swedish way of being' (31 year old Swedish male receptionist).

Something similar took place with Danish audiences and their engagement with what they perceived as the authentic values of the amateur series. Typical for viewers was the following comment: 'the Danish version is kept much more down to earth. They try to keep it a fair competition that fits the Danish segment of viewers' (33 year old Danish female teacher). Such a tone connects with the treatment of ordinary people in the studio kitchen: one manager noted 'the best thing about this is to try to help them to become their best' (Hill and Askanius 2015). In one example, the makeup artist, who worked on over 300 episodes, always checked to see if contestants had food in their hair: 'my primary task is to make them feel good about themselves' (Hill and Askanius 2015). Another producer noted 'it is important to see the person that is in front of you and to understand there is a lot at stake for them' (ibid.). A contestant reflected on their treatment in the series: 'I do think *MasterChef* is a positive programme. The people who do not go through to the next round are not exposed … you maintain this level of mutual politeness. To me, that is very important' (42 year old Danish female actress and participant). Audiences were aware of this caring attitude towards contestants: 'they made it typically Danish … the judges always think of something positive to say even though it may not have tasted that good. It is a matter of respect I think' (32 year old Danish female unemployed).

Such respect for ordinary participants stands in contrast to the celebrity version. Viewers easily related to the amateurs because they could imagine themselves in the authentic storytelling of the format: 'it is much more interesting watching the amateurs because I can relate to them more than the celebrities … they have eaten in fancy restaurants' (32 year old Danish male shop assistant). 'The amateur version is better because it is people like myself' (33 year old Danish female teacher). Once again, we see a reflection of the down-to-earth and Danish feeling of the format for regional audiences:

> I get a positive feeling. It is not like people throw their aprons off and say 'fuck!' when they are out. It more like 'oh, that is too bad'. None of them

cross the line in how to behave or react. It is not too much ... it is still just food.

(47 year old Danish male engineer)

Such a comment signals the balancing act of connecting the entertainment spaces of television, in the form of the competition, with the real-word spaces of Danish audiences and their perception of how contestants ought to present themselves – no temper tantrums, no fake tears, a controlled emotional performance that demonstrates cooking skills.

What is striking about the transregional audiences for *MasterChef* is a similar appreciation of the format as an invitation to an event that feels local in tone and flavour. In Britain, viewers praised the brand as an invitation to a dinner party at the BBC, where everyone is trying their best to be sociable and to compliment the food:

MasterChef is an invitation to dinner, really. When you invite people to dinner and you make something really nice for them, you make the effort, the look on their faces just says it all ... Feeding people is something very important.

(46 year old British female public health consultant)

In this local context, the British *MasterChef* amateurs series was perceived as a pro-social brand, something that represented the BBC's ethos of entertainment for the public good. Such an evaluation might be connected to the public service remit of the broadcaster, but we see transregional audiences watching on commercial channels describing their experience in similar ways. Danish and Swedish audiences expressed criticism of what they described as emotional porn from commercial broadcasters, and yet they look to *MasterChef* as authentic. One person described *MasterChef* as 'a sense of invitation' (60 year old Alaskan female teacher), and this perfectly sums up the ability of the format in particular regional settings to embody a pro-social idea that talent and success in food culture comes not from social standing and elitism, or through bullying, shouting and aggressive competition, but from a fundamental belief in food as a unifying force. This moral evaluation of food talent formats stands in contrast to Oren's (2013) analysis of other food television in different regional contexts that teaches audiences to participate in food criticism and an online critique economy. In this case transregional audiences negotiate the commercial drivers of the format and reality genre in the situated context of their culture and what is thought to be good television, good food, and pro-social values in life.

Food culture: 'decent and honest food'

For viewers, food comes first and the competition second in their engagement with *MasterChef*. This means that the real world values of food culture play a significant role in shaping the overall experience of this talent show for regional

FIGURE 8.4 Playing with *MasterChef*
Source: Photograph Tina Askanius.

audiences. On the value of food, a key issue is that the programme promotes 'decent and honest food' (30 year old Danish male self employed). For example, this woman explained: 'the food is the most important part to me … It is not what kinds of funny things are said along the way, it's the result on the plate you could say' (45 year old Danish female secretary). In the Danish version of the format this was connected with 'nose-to-tail' eating, or cooking with leftovers. For example one contestant noted 'We care a lot about not wasting food' (42 year old Danish female actress and participant). Another person at the auditions was there to support their daughter, and they explained how they had passed on Danish cooking skills to their children: 'I'm good with leftovers' (69 year old Danish female, retired). For audiences, the appeal of this kind of food television is 'they show you how to cook something great from nothing and that is really fun to watch' (48 year old Danish male IT consultant).

A key explanation of the connection between the televised space of the format and the real-world spaces of audiences is the way the series is embedded in everyday routines. The scheduling of the amateur series during weekday nights is a major factor in its popularity with families, working people and younger audiences. This reflects the overall demographic ratings for this series where more females, and viewers aged 25–50, watch regularly (Hill and Askanius 2015). For example, the scheduling of the series on TV3 in Denmark during weekday nights matched the rhythms of people unwinding after a busy day. The typical term used to describe

MasterChef was cosy, or '*hygge*' TV. The metaphor of actually eating *MasterChef* was common in viewers' discussions, for example snacking on the show, a midweek treat, something nice and delicious. Here, audiences described eating with *MasterChef*:

> I get home, I take some food and I go to my bed with the iPad and then I watch. I do that almost everyday.
>
> *(10 year old Danish schoolgirl)*

> I take dinner with me onto the couch and sit in front of the TV. It is easily digestible television.
>
> *(33 year old Danish female teacher)*

> I schedule my evening to be able to see it after dinner. I don't have any specific rituals but if I miss it one evening I make sure to catch the six o' clock rerun.
>
> *(57 year old Danish female unemployed)*

The tone of the format as an invitation to dinner is so important to the way audiences experience this food show as social ritual; it's a friendly space within which to eat and relax and feel you are not alone.

MasterChef is a marker point in everyday family routines, signalling a quiet moment when parents and children can unwind together: 'It is all about timing ... we've finished eating and the kids are running around like wild dogs, we can put this on and sit down. It fits into the rhythm of the family' (47 year old Danish male engineer). The power of scheduling is clear to see: 'just after dinner when the kids are running around frantically. Sitting down and watching this with them is just the right thing to do at this point in the evening. It calms everybody down' (42 year old Danish female actress and participant). These routines allow families to connect: 'I have a boy who is completely crazy about it. He'll be seven soon and he loves watching it with me. So that just makes it even nicer, the two of us together on the couch' (32 year old Danish female shop assistant).

A similar experience of television as social ritual can be found in Sweden. For some busy working parents *MasterChef* is their private relaxation time, for example one woman watched it in the bathtub. Working people timed their meals so they could eat with *MasterChef*: 'I usually eat during, so I make sure to have the food ready on time. I suppose that's a sort of ritual' (30 year old Swedish female freelance journalist). Nurses described coming off shift and watching *MasterChef* to relax after an intense day at work. Families perceived the show was one of the few kinds of entertainment they watch on TV4 together. *MasterChef* phrases had become part of everyday dialogue in the family home, for example one father described how his son commented on his cooking: 'You've nailed the flavours, Dad.'

The social ritual of watching carried over into creating dishes inspired by the series. A contestant on the Danish *MasterChef* reflected on how the series had been a catalyst for cooking: 'I have always sucked at cooking ... it's actually because of the programme that I've become good at cooking, I learned through TV' (18 year old Danish female waitress and participant). Another woman explained: 'the food element is really important ... I went straight to the kitchen to make pancakes and I snap-chatted everyone "hey I'm eating pancakes"' (33 year old Danish female teacher). In this case the inter-generic spaces of reality television connect across the television studio, the viewer at home in their kitchen and social media; in such a way an engagement with food culture is taking place across the mediated and real-world spaces of audiences.

In the Swedish context, younger viewers linked the social ritual of television with food culture. This student explained: 'all my friends watch the show, so we usually watch together. I live next door to my best friend, so we usually say *Mästerkock*, eight o'clock tonight!' (22 year old Swedish female student). Younger viewers described the show as a resource for healthy living:

> A lot of my friends have become interested in cooking good food. Proper food. Not just pasta and meatballs. Actually trying things. And I think that *Mästerkock* ... this thing of cooking good food feels like it comes along with it, taking an interest in what you eat. And we cook it properly, from scratch, by ourselves. Maybe there's a link there.
>
> *(22 year old Swedish female student)*

Viewers also described growing out of trashy reality entertainment and growing into shows like *MasterChef*: 'I was more into reality TV before, but I lost interest in them ... some reality shows feel brain dead ... when instead we can have a show about people who compete by cooking together' (31 year old Swedish male receptionist). Their comments highlight how *MasterChef* stands for a refined palate for good food and entertainment.

Danish contestants and viewers talked at length about why food matters to them, both personally in relation to their family experiences, and socially in relation to their communal experiences. This participant reflected on growing up and learning about home cooking:

> When I was really young we would have traditional fare, and when my mum was playing bingo my dad would cook. It was either pizza or he would try to make these hamburgers that were always really dry and not very nice to eat. So I asked my mother if I could learn how to cook my favourite dish. That was when I was nine .... when my mum was playing bingo we would eat some proper food. I had to throw my dad out of the kitchen, which he didn't like very much, and he started to have an interest in food as well. He can actually cook now.
>
> *(30 year old Danish male, self employed and participant)*

His comment highlights how reality television is a space for people's memories of food culture, and of sharing skills in cooking. A female viewer commented on watching with her seven year old son:

it is in our culture to share good meals ... I hope it will bring back a focus on food as a unifying force that will get us together around the table, so we can talk about our day, our thoughts and feelings.

(32 year old Danish female shop assistant).

In another example (see also Chapter 2), one father explained:

Food means a lot to me. It really does. It has to be proper food and by that I mean good ingredients. It doesn't have to be gourmet or fine dining but it has to be honest food. And that means something to me because I know that everything we put in our mouths matters. If you put diesel in a car that runs on gas, that doesn't work either. It needs to be suitable for us humans. I just had a boy and I think a lot about what he eats. Food is what sows the seeds for everything we do and become. That's what it means to me.

(48 year old Danish male IT consultant)

They describe food as a moral issue: it must be 'honest', that is to say good food cooked from scratch; and they describe food as life politics, the family kitchen a place to learn about 'everything we do and become'. Although they look to the future in their relationship with their children, they are also shaping a legacy of food memories and recipes to be shared throughout generations.

Conclusion

The talent show discussed in this chapter uses the inter-generic space of reality television to balance the construction of entertainment with the real-world spaces of creative labour and food culture. The widening of these inter-generic spaces across entertainment and everyday life produces varieties of performance for contestants in the series and invites a spectrum of engagement by audiences, including positive and negative engagement. In the audience research, the critical and moral judgements about *MasterChef* as reality entertainment, such as its commercialisation of emotions and celebrities, transforms into positive engagement with the show as a place for authentic storytelling about food culture, and a space to reflect on life politics.

The focus on food within a competition is crucial. Audiences positively engage with the hard work of ordinary people cooking, literally a labour of love, often described by viewers as the experience of seeing their 'heart on a plate'. This physical and emotional labour is shown taking place in the television studio and in restaurants, schools or office buildings; in these contexts ordinary people demonstrate their culinary skills in relation to professional chefs and customers, and they are expected to put all their hard won skills into practice by making good food from simple ingredients. Roland Barthes (1979: 124), writing about the performance of singing and dancing in music halls, describes this as a 'subtle artifice', where the hard labour of an apprenticeship, long hours of training, and many instances of failure, is recreated in the moment of a performance. He describes this creative performance as 'the aesthetic form of work'; creative labour is 'memorialised and sublimated' in the spectacle of entertainment (1979: 124–125). Although Barthes is talking about live performance, there is a subtle artifice in the performance of affective labour and practical skills in food talent shows. People's hard work, dedication to their craft, and desire to improve is presented as a virtue; this is why audiences use a phrase like 'heart on a plate' to signify the pro-social values of a talent show such as this.

What we see from the audience research on this talent show is that people make the local version of the format their own, turning it into as a social ritual, treating it like a dinner companion, showing how food plays a part in bringing people together, a sharing of memories and skills, passed on to friends and family. Beyond engagement, we see how audiences experience food culture as something to nurture, to nourish as a virtue in life. One woman reflected on the value of food culture as a legacy: 'When I die, in my will I will leave someone my recipes' (46 year old British female public health consultant). Such a sentiment highlights how a cookery talent show can be about so much more than food consumption.

Notes

1 See *Daily Express*, Roxanne Huges, 3 December 2017, https://www.express.co.uk/showbiz/tv-radio/887568/Strictly-Come-Dancing-Fans-accuse-judges-semi-final-FIX-Debbie-McGee-Alexandra-Burke-ITV, accessed 29 January 2018.
2 See *The Telegraph*, Michael Hogan, 31 May 2017, www.telegraph.co.uk/tv/0/britains-got-talent-biggest-controversies-all-time/, accessed 29 January 2018.
3 See the fan community for Buttery Biscuit Base, https://www.facebook.com/pages/Swede-Masons-Buttery-Biscuit-Fanbase/295401110487031, or this ten hour dance remix of the original: https://www.youtube.com/watch?v=agx4re1_rWk
4 See for example this slash fiction *Masterchef Slash*, http://masterchefslash.livejournal.com
5 Sullivan, Caroline (2017) 'James Arthur Review', *Guardian*, 26 November 2017, https://www.theguardian.com/music/2017/nov/26/james-arthur-review-x-factor-wembley-arena, accessed 3 February 2018.

9
WARM UP ACTS

> Warm up trains someone not to be a star.
>
> *(Jeff Stevenson)*

Typical of television entertainment is the live show, a spectacular with hosts, contestants and professional performers entertaining a large studio audience and live public who watch, talk about, vote and interact with the main screen and related social media. This sense of reality entertainment with shows such as *Strictly Come Dancing* (BBC) or *Got Talent* (Syco, FreemantleMedia) as live spectacle is familiar; picture the roving camera shots of crowds and close up reactions of audiences to the drama on stage. But what is missing from this picture is the warm up act who routinely performs before the televised show and during breaks in it, inviting live audiences into an interstitial space of reality television (Grainge 2011). Shiny floor shows, panel shows and sitcoms have live studio audiences, and the warm up act is the cultural intermediary between the audience and the studio show.

Warm up acts offer a craft of live audience management that is hard won through years of creative and precarious labour practices (in stand-up comedy, variety, theatre, television and leisure industries), and yet they are invisible in media industries and academic research. Why are warm up acts denied recognition? This research builds on production and audience studies, using a qualitative approach to explore the hidden work of warm up acts. Much attention has been given in academic research to live television and mediated events, in particular the care structures within a live event and the power of 'liveness' for audiences watching at home (Scannell 2014). This research pays attention to the warm up acts and their audience, those affective moments when the staging of a live event involves a more intimate performance tailored to a studio audience.

The empirical data include interviews with five British warm up acts; observations of warm up performances during the filming of a live reality talent competition (*Got*

FIGURE 9.1 Live reality entertainment
Source: Photograph Tina Askanius.

to *Dance*, Princess); and participant observations of live audiences of reality events with crowds of up to 6,000 (see Chapters 4 and 7 for further work from this case study). The data are used to recognise the value of warm up acts in the shaping of the affective structures of live entertainment. What we shall see is that the skills and experience of the warm up act are of immediate value for audience participation, but this value can be counteracted when the work of the warm up professional sometimes hinders the professional entertainers from developing careers as stand-up comedians or television presenters; warm ups stand in the shadows, so to speak, part of a paradoxical profession that trains entertainers to not be the star of the show.

Recognising warm up acts

If you go to a recording of entertainment television it is likely you will see a warm up act engage with a live studio audience. Light entertainment and reality television is everywhere in the schedules, from daytime programming to peaktime weekday evenings, and the all important weekend blockbuster shows. To get a ticket to a recording of a panel or quiz show, a lifestyle or talk show, a sitcom or stand-up comedy show or a variety and reality entertainment event, usually entails signing up to a company such as Applause Store and waiting in a queue for the allocation of free tickets. That particular television audience company operates in the UK, east- and west coast America (LA and New York), Canada, Australia and

New Zealand.[1] Some shows are all booked up long in advance – *Top Gear* (BBC, 2002, in its old form) had a waiting time of five years, and most talent shows involve planning in advance, but other shows, especially panel shows on digital commercial channels, are actively looking for audiences and you can browse the list and sign up to recordings. There are also companies that deal with radio recordings of panel shows and comedy series that need live audiences and offer tickets to shows. Another way you might get tickets is by being a VIP client, including corporate and media industry professionals, or as a customer loyalty reward offered by a broadcaster or subscription service.

People working for Applause Store chatted during their coffee break at a live reality talent show, explaining how they liked working on the most sought after shows because audiences treated these events as a mini holiday, getting dressed up, booking into a hotel and making a night of it. These audiences were fun to work with, ready to be entertained twice, first by the warm up act and then by the main event. Warm up act Andy Collins (2015) noted how audiences made the screening a big occasion, especially outside of London, taking time to enjoy themselves and have 'a bit of a holiday'. For Applause Store employees the most difficult shows involved large events; sometimes audiences would not show up – for example on this particular day it was raining cats and dogs – and then the staff would have to venture into the local streets and shopping centres, giving away free tickets to deliver the essential live audience to the producers. Also tricky to work for were pilot panel shows and sitcoms, unknown to audiences and therefore requiring some creative thinking on behalf of the production company or Applause Store to entice an audience to the filming; one warm up described a pilot talk show with empty seats where he took people from one television screening and moved them two studios along to do double time as a live studio audience.

Alongside employees of Applause Store, the warm up act will assess the audience before they enter the studio, by speaking with the ticketing person about who is coming along, enquiring about large group bookings from particular regions, and watching people as they come into the venue. A warm up act knows their audience beforehand; it's their job to understand what kind of humour and style of performance (for example physical street theatre, friendly conversation, or musical participation) will work with this crowd, at this moment in time. Even the weather outside will make a difference to their performance, from the jokes they might use to the way they will cheer up a damp and disgruntled crowd. When audiences arrive in a studio and take their seats the first person they meet is the warm up who greets them, explains the recording process, and shapes the affective structure for the live screening, in essence creating a convivial atmosphere. Stuart Holdham is the warm up act for shiny floor shows such as *Strictly Come Dancing* (BBC1, UK 2004–). He explains: 'My job primarily is to get the atmosphere going … it's making sure audiences are looked after in terms of anything that happens, but mainly it is about having fun with the audience. I think I have as much fun as they do' (Holdham 2014).

In British television, warm up acts can earn between £50,000 and £100,000 per year, taking into account a variety of gigs from television to live entertainment, corporate events, pantomime, and cruise ships. Warm up acts in American television can earn $4,000–$6,000 a day for labour-intensive sitcom work, where there are long hours in front of a live audience (Locker 2015). Warm up acts will usually have an agent representing them as a comedian, actor and presenter as well as a warm up. Collins described the variety of work in his week:

> Every day I go with the flow and see what happens. I have a flexible act. For example, this week, Sunday night was a variety show in front of 2,000 people; Monday night was a talk show with an older audience, we talked about the war and playing bingo; tonight is a younger audience of 500 people, more of an Ibiza crowd.
>
> *(Collins 2015)*

Collins also runs an agency for warm up acts, operating with a select group of performers and providing this specialist service for floor managers, producers and presenters in the entertainment industry.

A warm up act will have behind the scenes information that helps them shape their performance, such as knowledge of the production crew, the filming schedule, and the breaks in filming – the dead time, when the warm up is most needed. Their relationship with the floor manager is central, and a tight group of light entertainment floor managers will often work with the same warm up acts, establishing an inner circle for live entertainment. Collins (2015) explained how a large part of his job is this relationship work: 'I get to know everyone, from Ethel the cleaner to Terry the head lighter. It takes me twenty minutes to say hello to everyone to get in the studio.' He described the frontstage persona for a warm up act and the backstage politics of the job: 'It's about being able to perform and play the game. Your stage presence is one thing, the offstage side is harder' (Collins 2015). What Collins notes is the impression management of the warm up act, where the frontstage persona is of most value to the audience, but the backstage diplomacy is of most value to the production company (Goffman 1959). Trust between the warm up and the floor manager is important, with weight placed on the warm up knowing their role in the hierarchy of the entertainment industry.

Alongside the floor manager, warm up acts have a relationship with the presenters, judges and other acts on stage. Frances Bonner (2011), in her research on television presenters, writes about the legendary Bruce Forsyth, his long career in variety and television, presenting for *The Generation Game* (BBC1, UK, 1971–) and *Strictly Come Dancing*. Bonner notes his ability to work the house, making a connection with the live and at-home audience. But most of the presenters discussed in Bonner's book have warm up acts who generate the convivial atmosphere necessary for them to shine as television personalities and stars. Warm up acts describe working for years as 'the' warm up guy for presenters like Forsyth (Jeff Stevenson, Stuart Holdham amongst others), or Jerry Springer (Andre Vincent); in this situation the warm up act becomes part of the family, showing up for every screening, day in and day out, representing the brand to live studio audiences.

Although warm ups are seldom celebrated, presenters cannot do without their skills and emotional labour. Indeed, so integral are they to the job of presenters and comedians that tensions can arise if the warm up is thought to overstep the mark with their audience. For example, Forsyth respected the job of the warm up, but was known to call them into his dressing room for a dressing down if he felt they delivered too many jokes rather than gently warming up the crowd for the real star.

Warm ups acts are workers with an 'absent presence' in the entertainment industry (Mayer 2011: 27). They are present in physical form, in their relationship with the audience and the floor manager, for example, but they are also the person who leaves the stage just as others take centre stage. Although they are not the kind of below-the-line workers that Mayer writes about (2011: 27), such as volunteers, extras, and factory workers, warm up acts have 'destabilised professional identities', unequal positions in production cultures, and an odd invisibility as creative performers. They are denied recognition of their labour; Bonner (2011) writes about presenters as cultural intermediaries, Bennett (2011) writes similarly about the value of television personalities – are not warm ups also valuable cultural intermediaries between the television show and audiences? The warm up is rendered invisible through the lack of recognition given to this kind of profession.

The warm up profession

In Frances Bonner's book *Personality Presenters* (2011) she asks: where do television presenters come from? She charts how presenters acquire the skills necessary to be cultural intermediaries between a television show and audiences at home. Producers are looking for a specialised knowledge of performance styles, an appearance that will suit their show, the technical skill of speaking confidently through the camera to the viewing audience; most presenters carry over these skills from other work, in particular stand-up comedy (Bonner 2011: 34). We can ask the same question for warm up acts – where do they come from? Often talent spotted as stand-up comedians in working men's and comedy clubs, they try out the job and a few stay for the course, perfecting their skills in the warm up profession. The experience of stand-up and variety work is good training for a warm up act, as they learn how to balance scripted material with spontaneous audience interaction; this means they develop the confidence to handle situations as they develop, an important part of the warm up's job in a live event.

There is a history of warm up acts working in music hall, variety, comedy and light entertainment. Andre Vincent, writing about the history of stand-up, highlights how the music hall circuit in the late nineteenth and early twentieth centuries incorporated multiple spots for artists in each evening performance, but this gradually changed in the interwar years in Britain into one single spot. He writes:

> in the early 1930s there were so many theatres to play, an act could be contracted for a different show every night for two years before completing the

venue cycle. Morecambe & Wise famously used the same thirteen minutes of material in the first ten years of their career on the variety circuit.[2]

After the Second World War stand-up comedians found their way onto the comedy circuit through variety, the British Armed Forces (within ENSA, the Entertainment National Service Association), student societies (the Cambridge Footlights), and in the 1970s community theatres and comedy collectives such as the National Theatre of Brent, which influenced a different style of stage comedy. The rise of 'alternative comedy' during the 1970s and 1980s helped bring stand-up comedy into commercial entertainment, in particular television and radio.

Another route to warm up work was through Butlins holiday camps, famous as a talent pool of variety performers. Holiday camps like Butlins and Pontins were a distinctly British tradition of seaside holidays at coastal resorts such as Skegness or Bognor Regis, offering low-cost holidays for working-class families where the accommodation and entertainment came together in one place. At Butlins, the 'redcoats' in their red blazers were entertainers who shaped the affective structure of the holiday, from 'wakey wakey' calls on the Tannoy in the morning, to cheeky daytime events such as the knobbly knees competition or glamorous granny contest, and ending the evening with a variety show or talent contest. To be a redcoat was to provide the typically female labour of emotional work (see Hochschild 2003), ensuring a convivial atmosphere for a family holiday, making people feel cared for and encouraging audience participation. Redcoats used this experience to launch careers in variety, stand-up comedy and television presenting; Bruce Forsyth was a redcoat, for example. Perhaps one of the most significant aspects of this route to warm up is that the skills relate to the affective practices of audience management, and the feelings of audiences themselves in an entertainment experience – the emotional labour of ensuring people have a good time whilst on a mini break from everyday life.

Warm up acts tend to have a background in working men's clubs, social clubs and variety theatre aimed at popular audiences. For example Jeff Stevenson described how he started in the entertainment industry as a young actor and comedian. The route into this industry was not easy. A working-class teenager with an after-school job in a greengrocers in East Acton, London, Stevenson dreamed of something other than 'humping horrible bags of vegetables. I get nightmares thinking about having to go back to that kind of manual work' (Stevenson 2015). One day after work he was walking past a stage school and heard laughter from inside; there and then he decided to walk in and audition, and his impromptu decision paid off as he was offered a fee waiver and stipend to join the school. The next day he informed his headmaster that he was leaving to join a stage school and he heard the man mutter: 'another boy with a dream' (Stevenson 2015). Such lack of encouragement for a working class-boy did not stop Stevenson from pursuing a career. Whilst learning the craft, he went to Butlins and entered talent contests, borrowing his father's dinner suit and doing stand-up. He recalls seeing Michael Barrymore as a redcoat and judging the contests, and later on being

Barrymore's warm up guy. Stevenson (2015) got the bug for comedy and dreamed of a future in entertainment: 'When we were at school we used to talk about our ambitions. Who will be on my show first?' While performing as a stand-up Stevenson was headhunted as a warm up man for variety shows such as *Sunday Night at the London Palladium* (ITV, UK 1955–69); he became a warm up comedian in the 1980s and 1990s and worked for many of the landmark light entertainment shows.

Andre Vincent recalled how he dreamed of becoming a comedian from a young age. His family were in the entertainment business; his great-grandfather and uncle were acrobats, his grandmother an opera singer; Vincent's family wanted him to follow in the footsteps of his grandmother, but from the age of five he knew he was going to be a comic:

> The first laugh – I was in school and there was an automatic pencil sharpener and I stuck my little finger in it and it came out bleeding. It got such a big laugh, even though I was in pain and the teacher was furious, and that was the moment for me. It was a real buzz of acceptance, I suddenly had the adoration of a room full of strangers.
>
> *(Vincent 2015)*

Vincent joined a circus school in Paris at eighteen, and travelled around Europe, America and Canada as a street performer, improvisational actor and stand-up comedian. Whilst performing he was asked to try out warm up. This would start a long period where Vincent worked on some of Britain's main sitcoms and panel shows.

In every generation there are a handful of men, and a few women, who are the warm up acts for most regional entertainment television or radio, working exclusively for certain shows and brands over a period of time. For example, Collins (2015) recalled how he got into warm up after working in the armed forces and continuing as a stand-up comedian in Britain's clubs. He noted how at the time in the 1990s, 'TV warm up was a closed shop; there were a few people, for example Ted Robbins and Jeff Stevenson.' Ted Robbins is a stand-up comedian, actor, after-dinner speaker and former warm up; he presented game shows such as *Quiz Night* (ITV, 1988–95), was a warm up for *Birds of a Feather* amongst other sitcoms, and starred as an actor in Peter Kay's *Phoenix Nights* (BBC, UK, 2001–02); now he hosts an afternoon radio show for BBC Manchester. Jeff Stevenson is a stand-up comedian, MC, and former warm up comedian. He came to warm up through comedy and variety, and for a period in the 1990s worked as one of the main warm up acts in entertainment television: 'I was doing the warm ups for *Barrymore, Pebble Mill at One, Style Challenge, This is Your life, The Generation Game*. One week I did 25 warm ups for daytime and late night shows' (Stevenson 2015). Then the work disappeared due to the precariousness of the television labour market: '*This is Your Life* got dropped, *Pebble Mill* was dropped, Jim Davidson fell out with the BBC … I lost all these series in three months. I watched my diary go from ink to snow blindness' (Stevenson 2015). Stevenson now works across the entertainment business, often as a stand-up comedian with the alter ego of Harvey Oliver. He also performs on cruise ships such as the QE II, which has a large theatre styled on the London Palladium, complete with royal boxes; he regularly does over 40 cruises a year, writing his own scripts and appearing as the headline act.

To reflect on where warm ups come from, within television there is a low cultural value accorded to light entertainment, which includes a judgement of performers in this genre and of popular culture and mass entertainment in general. Quite why light entertainment is seen as having little socio-cultural value is somewhat of a mystery. With a rich history in music hall and variety, tourism and television, light entertainment is a significant source of pleasure and collective cultural experiences, and yet is often overlooked as an object of study, dismissed as lightweight, a taken-for-granted type of family entertainment. For performers choosing to work in this genre there is the risk of a double negative: the negative value of the precariousness of labour conditions in theatre, television and the arts, and the negative attitudes to this kind of popular entertainment.

Another issue relates to the dominance of the warm up 'guy' (see the title of Bob Perlow's 2016 tell-all book about being the warm up act for American talk show host Jay Leno). There are few female warm up acts. The closed shop for warm up acts, the route to warm up through comedy, and the over-representation of male presenters and comedians in entertainment television all work to ensure that female warm up acts remain marginal. Male presenters, comedians and talk-show hosts tend to hire male warm up acts. This closed shop is similar to how women have struggled to be recognised and booked as stand-up comedians, with a historical background that indicates the structural barriers to their professional development in a male dominated area. There are some female comedians, presenters and light entertainers who are visible and successful – think of the late Caroline Aherne (1963–2016), the British comedian, actress and writer who wrote and performed in the sitcom *The Royle Family* (BBC, UK, 1998–2000 and 2006–2012) and as a chat show host in her persona as *Mrs Merton* (BBC, UK, 1993–1998); or consider Leslie Jones, stand-up comedian, actress, writer and performer for *Saturday Night Live* (NBC, USA, 1975–) with a successful sideline in live tweets for *Game of Thrones*. Given the range of comedy, light entertainment and reality television aimed at women, it would be sensible to extend the hiring of women in all these professions, from warm up acts through to comedy and television presenting, if television wishes to further engage female audiences.

Other notable exceptions include Jo Caulfield, a female warm up for Graham Norton who now works as a stand-up comedian, writer and actress. Comedian and presenter Ellie Taylor also worked for Norton:

> My agent was saying they needed some new people and asked whether I wanted to do it … When I've been on shows as a guest, I'm backstage, so I don't usually hear what the warm-up is saying, so I went and watched a couple of people do it and thought, 'Actually, I reckon this is do-able.' The audience is usually excited to be there; it's just getting a good chat with

people. It is well paid compared with going down to a pub and getting £50 to headline … but I didn't get into comedy to do warm-up.

(Gilbert 2015: 1)

Her comment on the route from stand-up comedy to warm up highlights both where warm up acts come from and also how this is a source of tension for the identities of performers as comedians and warm up acts. As one of the few female warm up acts, Taylor notes the difficulty of moving between warm up and presenting, or stand-up comedy. What we can see is that female warm up acts come through the same route as male warm ups but are quick to seek an exit from this work; perhaps an awareness of the difficulties of being a female stand-up comedian or presenter mean they are wary of creating further obstacles in their path through the entertainment industry.

If we know something of where warm up acts come from then we must ask where they go as their careers develop. Most do not choose warm up as a career in itself but come across it on their way to somewhere else, perceiving the job as a temporary position where they can network in the green room, making contacts for further comedy spots or presenting jobs. Well known examples of warm up acts who have gone on to become television stars and headline comedians include comedian Jimmy Carr; and Steven Amos, who worked as a warm up in light entertainment television before starring in his own comedy show on BBC2 in Britain, writing books and headlining live tours. But, although there are opportunities for television presenting, appearances on talkshows, headlining in comedy clubs or writing for television and radio, many find themselves returning to warm up work. There is also another ceiling in warm up work that relates to age – a misconception that age equates with tired material that contributes to the precariousness of the profession. We will return to this issue later in the chapter, after analysing in more detail the craft of making audiences warm, but not too warm, in live television.

The craft of warming up audiences

What are the qualities of a warm up act? Bonner (2011) adapts Richard Dyer's ideal qualities of entertainment for the profession of television presenters; she argues that these qualities include abundance, energy, community and risk. For example, the presenters of *Strictly Come Dancing* exude an abundance of emotions and energy and have a rapport with the live and at-home audience that makes the show feel like an invitation to a party, a community of viewers and fans who can be sure to have a good time. The judges and experts in this talent show evaluate the performance skills, while the presenters must manage the risks that come with live shows where no amount of training can rule out a costume malfunction or an attack of nerves in the live moment itself.

Jane Goodall's (2008) analysis of stage presence highlights the affective structures and performance styles of live variety. She discusses what gives entertainers stage

FIGURE 9.2 At the auditions for *Got to Dance*
Source: Photograph Tina Askanius.

presence, that mysterious quality which is hard to capture in words and yet is something people feel in the moment of a live experience. For example, she notes the lightness of touch of music hall performers of the past: 'those that have the genius of lightness, there is a quicksilver energy that seems inexhaustible and operates at lightning speed, lifting boredom to amusement, amusement to exuberance, exuberance to outbursts of hilarity and elation' (Goodall 2008: 137, cited in Bonner 2011: 117). The qualities of stage presence are related to performance and skill, experience with live audiences, and an instinctive sense of time and energy, the temporal and affective relationships that are so essential for positive live experiences.

We can say the qualities of a warm up act include conviviality, care, community and risk. Conviviality is the quality of being friendly and lively, being a convivial host, and at the same time showing a willingness to work together, to overcome problems to ensure the event runs smoothly. Another quality is that of care, that is to say the visible care that warm up acts take in ensuring audiences feel relaxed, informed and taken care of in the studio or venue; and they have a quality of community: in this case the ability to connect with their live audience and have some fun. There is also the quality of being prepared to risk those moments when live audiences talk back, heckle, or ignore a warm up, and those times when performances by presenters, participants, actors or guest celebrities can go wrong, which may mean the warm up is called onstage to work with the audience whilst problems are being rectified.

The qualities of a warm up act can be seen in the different styles of performance they use for certain genres and audiences. Stuart Holdham needs to appeal to a cross-generational audience for *Strictly Come Dancing*, one of the more challenging shows he works on because of the high expectations of the audience, many of whom have been waiting several years to get a ticket to the eight hours of live recording. Holdham uses musical participation as one technique: 'you play something that everyone has heard of, that spans generations, something that can pull on their heart strings, and get the people of a more mature generation on their feet, moving and grooving' (Holdham 2015). He also incorporates audience participation, inviting older couples to 'dance on the sacred dance floor; they will always remember dancing on the show'; and he uses physical comedy – the costume designers made him a disco suit with 3,000 hand-sewn crystals to wear for his 'Disco Devil' routine (ibid.). Another style is that of the convivial host, developing a rapport with an audience through talking with them. According to Stevenson (2015) 'the art of doing a warm up is to make it look like a chat; the best warm ups have a chat with the audience, it doesn't look like it is scripted'. Collins (2015) reads his audience:

> I watch them come in and you can pick out the characters, get the vibe. Even as I'm saying my material I'm looking at the audience, seeing if they get it, and then I get my audiences to do wild and crazy things.

Whatever the performance style, warm up acts invest time and emotional energy into a short and yet intensive relationship with their audiences.

We can see how the warm up performer is one of the core workers in the management of care structures for a live experience. Paddy Scannell adopts a phenomenological approach, drawing on the philosophy of Martin Heidegger, to explore the dialectical nature of live experiences. He argues that electronic media organise the living moment for us and reduce the existential strain of existence (2014: xi). This way of organising the living moment is called care structures and Scannell urges researchers to consider the taken for granted expectations of live experiences, including the attention to mood and time in the visible and invisible structures of live moments. 'Care structures are concealed in the world of appearances' (2014: 77); there is the labour that helps to co-create our expectations of a live event, including the management of 'liveness' as spaces of interaction, and the affirmation of a shared experience. Scannell draws our attention to the experience of live television as a dialectical playoff between the mood of live events, the management of care structures that support this, and our individual and collective-social experiences.

Two issues come to the fore in an analysis of warm up acts and live television. The first is the mood of a live experience and the second is the organisation of time. In a discussion of event television, Scannell (2014: 178) notes how Heidegger's insight on the phenomenology of mood underpins a definition of an event: 'whatever it was, or wasn't any event is defined by its mood. Mood is not some value added to occasions … it is the sake for which they were made to happen'. Care structures are the invisible management of the mood of an event. Time is also crucial: 'The time of the event, the time of television and the my-times of countless viewers all converge in the experiential, living enunciatory now of the event as it unfolds in a shared, common public time' (ibid.). Care structures, then, can be characterised as the hidden labour in the production of a live television event, both the labour of professionals in the industry, the labour of people participating in media production, and the labour of audiences in the co-creation of the mood and time of a live experience.

In relation to warm up acts, we have to take into account that care structures are made visible in their profession, that is to say visible within the production company and to audiences at the event. Although hidden from the experience of audiences watching at home, live and in tune with the time of the televised event, they are significant for the management of mood and time within the care structure of the overall event. Thus, the warm up act indicates that the sense of care structures as hidden needs to be rethought for this type of labour. Indeed, a talent show makes visible some of the hidden labour in the creation of mood, and the value of audiences as participants in the management of mood. According to the psychologist working on the series, Cynthia McVey (2014), 'care cascades down' through the practices of producers. Care also flows from below. The show invites audiences to be at a live venue, or to perform as contestants, and to interact and vote for winners, all of which brings into the spotlight the care structures of a live talent show (see Hill et al. 2018 forthcoming). As Bolin (2009: 42) notes in his analysis of live television, the studio audience provides visual background, atmosphere and serves as a focus for identification with audiences. The warm up act is the person ensuring that the studio audience is generating a warm and caring atmosphere that goes through the screen to people watching at home.

In addition, Bolin (2009: 45) highlights the spatial and temporal construction of liveness. There is the placement of multiple cameras and stages, and the positioning of the live audience, and there is the time management, including the scheduled time of the show, transmission time on television, commercial time within the breaks in the show, and the overall programme time with all the related ephemeral media and paratexts, such as extra shows, or live social media. Warm up acts are very aware of this spatial and temporal construction of liveness. They appear on stage, but are not limited in their movement by camera positions or lighting, so they can move around the stage and amongst the audience. They can also move the audience from the back of the venue to the front, or the top tiers to the front stage, as long as they return to their seats when filming starts. The warm up act usually offers information about time management, marking the build up to filming, the advert breaks, or the different segments in the filming of a sitcom or panel show. When a talent show like *Strictly* can run for eight hours, the audience needs to know about time management (breaks, catering, and so forth), and this is yet another way in which the warm up act makes visible the care structures for a live event.

We can see with warm up acts a difference between the time of the television programme being filmed, set alongside the experiential now of the live event, and the shared, public time of the transmission of the event broadcast to audiences at home. The warm up act features as part of two of these temporal dimensions but is absent from the sense of public time of the recorded event. This creates an uneven value chain in the production where the warm up is vital in making visible the care structures for audiences and their live experience, but undervalued in how this positive mood is carried through the screen to the broadcast public. Vincent noted how some producers seemed unaware of just how significant the warm up is to generating a good mood for the overall live experience: 'Sometimes I will ask a floor manager have you got any music to play while they are coming in, just to give the place a bit of atmosphere? And they will say "Well, you will do that in a minute." I know I'll do it in a minute but at the moment it is horrible' (Vincent 2015). What he describes is the fragility of the social situation in a studio where a lack of care can create a negative atmosphere. As he noted, 'if you have the warmth of everyone in the studio, then you will have the people at home' (ibid.).

In Lunt and Stenner's research on *The Jerry Springer Show* they describe how the audience acts 'as both the barometer of the affective climate in the studio, and its amplifier' (2005: 67). The presenter, the bouncers, the staging of the encounters all work together to make visible emotional expression and audience participation, walking a thin line between strong emotions and a spectacle of excess. The audience does not go from disinterested to emotionally expressive as soon as the cameras roll, indeed Springer will be working closely with his warm up act and needing their skills in audience participation. Lunt and Stenner (2005: 64) show how a volatile affective climate signifies 'a fragile social situation'. Warm up acts manage this affective climate, handling the audience when they are in these unusual social situations. Vincent was the warm up comedian for Springer when he came to work in Britain. He recalled early screenings when the production was feeling their way into this local adaptation of an international brand. One of the problems was the quietness of the British audience, which was not used to emotional expression of the kind that had become notorious in America. Vincent explained: 'At the start the American version did not work and you could feel it. He was expecting the audience to shout "Jerry! Jerry!" and instead they would clap and say "Well done Mr Springer, you've told them."' He used his skills as a comedian and improvisational performer to work with the audience, and he described how Springer gave him freedom to take risks with the type of humour he used. Vincent (2015) was trusted to 'create the moment'. This labour highlights the pressures of emotional expression, the opportunities of participation and the risks of emotional imbalance that Lunt and Stenner describe in their analysis. In this case, there was the risk of too few emotions, the British reserve threatening the very kind of emotional excess the talk show needed to make it part of the Springer brand.

Warm up acts for reality talent shows

Of the 6,000-strong crowd at Earl's Court in London for the live screening of talent show *Got to Dance*, many were from local communities, dance schools, and general supporters of the dancers on stage. Another large group were people who regularly went to live filming of reality talent shows, getting tickets through Applause Store for an annual round of all the main television entertainment events. The mood of an event started in the queues, where people mingled while waiting for hours before the doors opened. Some families picnicked at the side of the road, like a day out at the beach, bringing chairs, flasks of tea and sandwiches. Once inside, crowds wandered around the venue, taking pictures in front of cardboard cut-outs of the judges, popping into the *Got to Dance* photo booth for a memento. It was an example of live audiences taking a mini holiday at the television event.

It was the job of Stuart Holdham to entertain the audience before the filming of the live event and during the advert breaks. He had worked on this show from its inception; for season five (2014) he worked during the auditions at the London Roundhouse entertaining the participants and their families in a more intimate setting; several months later he worked the live events during August at Earl's Court where he performed in front of large crowds. He prepared in advance, building up material from popular culture and tweaking his gags for this kind of reality TV audience. For *Got to Dance*, musical participation was the most

FIGURE 9.3 Behind the scenes at *Got to Dance*
Source: Photograph Tina Askanius.

significant performance style he used to appeal to the family audiences and aspiring child dancers. He explained:

> my preparation is the music, what is going to get that crowd going, what is going to have the biggest wow factor. Atmosphere is everything in a big stadium, if you do not get that crowd up it will have a massive impact on the show.
>
> (Holdham 2014)

How does a warm up act prepare for a live crowd? The ritual of putting on the suit is part of his preparation to get in character:

> When I put my suit on and my sparkly tie with diamantes on it, I become Stuart the Entertainer. Something comes over me, you just feel … I put my shiny patent shoes on and before I go out I will look in the mirror, straighten my tie, make sure the suit is hanging right, then if I feel good I perform a lot better.
>
> (Holdham 2015)

With a different suit for every performance, Holdham invests in his appearance in order to become Stuart the Entertainer. The shiny shoes, the sparkly tie, the final check in the mirror bring out his frontstage performance as a professional entertainer.

Holdham's performance for the live events typically involved greeting the audience: 'Welcome to *Got To Dance*, make some noise', filling the stadium with energy and then feeding off that energy during the first warm up moment. He worked the different spaces of the stadium, moving around the audience at the front of the stage, making jokes that invited those in the top tier seats to engage with the event. When he played a song he would invite children to dance in the aisles, giving away T-shirts to a selection of dancers – 'She's got it, he's got it!', pointing them out to the rest of the audience, recognising these young participants as stars in the making. During the advert breaks he would play another song and encourage people to dance, to fill the venue with energy, movement and laughter.

In another advert break hundreds of young children from the age of five upwards stormed the lower levels of the stadium to dance; they climbed over the barriers, ignoring security guards and pouring into the seating areas that led to the open spaces. These children could not wait to participate, some performing collective routines, others doing impromptu street dance, a few brave ones making acrobatic moves. Holdham could be heard taking in the mayhem, a short intake of breath and laughing at the sheer physical expression of happiness from these children; no sooner had they reached the open area and danced, then they had to run back to their seats just as the song ended. The advert break might be perceived as dead time between the real action, but at this live event these interstitial moments had more kinetic and improvisational energy than some of the acts on stage. Holdham understood that for a reality talent show such as this, the promise of dance participation is essential to its success. We saw the show in miniature, children passionate about dance hoping to be spotted for their talent and to make it in the entertainment industry, to be a star. These children expressed their emotions, their bodies literal examples of embodied meaning making. Holdham stood in for the judges and experts, a warm persona who made the audience feel invited to the party, channelling optimism and encouraging physical expression of those affective moments.

We might look at this moment and say the warm up act represents the brand and encourages children to participate in the new capitalism of the reality television industry. Families there to support their children dreaming of success as a professional dancer, and potential reality television celebrity, would certainly be aware of the opportunity a show such as this offers dancers to be visible, perhaps talent spotted for musical theatre or by specialist dance schools. The children themselves were fully aware of the training, ambition and luck necessary to be a professional dancer; many that we spoke to at the live events had started training from the age of five in various styles of dance, travelled long distances to their chosen dance schools, and were already auditioning and considering agents. The dance industry is a tough profession, requiring family support in the form of time, finance, transportation and emotional labour if a child dancer is to stand any chance of success. These participants of future talent shows were well aware of the opportunities that television offered for celebrity stardom and social media attention, and critical of the commercialisation of dance and the short-lived careers of reality talent show winners. These children took selfies for their Instagram feeds, filmed promotional videos, and critically reflected on the drawbacks of entering a talent show contest. The curse of the talent show winner is now a popular urban legend – whatever happened to the winner of *Britain's Got Talent*? Indeed, the winning ensemble of this season's *Got to Dance* disbanded after the series, and the lead dancer is now a fully trained barber, 'as seen' on a reality talent show. The optimism expressed through physical dance by these children is tinged with a pragmatic approach to the dance industry and the risks of participating in talent shows.

For Holdham (2015), that night was a good night: 'You always search for that round of applause, and when a producer comes up and says "good show" you feel a small, miniscule, part of the success of the show.' Other nights were more challenging. On one evening during the live events, the rain had dampened the atmosphere in the stadium. He had to work extra hard to warm up the crowd and his strategy was to remind himself of the audience's expectations:

> when they got their tickets through the post and they found out they were coming to one of the live semi-finals, they bought some clothes, they straightened their hair, you know, they put their best perfume and aftershave on and unfortunately they got drenched in the rain. That makes my job a little bit tougher because I have to make them forget all about that and to enjoy themselves. Yes, it was a bit humid because they are dancing around and there was steam coming off them as they were moving … But you know what, it was still a great atmosphere, although it was pouring down outside.

Holdham balanced the qualities of conviviality, care, community and risk essential for a warm up act, and a damp atmosphere was transformed into a good night out for this community of audiences and fans.

In fact, Holdham is an eternal optimist: the glass is half full, rarely half empty. He reflected on this optimism:

> Just when you think 'oh my God, I am really tired!' you look back and pick yourself up. I used to work with rubber Wellington boots, apron and gloves, facemask and carcinogenic chemicals, and you think to yourself 'This is so much better.' The buzz that you get, I mean, after tonight I won't go to bed until 2 a.m. because the adrenaline is pumping … If any warm up guy says they do not love it they are lying, because the power that you get, the satisfaction of all those people laughing at your routine, is the most empowering thing any human being can experience in their lifetime.

Yet despite this optimism and empowering experience, as a warm up act he occupies a rather invisible role in the production as seen by audiences at home. The effervescence of the front stage performance fades into the background of the politics of warm up work.

At the live event audiences approached Holdham to take a selfie, banter about the show, feeling a connection with Stuart the Entertainer. He had a particular performance style that appealed to the kind of working-class audience for *Got to Dance*: for example a good sense of humour, an ability to laugh at himself, an immediate warmth of personality that invited people from different backgrounds to develop a rapport with him. The contrast between these interactions with a regular *Got to Dance* audience and the VIP and industry guests only serves to highlight how his warm up persona is inclusive, adding to the qualities of conviviality, care and community already there in his audience participation skills. The more elite audiences on the final night did not laugh, or get up and dance in the advert breaks; they expressed a feeling of entitlement – 'Entertain me!' Seated in one part of the Earl's Court stadium, these elite audiences ignored the warm up performer, effectively creating a zone of ugly feelings (Ngai 2005), preventing him from shaping the affective structure of the live finale as a moment to remember. At the end of evening Holdham came out to thank the audience, a sign of the warm up's sensitivity to the care structures at live events, and a sign of the absence of the presenter who did not take the time to acknowledge the value of audience participation.

The paradox of warm up acts

The context of warm up acts and live experiences gives us a useful situation by which to understand the shaping of affective practice within a hidden profession. As we have seen, the way into warm up offers the chance of moving on from this work into presenting a television show or being a headline comedian, a possibility that is ever present and yet which is so hard to achieve in the competitive world of entertainment. This paradox of the profession highlights a cruel optimism at work. The idea of cruel optimism, as outlined by Lauren Berlant (2011) pays attention to the feeling of optimism and the moment of impasse. For Berlant all attachment is optimistic

> if we describe optimism as the force that moves you out of yourself and into the world in order to bring closer the satisfying something that you cannot generate on your own but sense in the wake of a person, a way of life, an object, project, concept, or scene.
>
> *(2011: 2)*

She describes optimism as ambitious, shaped by an affective structure that 'involves a sustaining inclination', something that 'ignites a sense of possibility' (ibid.). But at the same time, optimism can be cruel, making the thing you most desire just out of reach, impossible to attain and yet still a driving force in the unfolding of the present. Berlant focuses on liberal capitalist fantasies and how these take expression in aesthetic forms that register cruel optimism; genres attuned to the 'norms of self management' and forms that articulate different class, race, and gendered affective structures become the material through which she theorises the present way of living in American political culture.

Berlant's idea of cruel optimism can help us to see how a genre such as light entertainment, and its associated celebrity and stardom, shape an experience of optimism, and moments of impasse, the situations that arise which suggest the desire of recognition and stardom will be denied, just out of reach and yet still something to dream about.

Optimism and ambition are ubiquitous in the entertainment industry. There is a hunger for fame that the reality genre has used as a trope for its non-scripted narratives. This hungry 'celebrity in the making' has a long history in light entertainment and variety theatre. The Butlins holiday camp talent shows of the 1930s invited people to star in their own entertainment experience – what must it have felt like to win a talent contest during your family seaside holiday? Television talent shows in the 1970s and 1980s such as *New Faces* (ITV, UK, 1973–1988), *Strike it Lucky* (ITV, UK, 1986–1999) or *Opportunity Knocks* (BBC, UK, 1949–1990) all provided a narrative of optimism for celebrity stardom whilst showing us the disappointment of failed acts. Reality talent shows provide opportunities for visibility and recognition of performance skills and yet the journey of the competition is littered with those voted out of the show. Such is the ambition of this optimism for celebrity stardom that anti-reality television novels like *The Hunger Games* (Susanne Collins, 2008–), or surreal television satire such as *Black Mirror* (Channel 4 and Netflix, 2011), take this trope and turn it into a social and political critique of the entertainment industry and neo-liberal politics in late capitalist societies. Here, we see the cruelty of optimism enacted by characters caught in an entertainment show that promises opportunity for stardom and the good life, but is in fact a dystopian world where moral and social injustice rules.

To go into warm up work as a route to stardom is a risky manoeuvre. One of the main risks is that as a warm up act you enable others to be stars, and watch them achieve a success that is built on the collective labour of a production team, agency, marketing and publicity. Warm up acts can find themselves walking a tightrope, being attentive to the mood and timing of a live event, monitoring the line between audience boredom and amusement, creating a heightened mood, but not quite one of exuberance. One warm up act described this cynically as 'I'm just there to fluff up the audience.' If a warm up steps over the line, displays too much presence on stage, then they jeopardise their job. For example, Vincent (2015) explained: 'I will play the moment and I can sometimes get a bollocking when I chase the laugh. That might mean I never work for them again.'

Jeff Stevenson recounted his experience working as the warm up guy for comedian and presenter Mike Yarwood at London Weekend Television; it was a big live spectacle with a pit orchestra, and a dance troupe on stage. Stevenson worked a 10-minute spot and it went very well – too well: 'I'm getting big laughs; I thought, I had better pull back, this is not good news' (Stevenson 2015). His spot extended to 40 minutes until finally Yarwood took the stage. Afterwards, the producer explained to him: 'We had a big problem. What was the problem? You. Yarwood heard the laughs and got in his car and drove home, saying "I cannot follow that young comic, I should have another warm up act"' (ibid.). The producer warned Stevenson to pull back, reminding him that a good warm up knows their place in the hierarchy of the production and the television star system.

Stevenson's experience highlights the paradox of the profession: warm up 'trains someone not to be a star' (2015). After two decades in the business he felt it was time for a change. He explained: 'I was not ambitious enough, not ruthless enough. I was not the one to work the green room afterwards, I never treated it as a business after the show' (Stevenson 2015). He returned to comedy, starting afresh and retraining as an alternative comedian rather than a light entertainer. He took the stage name of Harvey Oliver, ironically referencing variety comedy, but with a different performance style, ranting about the absurdity of life. 'Now you go out with a smile on your face, now you are the comedian, not the warm up guy' (Stevenson 2015). Stevenson (2015) advises comedians to avoid warm up work:

> If you are going to be a star, you will find it quicker and with more respect if you do not do warm ups. Stay away from the TV studios and do as many live gigs as possible. Agents will find you. You will be in your dressing room, with your own show, and you will hear someone like me as the warm up.

The risks in moving into warm up suggest how someone can be visible on stage to live audiences but invisible to agents and producers in the industry. This absent presence can be seen in other hidden labour in the entertainment industry. A warm up occupies a similar position to that of the understudy and stand-in within theatre. Understudies typically learn the lines and physical movements of lead stars, taking on a smaller part in a play or musical theatre, but ready to step into the lead role if the star is ill or unable to perform due to other commitments. The stand-in learns the lines of smaller parts in a play and will rarely come to the theatre or take part in a live performance, unless someone is sick or the understudy has stepped into the lead part. There can be a risk of being perceived as only a warm up act, not as a stand-up comedian, or only a stand-in, rarely cast as an actor with a part in a play.

The absence of their presence in the filming process, or in the live theatre, blocks recognition in the industry. If you look for archival footage of warm up acts you will be disappointed; they are rarely filmed in the television studio or venue by the production company; occasional footage can be found by audiences attending a reality television screening, such as selfies on Instagram with the warm up, or amateur footage of the warm up act secretly filmed as a memento of the live event. The warm up act exists as a performance, with text in the form of comedy lines, information to audiences, and vocal and body gestures, combining a script with spontaneous audience participation. This means the warm up exists as a live performance, not a screen performance, in a medium where screen time is paramount and produces premium value for the production company and broadcaster in the form of sales, audience ratings, social media buzz and advertising revenues. If a warm up performs as a comedian and presenter at corporate events they are valued for their live presence and the way they manage the care structures for delegates within these industry experiences. But for television, an absence of screen presence devalues their work. The economic drivers of television undervalue this profession, the lack of text, their non-appearance in the show itself a crucial and unfair indicator of the regard-system at work in light entertainment. Warm up acts stand in the shadows of screen culture, denied recognition by the very industry they work in.[3]

Conclusion

Recognition of the creative value of warm up acts is fleeting at best, with few oral histories of warm up acts, little archival material, ephemeral evidence created by audiences at live television events, and an absence of industry and academic research on this profession. The actual value of the warm up performers and their relationship with live audiences is lost in industry obsession with celebrity stardom, ratings and social media buzz for live spectaculars. It is as if the job title of warm up act blocks them from being recognised for their work as professional entertainers. They are the absent presence in the television industry. Similar invisible jobs include the stand-in for film and television, or the theatre understudies and stand-ins who replace lead actors if they are sick or unable to perform. As one warm up act noted, the profession paradoxically trains someone not to be a star. But the warm up act is someone who creates a meaningful connection with crowds and makes people feel recognised and valued for their performances as audiences at a live event. Such a respect for audiences entails an undervalued knowledge of people's experiences of entertainment television; they offer an unusual example of situated affective practice in research on production labour and the live audience experience. It is a cruel twist of irony that the warm up person shines a light on audiences in the entertainment industry and in doing so blocks their own path to fame.

Notes

1 See the official website of Applause Store, https://www.applausestore.com/
2 See Andre Vincent and his online publication on the roots of English stand-up, https://www.mislaidcomedyheroes.com/history, accessed 3 June 2018.
3 My thanks to Paul McDonald, Julie Donovan, John Corner and Ed Vollans for their insightful comments on warm up acts.

10

AUDIENCES AS PATHFINDERS

> We are co-creative and embrace our creativity.
> *(51 year old female Swedish office manager and fan of* Bron*)*

This book has travelled across people and popular culture, exploring the pathways to engagement and the various ways in which we shape and are shaped by the media landscapes through which we move. This exploration has included the voices and bodies, sights and sounds of audiences as they experience entertainment through television drama, reality TV, at live events, and within digital television itself as actors, participants and producers. And this exploration has been about the people who create the drama, live events and reality entertainment that we experience. Thus, the book has explored and charted the relationships between producers and audiences in shared places, what we might call places of the imagination.

The tracks within this book criss-cross the many print-trails of others; these include the way creative producers have imagined alternative landscapes of the mind in television drama, or the ways entertainers have created affective climates for our laughter and tears. These print-trails also include the ways audiences have imagined their social realities through modes of narration, or how performers embody meaning making through their physical expressions. The case studies of Nordic noir drama *The Bridge*, cult conspiracy thriller *Utopia*, reality entertainment *MasterChef*, warm up acts, and the live events of *Got to Dance*, all are places within a media imagination (Chambers 2016) that connects television storytelling with audience engagement and the textures and contours of people's lived realities.

One of the main ways of understanding the connections and contradictions between media producers and audiences is through the concept of a spectrum of engagement; this includes focus on the industrial contexts of engagement and the shifting and subjective practices of engagement with a range of genres, artefacts and events. Media producers can no longer assume a mass audience with which to

FIGURE 10.1 Pathways: on the set of *Bron/Broen*
Source: Photograph Tina Askanius.

engage, but rather are scrambling to keep up with audiences on the move, from live audiences, catch up viewers, 'piracy' and informal access to content, fans and anti-fans, contestants and participants, performers and producers. Audiences engage with media across a spectrum of identities and emotional and cognitive practices. In this way, engagement is experienced in myriad ways, and extends across an emotional range so that people switch between positive or negative engagement, and disengagement. A spectrum of engagement also works across different contexts, such as time, including fleeting engagement with a live event, or long form engagement with a brand on broadcast schedules and streaming services; and space/place, including live venues, distribution and digital spaces, and the spaces of everyday life.

Another way of understanding the engagement and experiences of audiences is to picture them in topographical terms, using the notion of roaming audiences to suggest the ways people traverse the media landscape. This approach builds on the work of Charles Taylor (2004) and the social imagination, exploring situated affective practice in audience research, and how audiences imagine and constitute themselves within the current media landscape. This notion of roaming audiences also connects with work on the physical act of walking and wayfaring, highlighting both the landscape of the mind, and the material elements of landscape and the body (Ingold 2011), in this case relating to the physical act of being at a live event, or how people organise their time and daily routines to make space for media, to embed it in their lives.

When we traverse the media landscape we can see the media industries as pathmakers, creating content within different genres of fiction and non-fiction, marshalling infrastructures of distribution and access, organising institutional time zones for the scheduling of national content to audiences, rearranging access to missed shows through catch up services, digital archives and consumer products. To see the media industries as pathmakers and ourselves as path-followers is the most common view of the relation between producers and audiences. But paths connect, and are 'acts of consensual making' (Macfarlane 2012: 17). Thus, we can also see audiences as pathmakers, creating their own content and sharing through social media, organising their own time zones to make personalised viewing schedules, reopening pathways previously considered closed. Pathmakers and path-followers are co-present in the media landscape filled with 'letters, words, texts, songs, signs and stories', flickering with the life of myriad peoples, the paths spreading and patterning, 'bringing alignments and discrepancies' (Macfarlane 2012: 394).

One of the most striking examples of the alignments and discrepancies of creative producers and roaming audiences is the case of the drama series *Utopia*. The writer, director and creative team started a geo-political dialogue about environmental destruction and population control. The mode of narration asked audiences to question a 'false social imaginary' (Taylor 2004: 143), constructed by powerful elites in shadow democracies. Transnational audiences and fans engaged with the drama, questioning the 'all pervasive order' (ibid.) of ruling elites putting their needs above the needs of citizens. They articulated 'rights talk', a right to roam the storytelling of the drama through illegal access to the series on piracy sites; they wanted economic, temporal and geographical freedom to watch this content without restrictions, free from commercial culture, geoblocking and time delays. These intensely engaged audiences and fans were not measured by the media industry, and at the time of transmission the drama attracted low official ratings in its country of origin, ultimately leading to the cancellation of the series. But a more enlightened approach would have identified and highlighted the wide range of audiences and fans from diverse regional and cultural backgrounds. The move by Amazon in April 2018 to adapt the original drama and make a nine-episode series of *Utopia* is a response by streaming services to align themselves with roaming audiences, making the new series available in 200 countries for their 'Prime' customers. This new adaption is not free to air, but it does show some movement in thinking around access laws and opening up alternative routes for transnational audiences to engage with content without geographical barriers in place.

Pathfinders

This conclusion to *Media Experiences* ends with a reflection on audiences as pathfinders within mediascapes. In the photograph shown in Figure 10.2, post-it notes on a whiteboard highlight the names of various characters in the original version of

Audiences as pathfinders 187

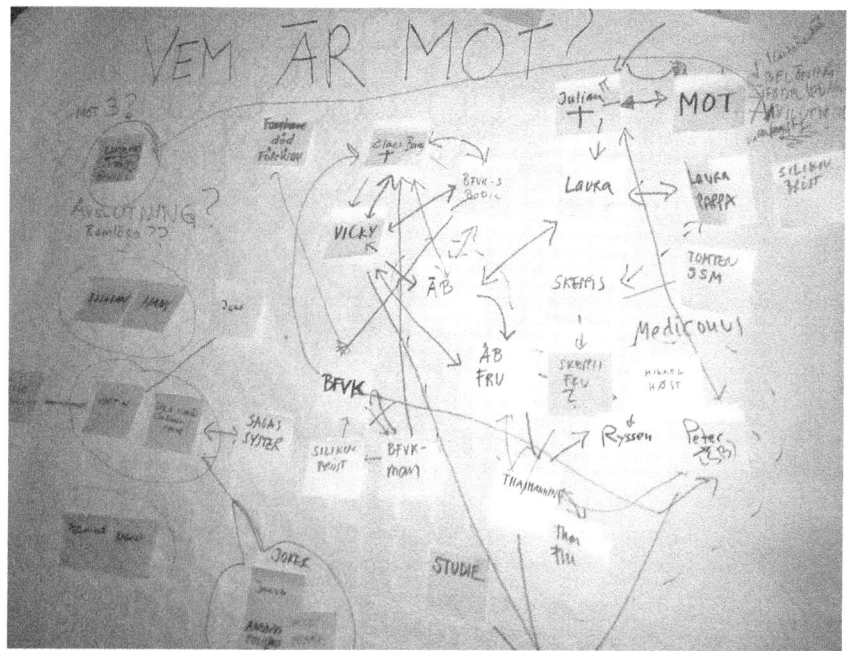

FIGURE 10.2 Pathfinders: mapping Mother of Three at *Bron/Broen* fan meeting
Source: Photograph Tina Askanius.

the crime drama *Bron/Broen* (season two), specifically all possible names of the mysterious MOT (Mother of Three), a character with no name in the narrative of this drama. The title on the board asks 'Who is MOT?' Colour coded notes run across the white board, and lines and arrows denote the connected lives of various characters. The whiteboard is in the home of a fan, one of the organisers of a dedicated fan community based in Stockholm. It is a material object that tells us how fans see this drama as a tapestry, with the narrative, characters and locations woven together in a tightly constructed whodunnit. The fans' regular gathering tells us how the threads in the drama connect the lives of these fans together, for these moments in time, meeting once a week for ten weeks during the transmission of the series in Sweden; they come together to debate the drama and affirm their relationship with it. It's an affective climate that allows for passionate engagement with the series and a feeling of inclusion: 'It's so goofy, but at the same time it's wonderful ... we are co-creative and embrace our creativity' (51 year old female Swedish office manager). The arrows point inwards and outwards, a topography of the narrative in the drama that runs through these fans and on into their lives beyond the drama.

As Wetherell (2012: 15) notes, sometimes patterns are imposed, and there are many ways by which the media attempt to push and pull audiences into established pathways. This push-pull dynamic highlights how the industry pushes audiences into branded places and hopes to keep them in one place by pulling them into specific kinds of storytelling. Take, for example, the case of Netflix; it imposes a temporal and geographical arrangement of media content, making available certain television series and films at particular times, in specific geographical zones. The ideal audience for Netflix might be binge watchers, becoming aware of a new television drama, say, through algorithmic recommendation, then arranging their everyday routines so that they can speed through each episode until there is no more to see; then the algorithmic recommendation for another similar drama leads viewers down a particular pathway within the branded world of Netflix ('because you watched …'). There is a situated affective practice within Netflix that invites audiences into an enclosed space, the password and subscription service only serving to underscore this bounded domain. The fact that audiences have figured out the geographical differences for Netflix in certain regions, and have become adept at using get-around services to watch content intended for national audiences elsewhere, is something the company is actively trying to block, along with other anti-piracy measures, such as friendly password sharing for accounts (Lobato 2017). Thus, audiences push back against Netflix and its bounded distribution.

This is one example of how media industries attempt to pull audiences into established zones by making commercially protected pathways for their customers to follow. However, audiences are also pathfinders, changing and refiguring their affective, temporal and geographical relations with media. Still with Netflix, the ability for audiences to watch a TV series within this branded space does not mean they will always choose to do so. As we saw in the discussion of *The Bridge* in Chapter 3, Scandinavian and British audiences who had missed the original transmission window for this Nordic noir drama on public service television caught up with the series on Netflix, but as soon as new episodes were shown live they reassembled themselves as public service viewers for weekly gatherings to watch when '*Bron* is on'. Younger viewers described their relief at not having to plough through all the episodes of a Netflix series, streaming and binging; they made sure not to download the latest series through piracy sites just so they could enjoy the unusual experience of watching live as a national audience. They called this experience 'old television', a retro television experience where audiences assembled themselves in order to enjoy drama as social ritual. They chose the collective social experience of live public service media over the dispersed and more personalised experience of streaming and binge-watching television.

Another way audiences become pathfinders is by constituting themselves as a live audience at an event. *RuPaul's Drag Race* is a reality talent show in search of the next drag superstar, originally shown on Logo TV from 2009, before moving to VH1 and gaining worldwide distribution through Netflix. Set against this top-down channelling of audiences through the commercial distribution of the series, there exist alternative ways to watch the show live at fan events, with screenings in Amsterdam, London and New York City, among other locations: for example in March 2018 *Time Out New York* detailed five different clubs, bars and move theatres where there were viewing parties for the latest season, including each 90-minute episode, and the spinoff behind the scenes series *Untucked*; these ranged from organised events with an MC and cast from the series and a promise of performances, screening and after party, to more informal *Drag Race* parties across the New York City (Goldberg 2018).

In the city of Copenhagen, a gay club shows the latest episode live to a packed house. Doors open at 8.30 on a Friday night to queues of fans waiting to get a table. The distributor is Out TV, an LGBTI brand that enables transmission beyond the American window. There is a large screen in the basement, and smaller screens scattered around other spaces in more intimate settings. The audio by the MC for the live screening can be heard around the different parts of the club, shaping an acoustic space for the duration of the show, across clusters of viewing upstairs and downstairs. The Drag House Collective helps to shape the affective climate for the live experience, where the combination of MC and stand-up comedian works to manage time in the event and manage audience engagement; people can call out, but there is a culture of attentive viewing during the episode and debate in the breaks, a key moment for audience reflection. This is a knowing talent show, an example of what Joke Hermes (2018) calls 'post television', playfully remixing other talent shows, critiquing and reproducing femininity, performing selves and constructing the 'best you', making cross-textual references to earlier shows and the media ensemble of the series and its paratexts. The mixture of the commercial enterprise of the show and its performers, and the affective scripts within the format that celebrate drag, all work to make the viewing of the tenth season a memorable live experience.[1] People deliberately do not check out what has happened on social media, nor do they secretly watch an episode, choosing to experience the live event as a performative space, a place of co-presence. Indeed, the club becomes a localised place for audiences to come together.

One of the reasons why clubs in Copenhagen started showing *RuPaul's Drag Race* was a creative response to the downturn in the use of these clubs for hook ups, as dating apps have changed the hook up culture of LBGTI communities. What we see is a cross-promotional enterprise between several of Copenhagen's entertainment economies: the clubs, the distributor Out TV, the drag collective, consumers, and the absent presence of dating apps that have privatised sex hook ups. This is the tenth season of *RuPaul's Drag Race*, it's a long established reality talent show with an extensive archive, but this is the first year of live screenings in Copenhagen, demonstrating how an old show can be found anew by audiences and fans. *RuPaul's Drag Race* is an example of how roaming audiences impact on media and entertainment industries, finding their own pathways to roam around the storytelling, and these pathways in turn become integrated into multi-faceted distribution and economic models by several connected entertainment industries.

Analysing the interfaces between creative production and audience practices helps us see the impact of audiences as pathfinders in media industries. According to Douglas Wood (Director of Research and Audience Insight at Endemol Shine), these interfaces allow producers for a drama such as *Utopia*:

to peel back the layers of audience engagement beyond the traditional boundaries to reveal a universe that is rarely explored or reported. It was a revelation to see how this rich content resonated with audiences who often sit outside established methods of linear TV measurement and how important the relationship between creator and viewer can be. This research adds to our collective knowledge about these increasingly diverse and mobile audiences who are consuming TV content in a more personalised and selective manner.

(Wood 2016)

The non-linear journey that criss-crosses the media landscape puts a premium on creative content and the power of storytelling, but poses all sorts of problems for audience measurement systems, licensing opportunities, and different revenue streams for creative content. As television critic Mark Lawson notes on binge viewing within streaming services, 'as is so often in the medium, creativity and commerce pull in opposite directions'.[2] But if we consider audiences as pathfinders then it shows how they are 'simply finding and fitting the content into their lifestyles, and those lifestyles have changed faster than many broadcasters have been able to keep up with'.[3] Certainly one of the outcomes of researching producer/audience interfaces is to highlight 'the dynamics likely to be at work in the future variegated network of media experiences and the challenges posed for the business models of the diversified media industry'.[4]

To reflect on roaming audiences, Tim Ingold argues in *Being Alive* that 'wayfaring is the fundamental mode by which living beings inhabit the earth' (Ingold 2011: 12). He explains that as an anthropologist this requires the skills of bringing together materials, bodies, and flows of human experience: 'coupling action and perception along paths of movement' (2011: 15). He urges researchers to follow what is going on, 'tracing the multiple trails of becoming' (2011: 14). Ingold's use of lines, following a Deleuzian philosophical way of thinking, is similar to Macfarlane's 'path-trails' (2012: 26) and the 'topographies of the self we carry within us' in his nature writing. For the study of audiences, this suggests attention paid to situated affective practices, the material conditions for engagement and experiences, and the path-trails that help us understand audience movements. Kristian Møller (2018) notes in his research that wayfaring means 'attunement to the ways biography and affect is not simply *there* to be found and made explicit, but arise in interactions between users and their digital media environments'.

There are ways of seeing movement and the act of wayfaring as a productive force with media audiences. Ingold writes about repositioning the meaning of the term 'production' from the activities of making and building to processes of hope, growing and dwelling (2011: 6). In the example of *RuPaul's Drag Race* live screenings, we can see the ways audiences constitute themselves as a productive force, connected both to making an event and to growing a local audience who can feel at home in the storytelling of this reality television experience. The interactions between live audiences and their physical environment transform dispersed sites of reception into concrete places where audiences can enact their embodied meaning making of this television series and perform the identity work that is such a significant aspect of popular culture (Hermes 2018). In this case, what we see is how roaming audiences assemble themselves into local cultures of viewing, where people perform being an audience, where displacement becomes emplacement.

Macfarlane writes about how some of the most interesting pathways are made in unofficial ways: 'in every town and city today, cutting across parks and waste ground, you'll see unofficial paths created by walkers who have abandoned the pavements and roads to make shortcuts and make asides' (2012: 17). Town planners call these improvised routes 'desire lines' or 'desire paths' (ibid.). Roaming audiences find improvised routes, creating 'desire paths', and these unofficial pathways invite a more enlightened access law; what exists at present are legal measures to restrict movements across the media landscape, but the opening up of desire paths may enable a wider range of communities to engage with media that is curtailed or censored in particular regions. These unofficial habits of roaming audiences tell us something about their movements and moments of stasis, or impasse, about the constitution of audiences in mediated spaces and in the physical places of homes, public settings and live venues (Ingold and Vergunst 2008: 1).

In audience research we all too often imagine people as fixed, or transfixed by, media content, stuck on the sofa or glued to a screen. But people generate movement and stillness, speeding up and slowing down, as they travel through the media landscape. This duality is apparent in the ways people describe their media experiences. Take this example, a viewing of *Bron/Broen* on a train journey in Sweden:

> I was on the train down from Stockholm, and there was someone in front of me watching on his computer. So I started watching between the seats, from behind. And I couldn't hear anything … I could only see the images, and thought: 'What the hell is going on here?' And I went home and finished watching the first episode. And then I watched the second one right away, and said: 'Well, we have to watch this, when's the next one on?' And then we were hooked. And that's something that you haven't experienced for years, just waiting for the next episode. You get so used to just buying the DVD-box or downloading it. But this is like it used to be, sitting and waiting.
>
> *(60 year old Swedish female editor)*

That long train ride initiated another journey through the storytelling of the drama series, beginning with streaming the first few episodes and then 'sitting and waiting' to watch at a fixed time and place.

If we return to Roland Barthes' (1979) discussion of the contrary freedom of eating in a dining car of a French train (see Chapter 3) this is particularly apt to the media experiences of roaming audiences. The idea of contrary freedom relates to the ways everything in the dining car is designed to transform contingency, displacement and movement into a 'mirage of solidity' (1979: 141). So, the heavy linen napkins, elaborate menu, and attentive waiters all serve to provide material objects and suggest an affective climate of a restaurant on the streets of Paris rather than a train travelling through the suburbs and small towns of France. Barthes notes how 'each constraint seems to produce its contrary freedom' (1979: 141). In the example of watching the crime drama on the train, we can see how the technological affordances of television and the internet offer people myriad ways of accessing media through dispersed sites of distribution and reception. But the woman on the train creates an illusion of immobility: she chooses to slow down time and find a fixed place to experience the drama. She eschews accessing the drama online, instead opting to wait and be part of the constituted audience for public service media. These old ways of watching television overlay the new ways of on-demand cultures of viewing. How ironic, then, that a crime drama such as *Bron/Broen*, which is about the mobility of people across borders, is given such solidity by audiences; people enhance the materiality of their media experiences, and slow down movement and time, to imagine and dream. It suggests the contrariness of media experiences, how we are scattered as well as affirmed by the places through which we move.

Notes

1 I am grateful to Kristian Møller for his observations and insights at this screening of the show in Copenhagen, and his encouragement to write about audience assemblage.
2 Mark Lawson in the *Guardian*, 25 May 2018, 'Box, Set and Match: How On-demand Became TV's New Battleground, https://www.theguardian.com/tv-and-radio/2018/may/25/box-set-and-match-how-on-demand-became-tvs-new-battleground, accessed 5 June 2018.
3 Ian Calcutt, email correspondence with author, 1 June 2018.
4 John Corner, email correspondence with author, 20 May 2018.

APPENDICES

Project team

The project team included: Professor Annette Hill; Julie Donovan, a creative content consultant with twenty years experience working in the media industry, and interests in the international formats business; Dr Tina Askanius, a Danish-Swedish media researcher with interests in social media; Dr Koko Kondo, a Japanese-British audience researcher with expertise in qualitative research; and Jose Luis Urueta, a Colombian-Swedish researcher with a passion for audience research.

The Project Advisory Group included Professor Göran Bolin (Södertörn Högskola, Sweden), Professor Raymond Boyle, (Glasgow University, UK), Professor John Corner (Leeds University, UK), Professor Jeanette Steemers (University of Westminster, UK), and Douglas Wood (Endemol Shine Group).

Julie Donovan has been working in the TV entertainment industry for over 20 years. She started her career in production at London Weekend Television (LWT), and worked her way up from researcher to producer on a number of shows for both primetime terrestrial and cable networks. In recent years, she has been involved in the international formats business, most recently within the Worldwide Entertainment Department of Fremantle Media as Senior Vice President responsible for International Format Development.

Dr Koko Kondo is currently working at the University of Westminster, UK. After working in the media industry in Tokyo for almost nine years (TV presenter, sales and promotion, and management), she did a Ph.D. on the subject of Japanese children and global media. Her post-doctoral research with Brunel University examined digital media at home for designing the interface of interactive TV. She has also assisted Professor Hill's work on paranormal media. Her current interests include viral marketing, social media and digital media use in higher education.

Dr Tina Askanius is currently working as a senior lecturer at Malmö University, Sweden. She is mainly involved in production and audience fieldwork in Scandinavia. Some of her current work in the Media Experiences project involves political documentary audiences and qualitative studies of crime fiction series and their fans.

Jose Luis Urueta is currently working as a visiting researcher at Lund University with Annette Hill. He was a full time research assistant in the Media Experiences project. Jose holds an M.A. in Public and International Affairs from the University of Ottawa.

Research notes: *The Bridge*

The case study of television drama format *The Bridge* (Filmlance International and Endemol Shine) needs some explanation. The format is based on the original crime series *Bron/Broen* (2011–2018, SVT and DR) located in the border territory of Sweden and Denmark, and has run for four seasons. There are two adaptations of the original series, set across Britain and France (*The Tunnel*, Sky; *Le Tunnel*, Canal 5, 2013–2016), and America and Mexico (*The Bridge*, FX 2013–2014); a further adaptation was made between Estonia and Russia (2018). The original *Bron/Broen* has aired in 157 countries around the world, and the third season won a Crystal award for the best TV drama series of the year in Sweden. To avoid confusion, I refer to the international drama format as *The Bridge*, the American–Mexican version as *The Bridge* (FX, USA), and the original drama as *Bron/Broen*, which means the bridge in Swedish and Danish.

The production research for *The Bridge* was conducted by Annette Hill and Tina Askanius, and the audience research was conducted by Hill, Askanius, Koko Kondo and Jose Luis Urueta. The research was designed by Hill; and the analysis of the interview data was conducted by Hill. My thanks to the research team for their excellent fieldwork and observations for this case study.

For season two of *Bron/Broen* the qualitative research was based on individual interviews, focus groups and participant observation of audiences, conducted during October 2013– January 2014. Production interviews took place with 10 executive and creative producers, script writers, and location managers. There were 47 audience participants, including 33 women and 14 men, aged 16–65. There were 35 Swedes, 7 Danes, and 7 Europeans. The interviews and participant observations were conducted in Swedish and Danish and the focus groups were conducted in English. Participants comprised graphic designers, teachers, administrators, supermarket workers, carers, retired persons, students and unemployed persons. Each audience interview lasted between 40 and 60 minutes and took place in homes and coffee shops and via Skype and telephone in southern Sweden, and western and eastern Denmark.

For season three of *Bron/Broen* the production research included interviews and observations during April 2015 at Filmlance and on location; there were also interviews during post-production with creatives during August and September 2015. Observations resulted in audio recordings, fieldnotes and photographs. Twenty-seven production interviews took place with executive producers, writer, director, editor, production, sound and costume designers, actors, location manager, PR and event organisers, and extras; there were 12 female and 15 male interviewees.

At the launch event for season three, 27 vox pop interviews took place at the venue with a range of fans comprising 6 males and 21 females. Observations resulted in audio recordings, fieldnotes and photographs, with follow-up interviews with selected fans for the audience research. For the audience research, 41 Swedes participated in individual and group interviews (2–3 persons) and two focus groups. The fieldwork time frame was October 2015–January 2016. This included 30 females and 11 males, aged 21–71, with a range of occupations comprising student, till operator, cinema worker, librarian, teacher, receptionist, lawyer, to retired. In terms of the Danish audience research, 25 Danes participated in individual and group interviews (2–3 persons). The fieldwork time frame was October 2015–April 2016. This included 15 females and 10 males, aged 23–71, with a range of professions comprising student, postman, truck driver, child carer, support worker, clerk, teacher, pharmacist and retired. Each audience interview lasted between 40 and 60 minutes and took place in homes and coffee shops and via Skype and telephone in southern and central Sweden, and western and eastern Denmark.

For season two of *The Bridge* (FX, USA), the fieldwork took place between 2014 and 2015. There are four production interviews with executive and creative producers at Elwood Reid Inc., Shine America. There were 15 interviews with viewers in America and Mexico watching season two of *The Bridge* (FX, USA). There were 7 men and 8 women; they were aged 23–62 years of age. In terms of occupation, respondents ranged from office assistant, unemployed and swimming pool maintenance worker to agricultural worker, IT specialist, business owner, academic, lawyer and marketing worker. The interviews were conducted in Spanish and English, by telephone and Skype, and these viewers accessed the series mainly on DVR and streaming services, which reflects the ratings for this series and its predominance of catch up viewers. This study of *The Bridge* started as exploratory research, with the intention to continue for season three, but FX cancelled the series during the fieldwork period. The production interviews were conducted by Annette Hill and the audience interviews by Jose Luis Urueta.

For seasons two and three of *The Bridge* in the UK, which was the original *Bron* aired on BBC4, the fieldwork took place between 2014 and 2016. For season two there were 30 interviews conducted with audiences, both individual interviews and group interviews, taking place in offices, homes and coffee shops, and lasting approximately one hour. There were 20 females and 10 males, aged 24–69 years old. Participants were mainly from the ABC1 social grade, lower to middle class and upper class, including writers, art curators, teachers, project managers designers, nurses, teaching assistants, self-employed people and retired people.

For season three in the UK the fieldwork took place between 2015 and 2016. There were 21 interviews conducted with audiences, both individual interviews and group interviews, taking place in offices, homes, and coffee shops, and lasting approximately one hour. There were 17 females and 4 males, aged 29–71 years old. Participants were mainly from the ABC1 social grade, lower to middle class and upper class, including teachers, nurses, tennis trainer, publicist, architect and beauty therapist, self-employed people and retired people.

Two participants observations took place at the fan event Nordicana, held in London in 2015 and 2016. Observations, short interviews and photographs were taken at the event in order to explore the branded tourism events taking place around Nordic noir and regional tourism, and fan activities arising from television crime drama. Koko Kondo conducted this fieldwork.

In sum, the audience research was focused on Sweden and Denmark, with a total of 140 respondents from Stockholm and southern Sweden, western and eastern Denmark; this regional focus is related to the production study with Filmlance International and its target audience for SVT and DR. There were 50 interviews with viewers in Britain watching *Bron/Broen*, from southern England and Wales; these viewers were watching season two and three, shown on public service broadcaster BBC4, and reflect a more middle-class, older audience that is the target group for this niche channel.

For a sample of the fieldwork questions please see the interview guide (below) designed for season three of *The Bridge* in Sweden and Denmark.

Questions for The Bridge *season three audiences*

Theme 1: social context

- Tell us how you watch *The Bridge*.

    a   Setting, preparation, any ritual, describe the atmosphere (at home) …
    b   Alone/together
    c   And how did you hear about it (for those new to the show)?

- Describe how you like to watch it.

    a   E.g. silence, chatting gossiping tweeting, updating online as the shows run
    b   Once per week or store up and watch in one big go (pros and cons to both experiences?)
    c   Live on TV, catch up on SVT play or DR-TV, etc.
    d   The Sunday night slot: what kind of TV do you prefer to be watching on a Sunday night? Entertaining relaxing versus complex storyline
    e   Unusual route, not SVT, DR etc. (for those in the grey zone)

Theme 2: storytelling

- Tell us about the story so far.

    a   How would you describe the narrative? Multilayered?
    b   From S2 to S3

- c Hopes, fears, reflections about S3 storytelling
- d Characterisation, Saga, the loss of Martin
- e New characters, – Henrik – returning characters – Hans

- Crime story

  a What about the crime plot?
  b Themes of morality, heroes, anti-heroes, when good people do bad things, bad people do good things
  c The complexity of the crime story – keeps you guessing, too complicated?
  d Genre issues in crime drama

- Family story

  a The characters, scenarios?
  b Dysfunctional families
  c Saga, her family, her work family, children, parents
  d Characters and their fate: Can they escape the past? Change the future?

Theme 3: understanding

- What would you say is your understanding of *The Bridge*?

  a Melancholy, tragedy, loss, light at the end of the tunnel, hope in the darkness
  b Saga struggles to understand people; who understands her?
  c Saga at work, at home – what makes her human?
  d Understanding of family issues, problems, gender relations
  e Emotional range, empathy, anger, rejection
  f Saga, Henrik, characters who are vulnerable
  g Different cultures – DK vs SE made explicit in the relation between Hanne and Saga for example?

- The political theme

  a What do you think of the political themes raised in this season?
  b The journey from S1 to S3: from welfare politics to climate change to gender politics?
  c What do you think about the story of contemporary Scandinavian societies?
  d What unites and separates us, our future?

- Challenging narratives

  a The complexity of the storyline and the plot
  b The political themes: how important are they to you?
  c Does this drama give you space to think and feel? How? details ...
  d What kind of audience are you for *Bron*? Dedicated, challenging, fickle?

Theme 4: craft

- What do you think of the way *The Bridge* is made?
- Tell us about the little details that make up the big picture.

  a Landmarks, bridge and the sea, city and countryside locations
  b Music, sound, overall emotional tone
  c Colour and lighting and weather
  d Writing and the script
  e Direction and overall tone of the drama
  f Editing and the visual energy

- Comment on the contrasts. For example image, sound, characters, cool contrasts, hot emotions.
- Different countries, languages

  a Emotional cracks
  b Political cracks
  c Moral ambiguity
  d Cultural difference
  e Cross borders

- How do you think *The Bridge* translates to other countries?

  a Made in SWE/DK, UK/FR
  b What translates/what doesn't?

Theme 5: drama

- What do you think of television drama right now?

  a Crime drama, other kinds of drama …
  b Are you watching more drama, compared to reality TV, or docs?
  c Do you make time for your favourites?
  d How are you finding out about new drama series? Recommendations, social media, reviews? Illegal downloads, catch up, Netflix, buying DVD box sets?
  e How do you find information, new seasons, storylines etc. – through social media, blogs, friends?
  f Does good drama make you happy?
  g Reflections on being an audience … what kind of audience, fan, user are you?

Finish: anything else?

Research notes for Utopia

The *Utopia* research used a qualitative approach to *Utopia* producers and audiences, drawing on individual and group interviews. A total of 77 interviews were conducted overall for seasons one and two. For the production research, there were interviews conducted face to face and via telephone and Skype during April 2015, many taking place at the offices of Kudos. Interviews resulted in audio recordings and fieldnotes. Twenty-one production interviews took place with executive and creative producers. These included the commissioner, and marketing team, executive producers, writer, directors, cinematographer, production design, composer, sound and costume designers, casting director, and actors; there were 8 female and 13 male interviewees.

For the audience research, 56 audience members and fans participated in individual and group interviews (2–3 persons). The fieldwork time frame was June 2015–April 2016. The recruitment method involved snowball sampling, primarily through social media and otherwise friends of friends. After the project was flagged on official *Utopia* social media we received 4,000 views, and 1,000 likes; this led to 170 fans emailing and Skyping about the project. Many dropped out after learning that we would audio record the interview. Although we guaranteed anonymity, audio recordings made *Utopia* fans nervous due to their political beliefs, illegal viewing, and conspiracy theories regarding the cancellation of the television series. For every interview, the researchers needed to patiently build trust with these fans from around the world, conducting most interviews in the middle of the night due to time differences.

The overall sample of 56 participants comprised 15 females and 41 males, aged 16–38, with a range of professions from student, unemployed, artist, activist, musician, charity worker, graphic designer, teacher, translator and spacecraft operator. Fans were from the UK, Sweden, Denmark, France, Germany, Italy, Greece, Spain, Slovenia, Russia, America, Canada, Colombia, Argentina, Chile, Australia and New Zealand. Interviews were conducted in English and Spanish. Each interview lasted between 40 and 60 minutes and took place via Skype and telephone, or in homes and public places.

The production research was conducted by Annette Hill and Julie Donovan; the audience research was conducted by Jose Luis Urueta, with help from Koko Kondo, and designed by Annette Hill.

For a sample of the fieldwork questions please see the interview guide below designed for *Utopia* seasons one and two.

Utopia *audience interview guide*

Theme 1: social context

- How did you find *Utopia*?

    a How did you find out about it? Reviews, friends, fans? From the beginning, later on, only now?

    b How did you watch it? On TV, catch up, internet, disc, stick, cloud?

    c Watching through traditional TV, DVD, or illegal viewing.

- What kind of *Utopia* viewer are you?
    - a Regular viewer, fan, turn off?
    - b Who did you watch it with? Alone, friends, partner, family? Re watch, chat, tweet, blog? Re-mix?

If they mention cancellation discuss now and return to topic later.

Theme 2: content

- What is *Utopia*?
    - a Genre mix, black comedy, comic book, conspiracy thriller
    - b Storytelling, characters, setting
    - c Themes, e.g. network, resistance, population control, environment, family, politics
    - e Emotions, e.g. hilarious, heartbreaking, horrifying

- Who is *Utopia*?
    - a Characters, e.g. Wilson, Jessica, Arby, Mr Rabbit and Network, resistance, immersive world of *Utopia*

Theme 3: look and feel and sound

- How would you describe the *Utopia* world?
    - a Visuals, space, people, details
    - b Colour, emotions
    - c Hyper realism. The writer calls it 'reality round the corner'

- What about the sound and music?
    - a Sound and narrative
    - b Electronic sound, real sound.
    - c Sound and emotion. The director calls it 'sound seduction'

- What about the black comedy?
    - a Use examples of tone of *Utopia*, black comic absurdism
      Ask for memorable scenes, and/or show scenes such as season two, episode three, Lee kills Early Bird Joe; or season one, episode one and opening sequence in comic book store.

Theme 4: morality and politics

- What do you think about the political issues in *Utopia*?

    a   Population control, environment, fertility, family, corruption
    b   Violence, shocking scenes, political punch
    c   Could this happen? Blurring of fact and fiction, news and hyperreal drama. Ask for memorable scenes, and/or use season two, episode one as example

- What do you think of the moral issues in *Utopia*?

    a   Moral ambiguity, grey areas between good and bad
    b   Violence – makes us feel uncomfortable? Personal boundary?
    c   What would you do? Big moral question left for us to decide, approaching apocalypse? What we can do about it?

Theme 5: reflections

- What is distinctive about *Utopia*?

    a   How, in what way? story, style, visuals, sound, editing, overall feeling? Too complex, too simple? Love the details, too many details?
    b   Does it give you space to think? about characters, story, issues, politics, morality. Through the writing, directing, acting, performance, music and sound?

- How does *Utopia* compare to other content?

    a   Quality of *Utopia* as cinematic, winning music awards, director, writing awards, compared to other cult drama (*Breaking Bad, True Detective, The Walking Dead* …)
    b   Trend in high quality content, beyond television, how do you describe this kind of content? How do you get hold of it? For example friends recommend, download, stream, share?
    c   Watch and listen in other ways? For example prefer to watch with no adverts, or binge watch in your own time, or listen to music separately, comment, review, inspire …?

- What do you think are the reasons for *Utopia's* cancellation?

    a   Drama, summer scheduling, Channel 4, on demand, ratings for TV audience, illegal viewers …
    b   What happens next? In the story, any ideas as to network, resistance, Arby, Wilson?
    c   *Utopia* fan campaigns, bring back *Utopia*, crowdsourcing, the new version in America? …
    d   What message would you give the makers of *Utopia*? Anything else?

Finish: anything else?

Research notes for Got to Dance

For the production research, there were interviews and observations of the auditions, semi-finals and finals for *Got to Dance*, from May to August 2014. A team of four, including creative content consultant Julie Donovan, Annette Hill, Tina Askanius and Koko Kondo conducted the research, sharing the work across the different sites of data collection; 10 production interviews took place with executive and creative producers; 30 interviews were conducted with performers at the auditions, and 10 interviews at the semi-finals and finals, including family and friends there to support dancers. Observations took place front and back stage at the Roundhouse, London, and Earl's Court, London, during a two-week period, resulting in audio recordings, visual and aural data, and fieldnotes.

All of the team took part in participant observations, taking notes, keeping diaries, and taking photographs and short videos as visual aids for the analysis of the data; the team discussed the participant observations at several moments of reflection during and after each production day was over. This continual reflection and analysis of the ongoing fieldwork allowed for flexibility in the data design, as each day the participant observations would be attuned to the production environment and the different kinds of participant at the venues. For example, in relation to the live shows, participant observations involved shifting attention to the backstage rehearsal space for the dance groups alongside the spaces for friends and family which were semi-backstage, and the main venue for audiences. Production practices for the participants, family supporters, and crowd management worked across these production and reception zones. Such observations supported the theory building and analysis of the care structures within the production of a live reality event.

For the audience research, 50 individual and group interviews (1–5 persons) were conducted with live crowds at the semi-finals and finals, in the queues, coffee shops, and on the street, outside and inside the venue. Each interview lasted between 5 and 20 minutes. Recruitment was focused on a range of participants and audiences, including professional dancers, individuals and dance troupes, dance teachers, family groups, people at the live show who received tickets as Sky subscribers, and people who were there to experience the filming of a reality talent show. Interviews were conducted individually and in groups in order to ensure both one-to-one and group interactions. The interviews were designed with a topic guide, including social contexts related to routines surrounding attending the live show, or watching the series at home, and theoretically informed themes such as emotional and critical engagement with the series. Further follow up interviews were conducted with dance schools and at home audience, in order to explore issues raised by the fieldwork in August surrounding the final outcome of the series and its cancellation by the broadcaster. Participant observations of the live shows, where the venue accommodated audiences of 4,000–6,000 each day of filming, followed the same pattern of flexible and pragmatic design, with notes, diaries, visual and aural recordings building a nuanced picture of the experience of live reality television. The interviews and observations served as valuable sources of knowledge construction for live experiences.

For a sample of the fieldwork questions, please see the interview guide (below) designed for the auditions at the London Roundhouse.

Got to Dance, May 2014: notes for fieldwork for auditions

Interviews

Short interviews on the go, from 5 to 15 mins. If you follow up with someone, then take an email and contact again for another interview when the TV series is on air – in person, via Skype.

Mixed interviews with individuals, and groups of friends and dance troupes, famlies and so forth.

Get them to state their name, age, occupation, where they come from. This can be done for each recorded interview.

Consent forms – use these for children, young adults and adults. If you are interviewing anyone under the age of 18 years then ask for permission from a parent or accompanying adult, who can be present and also participate in the interview if they wish.

Key questions

1. What are your reasons for being at the *Got to Dance* auditions? Probe: personal motivations, friends/family urged them, the dance group leader etc.

2. What is your experience so far? Probe: what they expected, what they hope for, how keep up energy, prepare for the audition, support others in their auditions, etc. Are they doing this because of their passion for dance, or just to have a go?

3. Have they auditioned before? For *GTD*, for other reality shows? How do they know what to expect? Is there a *GTD* style of audition? Impression of other contestants?
   Probe: what is it like supporting your family/friends in their auditions? Stay positive, commiserate ...
   What's it like watching the auditions? The crowd, the judges, performances, etc.

4. What do you think of the TV series? Probe: what do they like/dislike? Comments on judges, presenter, other contestants, previous winners, styles of dance, etc. Do they vote, go online, share videos, etc?
   How does *GTD* compare with other talent shows?
   What they like and don't like ... Quality of dance, mix of styles of dance.

Participant observations

Take time to observe the look and feel of the crowds, how people interact, prepare for the auditions, handle nerves, make jokes. How do people interact with the production team? How do they react to other auditions? The venue, space, music, sound, emotions. When the auditions are running, sit and observe them, note the etiquette of the audience, when they cheer, clap, stand up or not, react to the producers, judges,

Research notes for *MasterChef*

The *MasterChef* UK pilot research was conducted from March to May 2014. The data included three interviews with executive producers at Shine on the global format, one production observation of *MasterChef* UK the celebrity version, and 10 audience interviews with individuals and groups of adults, aged 21–55 (social grades B, C1, C2) based in the UK, and website analysis of the official and unofficial *MasterChef* universe. The production interviews and observations were conducted by Julie Donovan and the audience research was conducted by Koko Kondo. The fieldwork questions were designed by Annette Hill.

The *MasterChef Denmark* research used a qualitative approach to producers and audiences, combining individual and group interviews, alongside participant observations. A total of 60 interviews were conducted overall. The fieldwork was conducted by Tina Askanius and the research was designed by Annette Hill.

For the production research, there were interviews and observations of the auditions and semi-finals for *MasterChef Denmark*, from September to November 2014. Thirteen production interviews took place with executive and creative producers. For participants, 27 interviews were conducted with performers at the auditions, and semi-finals, including family and friends there to support contestants. This included 14 males and 11 females, aged 6–69, from a range of professions, such as student, waitress, soldier, accountant, teacher, and pizza baker. Observations took place at the *MasterChef* studio in Copenhagen during a three-day period, resulting in audio recordings and fieldnotes. For the audience research, 20 individual and group interviews (1–3 persons) were conducted with viewers after the season had aired on TV3 in Denmark from April to August 2015. This included 14 females and 6 males, aged 6–69, with a range of professions from shop assistant, musician, engineer, teacher, to unemployed and retired. Each interview lasted between 40 and 60 minutes and took place in homes and coffee shops in western and eastern Denmark, and via Skype and telephone.

The *MasterChef Sweden* research used a qualitative approach to producers and audiences, combining individual and group interviews alongside participant observations. A total of 48 interviews were conducted overall. The fieldwork was conducted by Tina Askanius and the research was designed by Annette Hill.

For the production research, there were interviews and observations of week eight, and post production for *MasterChef Sweden*, from November 2014 to January 2015. Twelve production interviews took place with executive and creative producers. For participants, six interviews were conducted with performers during week eight during breaks from production; the interviewees comprised two males and four females. Observations took place at the *MasterChef* studio in Stockholm during the two-day period of 4–5 November, resulting in audio recordings and fieldnotes; and at the post production offices during 29–30 January, resulting in audio recordings and fieldnotes. For the audience research, individual and group interviews (1–3 persons) were conducted with viewers during and after the season had aired on TV4 in Sweden from March to June 2015. Interviewees comprised 23 females and 7 males, aged 18–50, with a range of professions comprising nurse, student, social worker, bartender, teacher, receptionist and unemployed. Each interview lasted between 40 and 60 minutes and took place in homes, coffee shops and workplaces in Sweden, and in a handful of instances via Skype and telephone.

For a sample of the fieldwork questions please see the interview guide below designed for *MasterChef* audiences in the UK, Denmark and Sweden.

Questions for *MasterChef* audiences

Theme 1: social context/viewing context

- Tell us how you discovered *MasterChef*.

    a Friends, family trailers, social media, reviews?
    b Point of contact with other media – e.g. the direct link between content and newspapers, internet, TV

- How do you watch it?

    a Setting, preparation, any ritual? Describe the atmosphere (at home)…
    b Alone/together
    c After dinner?

- Describe how you like to watch it.

    a E.g. silence, chatting, gossiping, tweeting, updating online as the show is on?
    b Once per week or store up and watch in one big go (pros and cons to both experiences?)
    c Live on TV, catch up?
    d Channel home for *MasterChef* – explore channel brand and context

Theme 2: the look and feel of MasterChef

Show clip: *MasterChef* (Professionals, Amateur, Celebrity)

- What do you like about it? Dislike?

    a General comments, open question, see what comes up
    b Likes, dislikes, love, hate, indifference

- c See one viewer who said only thing they disliked – 'can't taste the food'
- What is the look and feel of the show?
    - a Tone, mood, happy, positive?
    - b Music, colour
    - c Kitchens, studio and on location
    - d Editing, directing
    - e Different sections, e.g. invention test, eliminations, professional kitchen tests
    - f What do you think about when contestants are in the studio, compared to outside challenges, or on location?
- How does it make you feel?
    - a What emotions come up? Positive, negative …
    - b What kind of experience?
    - c Is it about comforting, relaxing TV, the story of the contestant and a life-changing moment?
    - d Or competition, professionalism, the winner of the series?
    - e How does it draw you in? Feels like an invitation to participate? Or a competitive cooking show?
- How would you describe *MasterChef*?
    - a Cookery, reality TV, competition show?
    - b Probe genre, and expectations of viewers

Theme 3: emotions

- Winner of 2012 *MasterChef UK* Shaleen said cooking was her 'heart on a plate'. What do you think of that comment?
    - a Passion for food
    - b Praise from judges, criticism
    - c Memorable moments?
    - d Big tears, big happiness … probe strong emotions in show
    - e The big taste – probe the moment of tasting the food, the reactions of judges and contestants …
    - f Does the show make you happy?
- Is this a show about cooking?
    - a Explore themes in *MasterChef* about fine dining, professional food, good ingredients. Or something else …
    - b About other values, e.g. achievement, praise, professionalism, competition, amateurs as good as professionals …
    - c Does the show feel authentic? As a cookery competition, as an overall experience? Probe what feels real, the emotions, the fairness of the judges, the skills of contestants, other?

Theme 4: personalities

- One viewer said of *MasterChef* 'it is a chance to see ordinary people shine in public' Comment?

    a   Explore amateur/professional chef contestants
    b   How are people represented?
    c   Diversity of contestants
    d   Probe gender, ethnicity, class, age
    e   Does it feel real? Does it feel performed?
    f   What about different contestants? Which ones are you attracted to? Compared to other cookery contestants? E.g. *Bake Off*?

- What do you think to the different personalities?

    a   Judges, in any version
    b   *Celebrity MasterChef*
    c   Attraction to personalities ...?
    d   Professionals, junior ...
    e   Open question, see what comes up across different versions.

Show clips from *MasterChef*

Theme 5: different versions

- Tell us about the different versions of *MasterChef*

    a   Open question, see what comes up for *MasterChef, MasterChef the Professionals, Celebrity MasterChef, Junior MasterChef*
    b   Explore different versions, compared with Australia and America
    c   Other countries? What have viewers seen around the world ...
    d   Does the show feel like home? Feel foreign ...?
    e   Mix of cuisines and cultures
    f   What about when send contestants to other countries?

Theme 6: food

- What do you think of all the TV cooking shows on offer right now?

    a   What are your favourite shows?
    b   How does *MasterChef* compare to these other shows?
    c   Do you make time for your favourites?
    d   Does it make you want to cook? Try out recipes, share tips with others?
    e   Go to restaurants, experience fine dining?
    f   Food as art?
    g   How are you finding out about new cooking TV series – recommendations, social media, reviews? Illegal downloads, catch up?

h   What about other kinds of reality shows?
i   What else do you love, or hate at the moment?
j   Probe television trends …

Finish: anything else?

REFERENCES

Agger, Gunhild. (2013) '*The Killing*: urban topographies of a crime', in *Journal of Popular Television* 1(2): 235–242.
Agger, Gunhild. (2016) 'Nordic noir: location, identity and emotion', in Garcia, Alberto N. (ed.), *Emotions in Contemporary TV Series*, Basingstoke: Palgrave Macmillan, 134–154.
Ahlgren, Camilla. (2015) Interview with Annette Hill, 10 June, for Media Experiences project, audio recording: Lund, Sweden.
Allen, Robert C. (1985) *Speaking of Soap Operas*, Chapel Hill: University of North Carolina Press.
Anderson, Chris. (2008) *The Long Tail*, New York: Hatchett Books.
Andrejevic, Mark. (2004) *Reality TV: The Work of Being Watched*, Lanham, MD: Rowman and Littlefield.
Arvidsson, Adam and Bonini, Tiziano. (2015) 'Valuing audience passions: from Smythe to Tarde', in *European Journal of Cultural Studies* 18(2): 158–173.
Askanius, Tina. (2017) 'Engaging with *The Bridge*: cultural citizenship, cross-border identities and audiences', in *European Journal of Cultural Studies*, online first 8 September 2017.
Athique, Adrian. (2016) *Transnational Audiences: Media Reception on a Global Scale*, London: Wiley Blackwell.
Austen, Patrick. (2014) Interview with Annette Hill, 22 January, for Media Experiences project, audio recording: Lund, Sweden.
Austen, Patrick. (2015) Interview with Annette Hill, 16 August, for Media Experiences project, audio recording: Lund, Sweden.
Bakare, Lanre. (2017) 'Paradise found: *Utopia's* remake is welcome dose of TV justice', in the *Guardian*, 24 April 2018, accessed online, https://www.theguardian.com/tv-and-radio/2018/apr/24/utopia-remake-amazon-gillian-flynn-channel-4
Banet-Weiser, Sarah. (2013) *Authentic TM: The Politics of Ambivalence in a Brand Culture*, New York: New York University Press.
Barker, Tim. (2015) Interview with Annette Hill, 21 April, for Media Experiences project, audio recording: London, UK.
Barthes, Roland. (1979) *The Eiffel Tower and Other Mythologies* (translated by Richard Howard), New York: Hill and Wang.

Baudrillard, Jean. (1983) *Simulations*, New York: Semiotext(e).
Bazely, Pat. (2013) *Qualitative Data Analysis*, London: Sage.
BBC (2017) BBC Sports news, no author cited, accessed online 27 April 2018, https://www.bbc.co.uk/sport/football/40483486
Bennett, James. (2011) *Television Personalities: Stardom and the Small Screen*, London: Routledge.
Berlant, Lauren. (2011) *Cruel Optimism*, Durham, NC: Duke University Press.
Bernstein, Carolyn. (2014) Interview with Annette Hill, 9 November, for Media Experiences project, audio recording: Lund, Sweden.
Bignell, Jonathan. (2005). *Popular Television Drama: Critical Perspectives*, Manchester: Manchester University Press.
Biltereyst, Daniël and Lennart Soberon. (2016) 'Formatting reality: on reality television as a genre, a meta-genre and a larger tendency in contemporary television culture', in Moran, Albert, and Jensen, Pia Majbritt (eds), *New Patterns in Global Television Formats*, London: Intellect, 47–62.
Biressi, Anita, and Heather Nunn. (2013) *Class and British Culture*, London: Palgrave Macmillan.
Blomgren, Lars. (2014) Interview with Annette Hill, 17 September, for Media Experiences project, audio recording: Lund, Sweden.
Blomgren, Lars. (2015) Interview with Annette Hill, 14 September, for Media Experiences project, audio recording: Malmö, Sweden.
Bolin, Göran. (2009) 'Television textuality: textual forms in live television programming', in *Nordicom Review* 30(1): 37–53.
Bolin, Göran. (2017) *Media Generations: Experience, Identity and Mediatised Social Change*, London: Routledge.
Bolin, Göran and Forsman, Michael. (2002) *Bingolotto, Produktion, Text, Reception*, Södertörn, Sweden: Södertörn Press.
Bollas, Christopher. (2003) *Being a Character*, London: Routledge.
Bonner, Frances. (2011) *Personality Presenters: Television's Intermediaries with Viewers*, London: Routledge.
Bowrey, Katherine. (2012) 'The manufacture of "authentic" buzz and the legal relations of *MasterChef*', in Hunter, Dan, Lobato, Ramon, Richardson, Megan and Thomas, Julian (eds), *Amateur Media: Social, Cultural and Legal Perspectives*, London: Routledge, 73–93.
Boyle, Raymond, and Kelly, Lisa. (2012) *The Television Entrepreneurs*, Aldershot: Ashgate.
Bruhn, Hanne. (2015) 'The qualitative interview in media production studies', in Paterson, C., Lee, D., Sahar, A. and Zoellner, A. (eds) *Advancing Media Production Research: Shifting Sites, Methods and Politics*, Basingstoke: Palgrave Macmillan, 131–146.
Buonanno, Milly. (2006) *The Age of TV: Experiences and Theories*, London: Intellect.
Calabrese, Andrew. (2017) 'Human need as a justification for communication rights', in *The Communication Review* 20(2): 98–121.
Calhoun, Craig and Sennett, Richard (eds) (2007) *Practising Culture*, London: Routledge.
Carpentier, Nico. (2011) *Media and Participation: A Site of Ideological-Democratic Struggle*, Bristol: Intellect.
Chambers, Deborah. (2016) *Changing Media, Homes and Households: Cultures, Technologies and Meanings*, Basingstoke: Palgrave Macmillan.
Childress, Clayton. (2017) *Under the Cover: The Creation, Production, and Reception of a Novel*, Princeton, NJ: Princeton University Press.
Coleman, Stephen. (2010) 'Acting powerfully: performances of power in *Big Brother*', in *International Journal of Cultural Studies* 13(2): 127–146.
Collins, Andy. (2015) Interview with Julie Donovan, 22 April, for Media Experiences project, audio recording: London, UK.
Corner, John. (1995) *Television Form and Public Address*, London: Edward Arnold.

Corner, John. (1997) 'Television in theory', in *Media, Culture and Society* 19(2): 247–262.
Corner, John. (2011) *Theorising Media*, Manchester: Manchester University Press.
Corner, John. (2015) Email correspondence with A. Hill, 15 March.
Corner, John. (2017) 'Afterword', in *Media Industries* 4(1): 1–6.
Corner, John and Roscoe, Jane. (2016) 'Outside and inside television: a dialogue on "value"', in *Journal of Media Practice* 17(2–3): 157–167.
Crisp, Virginia. (2014) 'To name a thief: constructing the deviant pirate', in Fredriksson, Martin and Arvanitakis, James (eds), *Piracy: Leakages from Modernity*, Los Angeles, CA: Litwin Books.
Crisp, Virginia. (2015) *Pirates and Professionals: Film Distribution in the Digital Age*, London: Palgrave.
Dahlgren, Peter. (2009) *Media and Political Engagement*, Cambridge: Cambridge University Press.
Dahlgren, Peter. (2013) *The Political Web: Participation, Media, and Alternative Democracy*, Basingstoke: Palgrave Macmillan.
Dahlgren, Peter and Hill, Annette. (forthcoming 2018) 'Engagement matters: mapping the dynamics of political and cultural engagement', unpublished journal article.
Dayan, Daniel and Katz, Elihu. (1992) *Media Events: The Live Broadcasting of History*, Cambridge, MA: Harvard University Press.
Deery, June. (2015) *Reality TV*, Cambridge: Polity.
De Kosnick, Abigail. (2016) *Rogue Archives: Digital Cultural Memory and Media Fandom*. London and Cambridge MA: MIT Press.
Deleuze, Gilles and Guattari, Felix. (1977) *Anti-Oedipus: Capitalism and Schizophrenia* (translated by R. Hurley, M. Seem and H.R. Lowe), New York: Viking Press.
Denison, Rayna. (2011) 'Anime fandom and the liminal spaces between fan creativity and piracy', in *International Journal of Cultural Studies* 14(5): 449–466.
Donovan, Julie. (2013) Interview with executive producer of *MasterChef*, 12 October, for Media Experiences project, audio recording: London, UK.
Doyle, Gillian. (2018) 'Television production: configuring for sustainability in the digital era', in *Media, Culture and Society* 40(2): 285–295.
Ellis, John. (1982) *Visible Fictions*, London: Routledge and Kegan Paul.
Ellis, John. (2000) *Seeing Things*, London: I. B. Taurus.
Endemol Shine. (2018) Official website, accessed 30 April, www.endemolshinegroup.com/about/
Enli, Gunn. (2015) *Mediated Authenticity: How the Media Constructs Reality*, New York: Peter Lang.
Eriksson, Maria, Fliescher, Rasmus, Johannson, Anna, Snickers, Pelle and Vonderau Patrick. (2018) *Spotify Teardown: Inside the Blackbox of Streaming Music*, Boston: MIT Press.
Esser, Andrea. (2010) 'Television formats: primetime staple, global market', in *Popular Communication* Vol 8: 273–292.
Evans, Elizabeth Jane. (2011) '"Carnaby Street, 10 a.m.": *Kate Modern* and the ephemeral dynamics of online drama', in Grainge, Paul (ed.), *Ephemeral Media: Transitory Screen Culture from Television to YouTube*, London: BFI, 156–174.
Forsberg, Uno. (2015) Interview with Annette Hill, 14 April, for Media Experiences project, audio recording: Stockholm, Sweden.
Frosh, Paul and Pinchevski, Amit. (2018) 'Media and events after media events', in *Media, Culture and Society* 40(1): 135–138.
Frosh, Stephen. (2011) *Feelings*, London: Routledge.
Gam, Søren. (2013) Interview with Annette Hill, 22 January, for Media Experiences project, audio recording: Lund, Sweden.
Garcia, Alberto N. (ed.) (2016) *Emotions in Contemporary TV Series*, Basingstoke: Palgrave Macmillan.
Georgsson, Henrik. (2015) Interview with Annette Hill, 2 July, for Media Experiences project, audio recording: Lund, Sweden.

Giddens, Anthony. (1991) *Modernity and Self-identity: Self and Society in the Late Modern Age*, Cambridge: Polity.
Gilbert, Gerard. (2015) 'The warm-up men and women: who do Graham Norton and Alan Carr rely on to get big laughs?', in *The Independent*, 29 August. Accessed online 7 April 2018, https://www.independent.co.uk/arts-entertainment/comedy/features/the-warm-up-men-and-women-who-do-graham-norton-and-alan-carr-rely-on-to-get-big-laughs-10476776.html
Goffman, Erving. (1959) *Presentation of the Self in Everyday Life*, New York: Anchor.
Goldberg, David. (2018) 'Where to watch the season premiere of *RuPaul's Drag Race* in NYC'. *Time Out New York*, 21 March, accessed online 30 April 2018, https://www.timeout.com/newyork/news/where-to-watch-the-season-premiere-of-rupauls-drag-race-in-nyc-032118
Goodall, Jane. (2008) *Stage Presence*, London: Routledge.
Gorton, K. (2009) *Media Audiences: Television, Meaning and Emotion*, Edinburgh: Edinburgh University Press.
Grainge, Paul. (ed.) (2011) *Ephemeral Media: Transitory Screen Culture from Television to YouTube*, London: British Film Institute.
Gray, Anne. (2003) *Research Practice for Cultural Studies: Ethnographic Methods for Lived Cultures*, London: Sage.
Gray, Duncan. (2014) Interview with Julie Donovan, 19 September, for Media Experiences project, audio recording: London, UK.
Gray, Jonathan. (2008) *Television Entertainment*, London and New York: Routledge.
Gray, Jonathan. (2010) *Show Sold Separately: Promos, Spoilers and Other Media Paratexts*, New York: New York University Press.
Gregg, M. and Seigworth, G.J. (eds) (2010) *The Affect Theory Reader*, Durham, NC: Duke University Press.
Grindstaff, Laura. (2013) 'DI(t)Y, reality-style: the cultural work of ordinary celebrity', in Ouelette, Laurie (ed.) *A Companion to Reality Television*, London: Wiley Blackwell, 324–344.
Gripsrud, Jostein. (1998) 'Television broadcasting flow: key metaphors in TV theory', in Geraghty, Christine and Lusted, David (eds), *The Television Studies Book*, London: Arnold, 17–32.
Grossberg, Lawrence. (1987) 'The in-difference of television', in *Screen* 28(2): 28–45.
Hall, Stuart. (1980) 'Cultural studies: the two paradigms', in *Media, Culture and Society* 2(1): 57–72.
Hammersley, Martin. (1992) *What's Wrong with Ethnography: Methodological Explorations*, London: Routledge.
Hansen, Kim Toft and Waade, Anne-Marit. (2017) *Locating Nordic Noir*, Basingstoke: Palgrave Macmillan.
Hearn, Alison. (2010) 'Reality television, *The Hills*, and the limits of the immaterial labour thesis', in *triple C* 8(1): 60–76.
Helin, Sofia. (2015) Interview with Annette Hill, 10 September, for Media Experiences project, audio recording: Lund, Sweden.
Heller, Dana. (2012) '"Calling out around the world": the global appeal of reality dance formats', in Oren, Tasha and Shahaf, Sharon (eds), *Global Television Formats: Understanding Television Across Borders*, London: Routledge, 39–55.
Heritage, Stuart. (2017) 'Netflix: which shows are being binged the fastest?' 19 October, accessed online 20 February 2018, https://www.theguardian.com/tv-and-radio/2017/oct/18/which-netflix-shows-are-being-binged-the-fastest
Hermes, Joke. (2005) *Re-reading Popular Culture*, London: Blackwell.
Hermes, Joke. (2018) 'Freedom and stricture in *RuPaul's Drag Race*', in Media Freedom international symposium, 15 March 2018, Lund, Sweden, unpublished research paper.

Hesmondhalgh, David and Baker, Sarah. (2011) *Creative Labour*, London: Routledge.
Hill, Annette. (2005) *Reality TV: Audiences and Popular Factual Television*, London: Routledge.
Hill, Annette. (2007) *Restyling Factual TV: Audiences and News, Documentary and Reality Genres*, London: Routledge.
Hill, Annette. (2015) *Reality TV: Key Ideas*, London: Routledge.
Hill, Annette. (2016a) 'Push-pull dynamics: producers and audiences for television drama *The Bridge*', in *Television and New Media* 17(8).
Hill, Annette. (2016b) 'Sense of place: *The Bridge* international drama format', in Moran, Albert, and Jensen, Pia Majbritt (eds), *New Patterns in Global Television Formats*, London: Intellect, 281–294.
Hill, Annette. (2017a) 'Reality TV engagement: reality TV Producers and audiences for talent format *Got to Dance*', in *Media Industries*, Volume 4, issue 1 May 2017: 1–17.
Hill, Annette. (2017b) 'Reality TV crime programmes', in Rafter, Nicole and Brown, Michelle (eds), *Oxford Research Encyclopedia of Crime, Media and Popular Culture*, Oxford: Oxford University Press, 1–17.
Hill, Annette. (2018) 'Saga's story: emotional engagement in the production and reception of Nordic crime drama *The Bridge*', in Hansen, Kim Toft, Turnbull, Sue and Peacock, Steven (eds), *European Television Crime Drama and Beyond*, Basingstoke: Palgrave Macmillan, 1–17.
Hill, Annette and Askanius, Tina. (2015) *MasterChef Denmark* and *MasterChef Sweden*, Internal Reports, Lund: Lund University Press.
Hill, Annette, Askanius, Tina and Kondo, Koko. (2018 forthcoming) 'Live reality television: care structures for live experiences', in *Critical Studies in Television*.
Hill, Annette and Steemers, Jeanette. (2011) 'Big formats. small nations: does size matter?', in Lowe, Gregory Ferrell, and Nissen, Christian (eds), *Small Among Giants: Television Broadcasting in Smaller Countries*, Gothenberg: Nordicom, 203–218.
Hill, Annette and Steemers, Jeanette. (2017) 'Introduction to media engagement', in special section of *Media Industries* 4(1): 1–5.
Hill, Annette, Steemers, Jeanette, Roscoe, Jane, Donovan, Julie and Wood, Douglas. (2017) 'A dialogue across industry and academia', in *Media Industries* 4(1): 1–15.
Hill, Annette and Turnbull, Sue. (2017) 'Nordic noir crime drama', in Rafter, Nicole and Brown, Michelle (eds), *Oxford Research Encyclopedia of Crime, Media and Popular Culture*, Oxford: Oxford University Press, 1–17.
Hills, Matt. (2002) *Fan Cultures*, London: Routledge.
Hochschild, Arlie. (2003) *The Commercialisation of Intimate Life: Notes from Home and Work*, Berkeley: University of California Press.
Holdham, Stuart. (2014) Interview with Julie Donovan, 26 September, for Media Experiences project, audio recording: London, UK.
Holdham, Stuart. (2015) Interview with Julie Donovan, 5 February, for Media Experiences project, audio recording: London, UK.
Holmes, Su and Jermyn, Deborah. (2003) *Understanding Reality Television*, London: Routledge.
Holmes, Su. (2004) '"But this time you choose!": approaching the "interactive" audience in reality TV', in *International Journal of Cultural Studies* 3(2): 213–231.
Holt, Jennifer and Sanson, Kevin (eds) (2014) *Connected Viewing: Selling, Streaming and Sharing Media in the Digital Age*, New York: Routledge.
Hu, K. (2005) 'The power of circulation: digital technologies and the online Chinese fans of Japanese TV drama', in *Inter-Asia Cultural Studies* 6(2): 171–186.
Hyde, Marina. (2016) 'Gregg Wallace falls out of the spotlight and into the deep fat fryer', in the *Guardian*, accessed online 29 October 2017, https://www.theguardian.com/lifeandstyle/lostin showbiz/2016/sep/01/gregg-wallace-falls-out-of-the-spotlight-and-into-the-deep-fat-fryer

Ingold, Tim. (2011) *Being Alive: Essays on Movement, Knowledge and Description*, London: Routledge.
Ingold, Tim and Vergunst, Jo Lee. (2008) *Ways of Walking: Ethnography and Practice on Foot*, London: Routledge.
Jackson, Lizzie. (2013) 'Participating publics: implications for production practices at the BBC', in *Public Media Management for the Twenty-First Century: Creativity, Innovation, and Interaction*, London: Routledge, 360–385
Jenkins, Henry. (2006) *Fans, Bloggers, and Gamers: Exploring Participatory Culture*, New York: New York University Press.
Jensen, Pia Majbritt and Waade, Anne Marit. (2013) 'Nordic noir challenging "the language of advantage": setting, light and language as production values in Danish television series', in *Journal of Popular Culture* 1(2): 259–265.
Jensen, Pia Majbritt, Nielsen, Jakob Isak and Waade, Anne Marit. (2016) 'When public service drama travels: the internationalization of Danish television drama and the associated production funding models', in *The Journal of Popular Television* 4(1): 91–108.
Johnson, Catherine. (2011) *Branding Television*, London: Routledge.
Johnson, Catherine and Turnock, Rob. (2005) *ITV Cultures: Independent Television over Fifty Years*, Milton Keynes: Open University Press.
Karaganis, Joe (ed.) (2011) *Media Piracy in Emerging Economies*. USA: Social Science Research Council.
Kaufmann, Vincent. (2002) *Re-thinking Mobility*, London: Ashgate.
Kelly, Dennis. (2015) Interview with Annette Hill, 21 April, for Media Experiences project, audio recording: London, UK.
Kilborn, Richard. (2003) *Staging the Real: Factual TV Programming in the Age of Big Brother*, Manchester: Manchester University Press.
Kissell, Rick. (2013) 'FX's *The Bridge* at the center of the DVR revolution', *Variety*, 2 October 2013, accessed online 20 October 2014,http://variety.com/2013/tv/news/fxs-the-bridge-at-the-center-of-the-dvr-revolution-1200688440/
Klinger, Barbara. (2010) 'Contraband cinema: piracy, *Titanic* and Central Asia', in *Cinema Journal: Society for Cinema and Media Studies* 49(2): 106–124.
Kohen, Melanie. (2013) '"This was just a melodramatic crapfest": American TV critics' reception of *The Killing*', in *Journal of Popular Television* 1(2): 267–272.
Landström, Anders. (2013) Interview with Annette Hill, 5 November, for Media Experiences project, audio recording: Lund, Sweden.
Landström, Anders. (2014) Interview with Annette Hill, 17 September, for Media Experiences project, audio recording: Lund, Sweden.
Larkin, Brian. (2004) 'Degraded images, distorted sounds: Nigerian videos and the infrastructure of piracy', in *Public Culture* 16(2): 289–315.
Lascia, J.D. (2005) *Darknet: Hollywood's War against the Digital Generation*, Hoboken, NJ: Wiley and Sons.
Lawson, Mark. (2018) 'Box, set and match: how on-demand became TV's new battleground', in the *Guardian*, 25 May, accessed online 1 June 2018, https://www.theguardian.com/tv-and-radio/2018/may/25/box-set-and-match-how-on-demand-became-tvs-new-battleground
Layton, Danny. (2015) Interview with Annette Hill and Julie Donovan, 22 April, for Media Experiences project, audio recording: London, UK.
Lee, Hye Jin and Andrejevic, Mark. (2014) 'Second-screen theory: from the democratic surround to the digital enclosure', in Holt, Jennifer and Sanson, Kevin (eds), *Connected Viewing: Selling, Streaming and Sharing Media in the Digital Age*, London: Routledge, 40–61.

Leonard, Sean. (2004) 'Progress against the law: fan distribution, copyright, and the explosive growth of Japanese animation', vol. 4, issue 2 of papers in the MIT Japan Program, Cambridge, MA: MIT Press.
Lindsay, Jeff. (2010) *Dexter Is Delicious*, London: Orion.
Llamas-Rodriguez, Juan. (2016) 'Tunnelling media: geoblocking and online border resistance', in Lobato, Ramon and Meese, James (eds), *Geoblocking and Global Video Culture*, Amsterdam: Institute of Network Cultures, 42–51.
Lobato, Ramon. (2012) *Shadow Economies of Cinema: Mapping Informal Film Distribution*, London: British Film Institute.
Lobato, Ramon. (2017) 'Streaming services and the changing global geography of television', in Warf, B. (ed.), *The Handbook of Geographies of Technology*, Cheltenham: Edward Elgar, 178–194.
Lobato, Ramon and Meese, James (eds) (2016) *Geoblocking and Global Video Culture*, Amsterdam: Institute of Network Cultures.
Lobato, Ramon and Thomas, Julian. (2015) *The Informal Media Economy*, Cambridge: Polity.
Locker, Melissa. (2015) 'Warm-up comics: the funniest people in TV who are never on TV: meet the people who get the crowd roaring before the cameras start to roll', in *Vanity Fair*, 8 October, accessed online 7 April 2018, https://www.vanityfair.com/hollywood/2015/10/tv-warm-up-comics
Lotz, Amanda. (2014) *The Television Will Be Revolutionized*, 2nd edn, New York: NYU Press.
Lunt, Peter. (2014) 'Reality television, public service and public live: a critical theory perspective', in Ouellette, Laurie (ed.), *A Companion to Reality Television*, Chichester: Wiley Blackwell, 501–515.
Lunt, Peter and Stenner, Paul. (2005) '*The Jerry Springer Show* as an emotional public sphere', in *Media, Culture and Society* 27(1): 59–81.
Macfarlane, Robert. (2012) *The Old Ways: A Journey on Foot*, London: Penguin.
Mann, Colin. (2016a) 'Australia: 66% of SVoD users also download illegally', in *Advanced Television*, 3 February, available at: https://advanced-television.com/2016/02/03/australia-66-of-svod-users-also-download-illegally/
Mann, Colin. (2016b) '25 per cent of Europeans stream illegally', in *Advanced Television*, accessed online 4 June 2016, https://advanced-television.com/2016/04/06/25-of-young-europeans-access-online-content-illegally/
Markey, Patrick. (2014) Interview with Annette Hill, 8 October, for Media Experiences project, audio recording: Lund, Sweden.
Marriot, Stephanie. (2007) *Live Television: Time, Space and the Broadcast Event*, London: Sage.
Massey, Doreen. (1994) *Space, Place and Gender*, Minneapolis: University of Minnesota Press.
Mattelart, Christian. (2016) 'The changing geographies of pirate transnational audiovisual flows', in *International Journal of Communication* 10, 3503–3521.
Mayer, Vicki. (2011) *Below the Line: Producers and Production Studies in the New Television Economy*, Durham, NC: Duke University Press.
Mayer, Vicki, Banks, Miranda, and Caldwell, John Thornton (eds) (2009) *Production Studies*, London and New York: Routledge.
Mazmanian, Melissa. (2016) 'Book review: *In the Meantime: Temporality and Cultural Politics*', in *ILR Review*, Cornell University, 69(2): 510–512.
McCabe, Janet and Akass, Kimm. (2007) *Quality TV: Contemporary American Television and Beyond*, London: I.B. Tauris.
McCormick, Rich. (2015) '*Game of Thrones* was 2015's most torrented TV show', in *The Verge*, 28 December, available at: https://www.theverge.com/2015/12/28/10672708/game-of-thrones-most-pirated-show-2015

McDonald, Paul. (2007) *Video and DVD Industries*, London: BFI Publishing.
McDonald, Paul. (2018, forthcoming) 'Pirate-states: US media industries and the geography of IP infringement', in special issue of *International Journal of Cultural Studies*, guest edited by Joke Hermes and Annette Hill.
McGrath, John. (2004) *Loving Big Brother: Surveillance, Culture and Performance Space*, London: Routledge.
McVey, Cynthia. (2014) Interview with Julie Donovan, 7 May, for Media Experiences project, audio recording: London, UK.
Meyrowitz, Joshua. (1985) *No Sense of Place: The Impact of Electronic Media on Social Behaviour*, Oxford: Oxford University Press.
Mittell, Jason. (2004) *Genre and Television: From Cop Shows to Cartoons in American Culture*, London and New York: Routledge.
Mittell, Jason. (2015) *Complex TV: The Poetics of Contemporary Story-telling*, New York: Routledge.
Møller, Christian. (2018) 'Methodological and ethical complications of mobile research', in Mobile Socialities International Workshop, 12–13 April 2018, Lund University, Sweden. Unpublished research paper.
Moores, Shaun. (2008) 'Conceptualising place in a world of flows', in *Connectivity, Networks and Flows: Conceptualizing Contemporary Communications*, Cresskill, NJ: Hampton Press, 183–200.
Moores, Shaun. (2012) *Media, Place and Mobility*, New York: Palgrave Macmillan.
Moran, Albert and Aveyard, Karina. (2014) 'The place of television programme formats', in *Continuum: Journal of Media and Cultural Studies* 28(1): 18–27.
Moran, Joe. (2013) *Armchair Nation: An Intimate History of Britain in Front of the TV*, London: Profile Books.
Morse, Margaret. (1990) 'An ontology of everyday distraction: the freeway, the mall, the television', in Mellancamp, Patricia (ed.), *Logics of Television*, London: British Film Institute, 193–221.
Munden, Mark. (2015) Interview with Annette Hill, 23 April and 30 April, for Media Experiences project, audio recording: London, UK and Forserum, Sweden.
Nani, Alessandro. (2018 forthcoming) Ph.D. thesis on public service television, audiences and crossmedia, University of Tartu.
Napoli, Phillip. (2010) *Audience Evolution*, New York: Columbia University Press.
Nelson, Robin. (2016) 'The emergence of "affect" in contemporary TV fictions', in Garcia, Alberto N. (ed.), *Emotions in Contemporary TV Series*, Basingstoke: Palgrave Macmillan.
Nestingen, Andrew and Arvas, Paula (eds) (2011) *Scandinavian Crime Fiction*, Cardiff: University of Wales Press.
Ngai, Sianne. (2005) *Ugly Feelings*, Cambridge MA and London: Harvard University Press.
Nowotny, Helga. (2018) *An Orderly Mess*, Prague: Central European University Press.
Oren, Tasha. (2011) 'Reiteration texts and global imagination', in *Global Television Formats: Understanding Television Across Borders*, New York: Routledge, 366–381.
Oren, Tasha. (2013) 'On the line: format, cooking and competition as television values', in *Critical Studies in Television* 8(2): 20–35.
Oren, Tasha and Shahaf, Sharon (eds) (2011) *Global Television Formats: Understanding Television Across Borders*, New York: Routledge.
Palmer, Gareth. (2003) *Discipline and Liberty: Television and Governance*, Manchester: Manchester University Press.
Pålsson, Adam. (2015) Interview with Annette Hill, 10 September, for Media Experiences project, audio recording: Lund, Sweden.
Parks, Lisa and Starosielski, Nicole. (2015) *Signal Traffic: Critical Studies of Media Infrastructures*, Urbana: University of Illinois Press.

Papacharissi, Zizzi. (2010) *A Private Sphere: Democracy in a Digital Age*, Cambridge: Polity Press.
Perlow, Bob. (2016) *The Warm Up Guy: Bob Perlow*, New York: Pelican Publishing.
Peterson, R.A. (2005) 'In search of authenticity', in *Journal of Management Studies* 42(5): 1083–1098.
Petrie, Alistair. (2015) Interview with Annette Hill, 31 March, for Media Experiences project, audio recording: Forserum, Sweden.
Plantinga, Carl. (2009) *Moving Viewers: American Film and the Spectator's Experience*, Berkeley: University of California Press.
Plunket, John. (2014) 'BBC4 goes weird and wonderful with abstract idents and new shows', in the *Guardian*, Monday 9 September, accessed online 30 April 2018, https://www.theguardian.com/media/2014/sep/08/bbc4-abstract-idents-new-shows-cassian-harrison
Price, Rob. (2015) 'Google gets 2.2 million piracy takedown requests every day', in *Business Insider*, accessed online 30 April 2018, http://uk.businessinsider.com/google-2-million-daily-piracy-takedown-requests-transparency-report-copyright-2015-11
Rath, Claus-Dieter. (1985) 'The invisible network: television as an institution in everyday life', in Drummond, Philip and Paterson, Richard (eds), *Television in Transition*, London: British Film Institute, 199–204.
Redvall, Eva Nordrup. (2013) *Writing and Producing Television Drama in Denmark*, London: Palgrave Macmillan.
Revoir, Paul. (2015) 'BBC iPlayer "watched by more than 60 million people outside the UK for free"', in the *Guardian*, accessed online 21 July 2015, https://www.theguardian.com/media/2015/jul/21/bbc-iplayer-uk-vpn-proxy-server
Rochlin, Margy. (2013) 'Border mystery, moved to a new border', in *New York Times*, 5 July, accessed 20 October 2014, www.nytimes.com/2013/07/07/arts/television/the-bridge-fx-series-is-set-on-us-mexico-border.html?pagewanted=all&_r=0
Rogers, Simon. (2015) Interview with Annette Hill and Julie Donovan, 22 April, for Media Experiences project, audio recording: London, UK.
Rose, Gillian. (2016) *Visual Methodologies*, 4th edn, London: Sage.
Sandvoss, Cornell. (2005) *Fans: The Mirror of Consumption*, Cambridge: Polity.
Scannell, Paddy. (1996) *Radio, Television and Modern Life*, London: Wiley Blackwell.
Scannell, Paddy. (2007) *Media and Communication*, London: Sage.
Scannell, Paddy. (2014) *Television and the Meaning of 'Live': An Enquiry into the Human Situation*, Cambridge: Polity Press.
Seale, Clive. (1999) *The Quality of Qualitative Research*, London: Sage.
Seale, Clive, Gobo, Giampietro, Gubrium, Jaber F. and Silverman, David (eds) (2007) *Qualitative Research Practice*, London: Sage.
Selznick, B. (2008) *Global Television: Co-Producing Culture*, Philadelphia, PA: Temple University Press.
Sennett, Richard. (2002) *Respect*, London: Penguin.
Sharma, Devika and Tygstrup, Fredrik (eds) (2015) *Structures of Feeling: Affectivity and the Study of Culture*, Munich and Boston: de Gruyter.
Sharma, Sarah. (2014) *In the Meantime: Temporality and Cultural Politics*, Durham, NC: Duke University Press.
Silverstone, Roger. (1999) *Why Study the Media?* London: Sage.
Skeggs, Beverly, and Wood, Helen. (2012) *Reacting to Reality Television: Performance, Audience and Value*, London: Routledge.
Steemers, Jeanette. (2016) 'International distribution of UK television content', in *Television and New Media* 17(8): 734–753.
Stevenson, Jeff. (2015) Interview with Julie Donovan, 28 May, for Media Experiences project, audio recording: London, UK.

Stewart, Kathleen. (2007) *Ordinary Affects*, Durham, NC: Duke University Press.
Strangelove, Michael. (2015) *Post TV: Piracy, Cord Cutting and the Future of Television*, Toronto: University of Toronto Press.
Szerszynski, Bronislaw, Heim, Wallace and Waterton, Claire (eds) (2004) *Nature Performed*, London: Wiley Blackwell.
Tapia de Veer, Cristobal. (2015) Interview with Jose Luis Urueta, 17 December, for Media Experiences project, audio recording: Malmö, Sweden.
Taylor, Charles. (2004) *Modern Social Imaginaries*, Durham, NC and London: Duke University Press.
Thompson, Marie. (2017) *Beyond Unwanted Sound: Noise, Affect and Aesthetic Moralism*, London: Bloomsbury.
Thornham, Sue and Purvis, Tony. (2005) *Television Drama*, Basingstoke and New York: Palgrave Macmillan.
Turnbull, Sue. (2014a) 'A suitable job for woman: women, work and the television crime drama', in *Continuum: Journal of Media and Cultural Studies* 28(2): 226–234.
Turnbull, Sue. (2014b) *The TV Crime Genre*, Edinburgh: Edinburgh University Press.
Vannini, Phillip, Waskul, Dennis and Gottschalk, Simon. (2013) *The Senses in Self, Society, and Culture: A Sociology of the Senses*, London: Routledge.
Vincent, Andre. (2015) Interview with Julie Donovan, 28 May, for Media Experiences project, audio recording: London, UK.
Vonderau, Patrick. (2014) 'Beyond piracy: understanding digital markets', in Holt, Jennifer and Sanson, Kevin (eds), *Connected Viewing: Selling, Streaming and Sharing Media in the Digital Age*, London: Routledge, 99–123.
Waade, Anne Marit and Jensen, Pia Majbritt (2013) 'Nordic noir production values', in *Academic Quarterly* 7(2): 188–201 .
Wells, Alex. (2015) Interview with Annette Hill and Julie Donovan, 22 April, for Media Experiences project, audio recording: London, UK.
Wenger, Piers. (2015) Interview with Annette Hill, 31 March, for Media Experiences project, audio recording: Forserum, Sweden.
Wetherell, Margaret. (2012) *Affect and Emotion: A New Social Science Understanding*, London: Sage.
Williams, Raymond. (1974 [2003]) *Television: Technology and Cultural Form*, London: Routledge.
Williams, Raymond. (1978) 'Structures of feeling', *Marxism and Literature*, Oxford: Oxford University Press.
Williams, Raymond. (1979) *Culture and Society: 1780–1950*. Harmondsworth: Penguin.
Williams, Raymond. (1981) *Culture*, London: Fontana.
Williams, Raymond and Orrom, Michael. (1964) *Preface to Film*, Ann Arbor: Film Drama and University of Michigan Press.
Wilson, Karen. (2015) Interview with Annette Hill and Julie Donovan, 22 April, for Media Experiences project, audio recording: London, UK.
Wood, Douglas. (2016) Interview with Annette Hill, 5 May, for Media Experiences project, audio recording: London, UK.
Wray Rogers, Bekki. (2015) Interview with Annette Hill, 22 April, for Media Experiences project, audio recording: London, UK.
Zelizer, Viviana. (2013) *Economic Lives: How Culture Shapes the Economy*, Princeton, NJ: Princeton University Press.

INDEX

affects 56–7, 69, 78; affective climate 175; affective patterns 61; affective practices 60–1, 65–8, 119
Agger, Gunhild 77
Aheme, Caroline 170
Ahlgren, Camilla 80, 83, 88, 91
Allen, Robert C. 78
Amazon 186
Amazon Prime 28
AMC 5, 97, 119
Amos, Steven 171
Andersson, Roy 112
Anti-Counterfeiting Trade Agreement 96
Applause Store 164–5, 176
Armchair Nation 32
Arthur, James 147
Arvidsson, Adam 125
Askanius, Tina 2, 7, 16–17, 19, 23, 39, 49, 73, 87, 122, 128–30, 139, 145, 149, 151–3, 156, 158, 164, 172, 176, 185, 187
Athique, Adrian 33–4
audiences: illegal audiences 94–120; imagining audiences 32; as metaphors 32–4; as pathfinders 184–92
Austen, Patrick 25, 76–7, 79–80, 82–3
authenticity 138–40, 150, 153; mediated authenticity 140–2; storytelling authenticity 151–5
Aveyard, Karen 21–2

Banjo, Ashley 65
Barker, Tim 113
Barrymore 169

Barthes, Roland 38, 50, 52, 72, 82–3, 93, 191–2
BBC 8, 22, 64, 96, 98, 133, 141, 147, 157, 163, 165, 169–70, 180;
BBC1 143, 165–6;
BBC2 150, 171;
BBC4 42, 47
Being Alive 190
Berlant, Lauren 180
Big Brother 8, 17, 62–3, 138, 143
Bignell, Jonathan 142
Bingolotto 15
Birds of a Feather 169
Black Mirror 104, 119, 180
Blomgren, Lars 26, 91
Bolin, Göran 174
Bollas, Christopher 75
Bonini, Tiziano 125
Bonner, Frances 143, 166–7
Borgen 76
Bowrey, Katherine 147
Boyle, Susan 65
Breaking Bad 5
Bridge, The 1, 5, 9, 16–18, 20–1, 26, 30–1, 39–40, 42–4, 47–8, 50–2, 72–3, 184, 188
Britain's Got Talent 64–5, 67–8, 141–2, 163, 178
British Film Institute 8
Broadcaster Audience Research Board 68, 134
Broadchurch 17
Bron/Broen 2, 5, 7, 12, 21, 25, 39–42, 46–50, 51, 72–6, 79–93, 185, 188, 191–2;

bootcamp 48–50; Larsson, Emil 92; Norén, Saga 12, 20, 40, 72–4, 78–9, 81–3, 87–91, 93; Rohde, Martin 79, 89–90
BT Sport 96
Buonanno, Milly 33
Butlins 180

Calabrese, Andrew 37, 101, 118
Calcutt, Alison 54
Calcutt, Ian 31, 55, 59, 69
Canal Plus 39
care structures 173–4
Carr, Jimmy 171
Caulfield, Jo 170
Chambers, Deborah 36
Channel 4 8, 27, 94, 106, 119, 180
character engagement 87
Cher 146
Christie, Agatha 75–6
Collins, Andy 165–6, 169, 173
Collins, Susan 180
construction of liveness 174
conviviality 172
Corner, John 28–9, 54, 58, 60, 71, 142
Cowell, Simon 53, 70
craft of warming up audiences 171–5
Crisp, Virginia 108, 110
cruel optimism 180

Dahlgren, Peter 58–60
Daily Mail, the 141
Daily Telegraph, the 141
Danes, Claire 88
Davidson, Jim 169
Dayan, Daniel 126
De Kosnick, Abigail 99–100
de Veer, Cristobal Tapia 104, 113–14
Deery, June 147
Denison, Rayna 99–100
Dexter Is Delicious 69
Donovan, Julie 8, 16, 24–5, 102, 129, 149
DR 39, 80
Drag House Collective 189
Dyer, Richard 171

Eco, Umberto 140
Ellis, John 75
emotions and genre 77
Encodi 100
Endemol Shine 8, 15, 17–18, 22, 24, 55, 102, 106, 144, 189; Endemol Shine Nordics 23, 26

engagement 28, 54–6, 58, 60, 68, 70–1, 101, 126, 138–9; audience engagement 148, 184–5; disengagement 62, 68; embedded engagement 121–37; emotional engagement 11, 64–5, 92; meaning of engagement 55; music and sound engagement 113; for reality talent shows 62–8; semantics of engagement 59; spectrum of engagement 6–7, 11–12, 28, 53–5, 62–3, 71, 185
Enli, Gunn 140
Eurovision Song Contest 121–2
Evans, Elizabeth Jane 35, 45, 130

fans 86–7, 99–100
Filmlance International 9, 18, 23, 26–7, 73, 78, 80–1, 87
FilmOn 100
Flynn, Gillian 28, 119
food culture 148, 150–1, 157–62
Forsberg, Uno 23, 26
Forsyth, Bruce 166, 168
Fox Mundo 5
freedom, contrary freedom 192; economic freedom, 37; geographical freedom 37
FremantleMedia 8, 163
Frosh, Stephen 58, 75, 126–7
Fox 64, 144
Foxtel 96
FX 5, 21, 39, 43

Game of Thrones 36, 40,53, 97, 170
Generation Game, The 166, 169
genre work 74
geo-blocking 98
geo-cultural paradox 21
Georgsson, Henrik 79–84, 88, 90–1
Gilbert, Gerard 170–1
glitchy palette 110-13
Goffman, Erving 49, 61, 153
Goodall, Jane 171–2
Got to Dance 9, 17–18, 20, 63–8, 71, 122–3, 128–37, 163–4, 172, 176–8, 184; Duplic8 67
Gray, Duncan 63
Grossman, Lloyd 143

Halvorsson, Kerstin 80–1
HBO 53, 119; HBO Nordic 40
Heather Scarecrow Festival 31, 53, 55, 59, 69–70
Heidegger, Martin 173–4
Helin, Sofia 78, 87–9, 93

Index 221

Henderson, Ella 146
Hermes, Joke 189, 191
Hills, Matt 99
Holdham, Stuart 165, 173, 176–9
Homeland 40, 88, 90
human constellations 91
Hunger Games, The 180

inclusivity 155–7
Ingold, Tim 190
ITV 8, 64, 133, 169, 180

Jackson, Lizzie 24
Jenkins, Henry 99
Jerry Springer Show, The 175
Jones, Leslie 170

Kantar Media 141
Katz, Elihu 126
Kaufman, Vincent 100
Kaurismäki, Aki 112
Kay, Peter 169
Kelly, Dennis 104–6, 115
Killing, The 42, 88; Lund Sara 88
Kodi 107
Kondo, Koko 17, 102, 129, 149
Kudos 9, 18, 94–5, 102, 104–5

Landström, Anders 27, 78, 80
Larkin, Brian 96
Lawson, Mark
Layton, Danny 106, 113
Le Tunnel (see also *The Tunnel*) 39
Lindsay, Jeff 69
Llamas-Rodriguez, Juan 37
Lobato, Ramon 36, 97–100, 108
Logo TV 101, 188
Lund University 9, 104
Lunt, Peter 139–40, 175

Macfarlane, Robert 1–2, 30–1, 191
Malmö Live 2
Mann, Colin 96
Marianne and Marcus Wallenberg Foundation 8
Markey, Patrick 44
Mason, Swede 145
Massey, Doreen 124
MasterChef 9, 13, 17–18, 21–2, 27, 138–162, 184; *Celebrity MasterChef* 149, 154; *MasterChef Australia* 147–8; *MasterChef Denmark* 17, 19, 25, 149, 152, 155, 159–60; *MasterChef Sverige* 138–9, 149, 152, 154–5

McDonald, Paul 99
McGee, Debbie 141
McGrath, John 63
McQueen, Steve 77
McVey, Cynthia 174
media, media engagement 6, 58, 60, 101, 126; media and entertainment events 126; media imaginary 3, 36; media landscape 2–3, 30, 38–9, 50–2, 185–6, 190–1
Meese, James 36, 98–9
Meyer, Stephanie 53
Meyrowitz, Joshua 32–3
Mittell, Jason 78
Motion Picture Association of America 96
Moore, Shaun 33
moral landscape 92
Moran, Albert 21–2
Moran, Joe 32
Mr. Bean 17
Mr. Robot 104, 119
Mrs. Merton 170
Munden, Marc 102, 104–5, 107, 111–14

narrative tapestry 83
NBC 170
Neave, Airey 115
Nelson, Robin 77
Netflix 40, 96–8, 100–1, 109, 119, 180, 188
Network 10 143
New Faces 180
Nimbus Film 18, 73, 80
No Sense of Place 32
Nordic noir 72–93
Norton, Graham 170
NTV 39

Office of Communications 8
Old Ways, The 1
One Channel 107
Opportunity Knocks 180
Oren, Tasha 147–8

Pålsson, Adam 91–2
Paradise Hotel 47
participation 58, 64, 175
pathfinders 186–92
pathways to engagement 1–4, 51, 184
Pebble Mill at One 169
performance of the self 61
Petrie, Alistair 19, 104–5

Phoenix Nights 169
Pinchevski, Amit 126–7
piracy 94–8; piracy and audiences 95
Pirate Bay, the 98, 109
Pirates of the Caribbean 98
places of imagination 184
poetics of television 78
Popstars: The Rivals 64
post television 189
power: power chronography 123–6, 136; power of cool 82–3, 89; power of time 123
Preacher 119
Preface to Film 57
Princess Productions 9, 18, 63, 65, 128, 164
Purvis, Tony 78
push-pull dynamics 4–6, 187–8

Quiz Night 169

Ramsey, Gordon 144
Real Housewives 138
reality TV 62–8, 128–37
Reddit 107, 110
researching media experiences 7–10
roaming audiences 1–4, 30–2, 34–5, 37, 45, 50–1, 94, 100–1, 121, 185–6, 190–1; for *The Bridge* 39
Robbins, Ted 169
Roddam, Franc 143
Roscoe, Jane 24
Rosenfeld, Hans 45, 80, 83
Royle Family, The 170
RuPaul's Drag Race 101, 188–91; *Untucked* 188

Salander, Lisbeth 88
Sandvoss, Cornell 86
Saturday Night Live 170
Scannell, Paddy 33, 61, 173–4
Seale, Clive 20
Sharma, Sarah 123–4, 136
Sherlock 96
Shine 9, 18, 64, 106, 149–50
Silverstone, Roger 33, 70
Sky 39, 96; Sky One 64, 128, 132
So You Think You Can Dance 64
social imaginary 2–3, 35, 52, 95, 114–18
social media blackout 44–8, 51
social rituals 40–4, 134, 159
Söderqvist, Johan 80

space, entertainment space 142–5; inter-generic space 142; world space 145–8
Spotify 98
Springer, Jerry 166
Stenner, Paul 175
Stevenson, Jeff 168–70, 173, 181; Oliver, Harvey 169, 181
Stewart, Kathleen 60
Strictly Come Dancing 64, 70, 141–2, 147, 163, 165–6, 171, 173
Strike it Lucky 180
structures of feelings 57–8
Style Challenge 169
Sunday Night at the London Palladium 169
Sundberg, Carl 80
SVT 41, 80; SVT Play 41–2
Syco 64, 163

Taylor, Charles 2–3, 35–6, 115–16, 185
Taylor, Ellie 170–1
temporal pluralism 124–5
Thatcher, Margaret 115
This is Your Life 169
Thomas, Julian 36
Thompson, Marie 114
Thornham, Sue 78
Time Out New York 188
Top Gear 165
topographies of the self 48–50
TorrentFreak 96–7
transmedia storytelling 35, 45
Tunnel, The 39
TV3 22, 150, 154–6, 158
TV4 22, 150, 155–6, 159
Twelve Years a Slave 77
Twilight 53

Urueta, Jose Luis 17, 102
USA Network 119
Utopia 9, 12–13, 17–18, 19, 27–8, 94–5, 101–20, 184, 186, 189

values of drama 46–8
values of production 22
Velling, Thomas 25
VH1 101, 188
Vincent, Andre 167–9, 175, 181
voices of piracy 106–10
Vonderau, Patrick 97–8

Walking Dead, The 97
warm up acts 163–183; the paradox of warm up acts 179–83; as a profession 167–71, qualities of a warm up act 171, reality talent shows 176–9
Wells, Alex 105–6, 115–16
Wenger, Piers 105
Wetherell, Margaret 10, 56–7, 60–1, 78, 119, 187
Williams, Raymond 57, 59–60
Wilson, Karen 106, 115

Wood, Douglas 8, 15, 17, 19, 24, 26, 55, 102, 189–90

X Factor, The 64, 66, 134, 138, 146

Yarwood, Mike 181
YLE 8

ZDF 80
Zelizer, Viviana 56